# Healing America

OTHER BIOGRAPHIES FROM W PUBLISHING GROUP

*A Man of Faith: The Spiritual Journey of George W. Bush*
written by David Aikman

*A Table in the Presence*
written by Lt. Carey Cash

*The Man Called CASH: The Life, Love and Faith of An American Legend*
written by Steve Turner, coming Fall 2004

* * *

OTHER BOOKS BY CHARLES MARTIN

*The Dead Don't Dance*

*Wrapped in Rain*, coming Spring 2005

# Healing America

*The Life of United States Senate Majority Leader*
*William H. Frist, M.D.*
*and the Issues that Shape Our Times*

Charles Martin

W Publishing Group
A Division of Thomas Nelson Publishers
*Since 1798*

www.wpublishinggroup.com

HEALING AMERICA



Published by W Publishing Group, a Division of Thomas Nelson, Inc., P. O. Box 141000, Nashville, Tennessee 37214.

*The people interviewed for this book have graciously given us permission to include their stories.*



Editorial Staff: Patty Crowley, Sheri Swanson and Ellen Anderson

Cover Design: Tobias Outerwear for Books
Photo section compiled by Rhonda Hogan.

Published in association with Yates & Yates, LLP, Attorneys and Counselors, Orange, California.

*Printed in the United States of America*
04 05 06 07 08 QW 5 4 3 2 1

*The very ablest youth should be reserved and educated not for the office of preaching, but for government. Because in preaching, the Holy Spirit does it all, whereas in government one must exercise reason in the shadowy realms where ambiguity and uncertainty are the order of the day.*

—Martin Luther

# Contents

# Introduction

In the months leading up to January 20, 2001, the winds of "compassionate conservatism" swept across the country bringing in a Republican president and a Republican majority in both the House and the Senate. Five months later—May 24, 2001—after reaching a late night deal with Senator Tom Daschle and other top Democrats, Republican Jim Jeffords left the Republican Party to declare himself an Independent and caucus with the Democrats. The ripple effects were many—(not the least of which occurred when Trent Lott passed the gavel to Tom Daschle (the South Dakota senator representing 530,000 voters) and work in the House and Senate came to a screeching halt.

For eighteen months, the Democratically controlled Senate, operating out of a one-vote majority, made every attempt to stall the Bush-led Republican agenda.[1] In the few times when the Democrats were unable to block a Republican initiative, Daschle spoke with disdain and frequently of the "partisan politics" that had come to dominate life in Washington, D.C. In contrast, Daschle himself became known as a wolfish partisan "whose strong opinions were only partially disguised by a lamb's demeanor."[2]

Having lost the majority, and control, following Jim Jeffords's decision—some might say defection—President Bush looked ahead to the November 2002 elections. In a strategic move to win back both, he asked a relatively unknown, first-term senator from Tennessee, Bill Frist, the son of a local country doctor and a gifted surgeon himself, to lead the GOP's Senate Campaign Committee, whose job it was, and is, to elect Republicans to office. Frist went to work, and on election night, November 2002, he quietly succeeded, and a shocked Daschle handed the gavel back to Trent Lott. Senator Lott promised the president and the American people that he'd immediately get to work on the Republican agenda.

Then came the one-hundredth birthday party for Senator Strom Thurmond.

The night was significant for several reasons. Strom Thurmond was one of the more notable figures in recorded American history. He had been a teacher, an athletic coach, and a superintendent of education. He studied law under his father, Judge J. William Thurmond, and became a city attorney, county attorney, state senator, and, eventually, a circuit court judge. Though exempt from serving in the military, Strom—who had already been an army reservist and a commissioned second lieutenant by the age of twenty-one—volunteered for active duty on the day the United States entered World War II. As a member of the eighty-second Airborne, he parachuted behind enemy lines on D-Day and helped secure the foothold for the Allies to liberate the European continent.

For distinguished service, Senator Thurmond was awarded five battle stars and eighteen other decorations, including the Legion of Merit with oak leaf cluster, the Purple Heart, the Bronze Star for Valor, the Belgian Order of the Crown and the French Cross of War.

After the war, Strom returned home to South Carolina. He was elected governor in 1946 and then ran as a Dixiecrat (a segregationist platform he later renounced) against Harry Truman for president of the United States. He lost, but was determined to serve America, so he ran for Senate in 1954 and became the only candidate elected to Congress by a write-in vote in American history. At the time of his birthday celebration, he had been reelected eight times since.

As a young man, he knew people who had seen Andrew Jackson, and he campaigned for the votes of men who fought in the Civil War. He and Herbert Hoover won their first elective office in the same year—1928. He served with about one-fifth of the nearly two thousand people who have been members of the Senate since 1789. And at the time of his birthday, he was nearly one-half the age of the United States Constitution itself. As a result of his long-standing service, it had been said that almost 70 percent of South Carolinians had met Strom Thurmond face to face.

As the celebration began, several senators came forth to offer their praise and congratulations. Obviously, much of his life had been praiseworthy, and admirers didn't have to look too far into his past to pay him a compliment.

When it came time for the newly returned Senate Majority Leader Lott to make his toast, he did: "When Strom Thurmond ran for president, we voted for him. We're proud of it. And if the rest of the country had followed our lead, we wouldn't have had all these problems over all these years, either."[3] And, when he'd finished, most people wished the man from the Magnolia State had never spoken.

Just what was Thurmond's lead? According to a 1948 speech, Thurmond said, "There's not enough troops in the army to force the southern people to break down segregation and admit the n—rance into our theatres, into our swimming pools, into our homes, and into our churches."[4] While history will record Strom's heroic contribution to America, it will also record the statement above: a paradox, and one the Republican Party of George W. Bush wants no part of. The events that unfurled over the next several days are best described as an "oil-in-water" reaction.

Lott's words were neither compassionate nor conservative. As soon as the words left his mouth, the president's compassionate agenda could be heard crashing upon the rocks, and the critics could be heard trampling over one another en route to the microphone.

But the Democrats had to be careful not to seem too eager, for they, too, were wrought with the paradoxes of politics. For among their ranks was one with a less-than-perfect race record. Senator Robert Byrd was once a member of the Ku Klux Klan, opposed the Civil Rights Act of 1964, and used the term "white n—rs" in a *Fox News Sunday* interview. In 1945, Byrd wrote to Mississippi's virulent segregationist Senator Theodore Bilbo that he would never serve in an integrated army. "Rather I should die a thousand times, and see Old Glory trampled in the dirt never to rise again, than to see this beloved land of ours become degraded by race mongrels, a throwback to the blackest specimen from the wilds." Confronted with the letter in 1999, Byrd said he didn't recall writing it. He said, "I will not dispute the quote, though I consider it deplorable." In 1946, at the age of twenty-nine, Byrd wrote to Imperial Wizard Green of the KKK: "The Klan is needed today as never before and I am anxious to see its rebirth here in West Virginia." He didn't dispute this letter either.[5]

The Republican senators and President Bush thanked Senator Lott for his distinguished service but told him that his comments were inappropriate, did not represent the sentiments they wished to express, and asked him to step down. Eight days later—December 20, 2002—he did.

The Republicans then met in a closed-door meeting to nominate one of the remaining ninety-nine members to take Lott's place. Someone who could lead alongside the president. Someone considered a moderate in the vein of George W with no ties to anything even remotely racist—some might even say, "difficult to pigeonhole," "an outsider," and "not a lifetime politician." While Nickles and Santorum threw their names in the hat—both deserving, able, and worthy senators—the president and the Republican Caucus had their eyes on another. A man who knew a good bit about veins. Before anyone left the meeting, Bush made a phone call and pointed him out.

Everyone knew he was speaking of the doctor—Bill Frist. Those who had thrown their names in the hat immediately withdrew them and stood faithfully alongside. Frist, who in fact had not sought the position of majority leader, was asked by the party if he would accept it. After counseling with Bob Dole and Howard Baker, he realized, that despite his own desires, he possessed an obligation to the body, to the institution, to the country. Despite the criticisms that he was an opportunist, he asked the members of his caucus for an evening to talk with his wife and his sons and pray about it.

As he had before on the evenings of his two previous elections, Frist and his wife, Karyn, drove to Two Rivers Baptist for a worship service. Midway through the service, the doctor, lost in his thoughts, thumbed through his Bible to an underlined passage he knew well. He could recall it from memory, but in times like this, he felt the need to reread it: "In his heart a man plans his course, but the Lord determines his steps."[6] Late in the service, the pastor publicly recognized the couple, called them forward and explained the gravity of the moment and their pressing need for strength, encouragement, and maybe most importantly, wisdom. The couple walked forward and knelt at the altar as the pastor told the congregation that anyone who wished could come forward as well and gather around the couple while he prayed. While his words were still echoing off the balcony, the pews emptied and the congregation, kneeling and standing, filled the altar around the doctor and his wife. Attendees would later remember that time as a powerful and poignant moment. The following day, Frist agreed to stand for a vote.

The count was unanimous.

In January of 2003, amidst great controversy and cries of racism and insensitivity, Senator William H. Frist, M.D., a mere second-term senator, assumed the role of majority leader of the Senate for the 108th Congress of the United States. Having treated tens of thousands of patients, he understood well the needs of the sick and dying and what it takes to bring health, wholeness, and healing.

Late in the afternoon on the day of his election to majority leader, longtime friend Dr. Karl VanDevender asked Bill, "How's it feel?"

Without hesitation, Bill responded, "Humbling."

Karl says, "That's where his faith has entered in. His humility impressed me then and now. Even now that he's in this position, Billy is trying to make decisions that impact this country not as a Republican or a Democrat, but as a man trying to do what is right. He has a servant's heart and when, like him, you reach the top of the mountain, the only place to look for guidance is up. He's got nowhere else to look but up and that's where he's looking."[7]

If Bill Frist, or "Fristy" as President Bush likes to call him, is to help heal the rift that divides America, then it will test every skill the good doctor ever learned. Many agree that while he's up to the task, he's got his work cut out for him. But to those who doubt, a word of caution: Bill Frist accomplished more by the age of forty than most do in a lifetime, lives by an uncompromising ethical code fueled by a quiet faith that is long on action and short on talk, possesses the gentle bedside manner of a country doctor and the skill of one of the best heart doctors the world has ever known, is supremely disciplined, and has never failed at anything he's set his mind to do. More importantly, he knows all too well that while he was the surgeon that transplanted more than one hundred fifty hearts, he's not the One who got them all started again.

This is Bill Frist.

# 1

THE INTERESTING THING about the three letters that appear in front of Bill Frist's name is that while he earned them, they are not the letters with which he most identifies. *SEN* might be what he does, but it's not who he is. To understand Bill Frist, one needs to look at the letters that follow his name.

First and foremost, Bill Frist is a doctor. And a skilled one, too. Being a doctor is the glasses—or prism as he likes to say—through which he sees life, and they color everything he says or does. His worldview begins with the idea that being a doctor is a high calling, one he answered as a boy. Having taken a leave of absence from his medical practice at Vanderbilt and is now in his second term in the Senate, he may well be one of the best heart transplant doctors in the world. His patients certainly think so. He's performed more than one hundred fifty heart and heart/lung transplants and countless bypass and various other emergency medical procedures. Even today as majority leader of the Senate, a stethoscope lies atop his desk as a sort of reminder, both to himself and to those with whom he meets.

But, when you think of the highly technological front-edge field of transplants, don't place "Billy" Frist in that egocentric world of Lone Ranger doctors and Billy the Kid gunslingers looking to be the fastest draw in the OR. Think of the neighborhood doctor your parents used to tell you about who'd come running at all hours of the night wearing a stethoscope, carrying a black bag, offering hope and a gentle beside manner. Even today, he keeps a black bag in the closet of his Senate office.

William H. Frist is an anathema in Washington, D.C. No insider, he's a conservative Republican, pro-life, fiscally conservative, and yet he's introduced legislation with Democrat Ted Kennedy, supports stem-cell research and increased funding for AIDS programs in Africa. Though he's a tireless supporter and constant ally of George W. Bush, even accused of being too much of a "yes man," he has friends on both sides of the aisle. He did not seek his party's appointment as majority leader, and yet when asked to throw his name into the hat, he did and was subsequently elected by his peers following Trent Lott's self-inflicted demise.

Lee Annis says that his initial instinct after watching Bill Frist debate Jim Sasser was to discount him as an idealistic but hopelessly naïve man much like Jefferson Smith, the movie character that Jimmy Stewart brought to life so movingly in *Mr. Smith Goes to Washington*. To Annis's surprise, Bill Frist was the only challenger to defeat a full-term incumbent senator in 1994. "What's more he knocked out Jim Sasser by more than 14 percentage points."[1] Others of high regard—such as former President Reagan's chief of staff, Howard Baker—tend to disagree with the Mr. Smith perception, saying Frist was a "well organized" man of "substance" with "a pretty clear view of what his job was."[2] The contrasting views of Bill Frist serve to reinforce the perception that "he's not easily pigeon-holed."

An admittedly tireless workaholic, Bill Frist has excelled at everything he's ever attempted. If he's faced a major failure in life, it's not been recorded. And if you're hoping to find skeletons in his closet, chances are good you're wasting your time. His friends claim that Bill Frist squeaks when he walks. Some have attempted to tie him to an investigation into the company his father and brother started, but that has been put to rest as a ridiculous witch hunt with regards to Bill. He graduated with honors more times than not, including Harvard Medical School; he's been elected class president or vice president more times than not, including three of his four years in college; he took courses that were not required, fearful that he might miss something; he earned the math medal in high school while also editing the yearbook; he played quarterback, although a motorcycle accident ended his athletic career and focused his sight on his and others' mortality; he earned his pilot's license at sixteen—even today, flying is a cherished hobby though seldom-seen escape. He's an avid marathoner—he's run seven and twice he's run the New York and Marine Corp marathons only eight days apart; he spends time as a medical missionary in Uganda and the Sudan—for years he's quietly spent a few weeks offering his talents in war-torn Sudan with Franklin Graham's Samaritan's Purse. He seldom drinks, and he loves his wife and kids—although he is the first to admit he spent far too much time away during the years he was building the Vanderbilt transplant center; he has waged a lifelong war against the idea of sleep—he often sleeps only three to four hours a night. He loves history, which helps explain the many books he's written—the most compelling of which is *Transplant*. He is seen as somewhat of a daredevil by nature and considers a picture of himself surrounded by more than a hundred of his transplant patients one of his most cherished possessions—"'They mean everything to me,' he says"[3]—and is cool as a cucumber under the direst of circumstances.

When in Tennessee, Sunday morning will routinely find Bill in church and, at times, a predominantly African-American church. As majority leader, his every move is scrutinized and picked apart for its political reasoning, but those closest to Bill will tell you that his attendance in church—no matter what kind of church—is certainly not political. He just seems to enjoy it, and further, they will tell you that he knows he needs it. This is understandable when you understand that if Bill Frist had not chosen to enter the field of medicine, chances are quite good that he'd have become a Presbyterian minister.

Like the president, he runs daily—wearing New Balance running shoes as Nikes don't seem to fit his wider forefoot. And on his bedside table as of late sits a book by Michael Deaver, *A Different Drummer: My Thirty Years with Ronald Reagan*.

Don't think for a minute that just because he became a senator that he's forgotten how to be a doctor. Hardly. Working at his desk on July 24, 1998, Bill was told that multiple gunshots had been heard coming from the steps of the Capitol Building. Bill immediately called the physician's office, who told him that two people had been shot by a lone gunman. Bill sprinted out of his office toward the Capitol where he soon learned there were four, not two victims. He knelt next to the first man, Officer J.J. Chestnut, who had been fatally shot in the head. Bill monitored Chestnut's heart, transported him by stretcher, and initiated CPR when Chestnut quit breathing inside the ambulance. Once the medics arrived and took over, Bill returned up the Capitol steps and attended to another man—who unbeknownst to Bill, was the alleged shooter. For Bill, that was immaterial. He told the media later, "I am trained to take care of the patient. I'm not the judge, I'm not the jury; I'm the physician." Bill stayed with the man throughout the ambulance ride to D.C. General Hospital and kept the man's heart and lungs working until they arrived and he turned the patient over to the emergency room physician.

And in January of 2003, as the newly elected Senate majority leader, Bill was driving along "Alligator Alley," thirty-five miles outside of Miami, en route to a family vacation home when a sport utility vehicle traveling the other direction blew out a rear tire, rolled over, and threw out all six passengers. Bill immediately rushed from his car and tended to the four survivors—including clearing a blocked windpipe and administering CPR—and established a makeshift triage while waiting on paramedics and firefighters. When they did arrive, he quickly communicated what they needed to know, thereby directing medics to those who most needed help and expediting their understanding of the scene.

Broward Fire-Rescue assistant chief Todd Leduc said, "The Senate majority leader was really instrumental in helping us treat the victims."

Bill responded later to the media, "As a doctor, my first instincts are to help, and I was privileged to offer my assistance today at the scene of this horrible accident. My heart goes out to this family which must face the start of a new year with this terrible tragedy."[4] Bill's identity was not known to those around him until sometime later when the police began writing the accident report.

Given what he's accomplished, Bill Frist has every right to be confident. He has excelled at Princeton and at Harvard Medical School; he trained under Dr. Norman Shumway—the inventor and father of transplantation—and performed medical operations and procedures that few human beings have ever attempted, much less thought of. Today, he is the sitting majority leader of the United States Senate, but despite his many titles and vast experiences, he is known as a man who possesses quiet self-confidence mixed with the much-needed humility of a quiet, bedside physician—one who is slow to speak and quick to listen. Those who know him well say that Bill Frist is the product of his parents' influence, rigorous training, experience, God-given talents, and deep-down drive.

Bill Frist has never shied from a leadership position, often putting him in the media spotlight and bringing accusations of "overly ambitious" from his critics. Those who know him disagree. Lifetime friend Barry Banker says, "I've known him thirty-seven years, and I'm here to tell you that there's not an ambitious, power-hungry sinew in his body. He is a leader, and when he sees a need, he leads. He feels a compulsion and need to serve mankind. Whatever he has accomplished, it's not about Bill Frist. There will always be the naysayers, but how do you argue against something like the Sudan?"[5]

Mass General colleague, Dr. Kim Jett, says, "Today, when so many are doctors of darkness and pessimism, Bill is a doctor of light and optimism. Even from an early stage, he was a natural-born leader."[6]

Bill Frist comes from a long line of doctors. His father, Thomas Frist, known as "Dr. Tommy" and a legend in Tennessee, may well be one of the most highly respected doctors ever to set foot in Nashville. To say he lived by a high moral and ethical code is an understatement. On the lapel of his coat, he wore a pin which his church had given him for attending Sunday school for forty-three years without ever missing a Sunday. Occasionally, Dr. Tommy took Bill with him in those all-too-often, after-dinner, late night runs to a patient's house. Evidently Bill was paying attention, because his patients will attest that his bedside manner is as good as any, and his style of communication is second to none.

Bill Frist has spent his professional life learning to overcome life-and-death circumstances. As a transplant surgeon, his success percentages were routinely ten points above the national average—placing the Vanderbilt program among the best in the country—and yet he is not one to blow his own horn. Throughout his life, he has allowed his actions to speak for him because that's what his dad taught him. Bill Frist once spent forty-five minutes in the OR massaging the heart of a gunshot victim until his hand cramped so badly he had to step aside, ask an assistant to step in, stretch his fingers for five minutes and then step back into place. Some critics have suggested, "Sure, he's a good doctor but he's only helped the people he wanted to, the people who were most able to pay and the people he liked." Nothing could be further from the truth.

For the record, yes, he transplanted hearts into people who could pay and people he liked—Bill Frist seems to like most everybody and most everybody seems to like Bill Frist—but his record tells the real truth. He's logged over eighty thousand hours in hospitals drawing blood, changing sheets, pushing gurneys, working in labs, filing paperwork, and caring for patients. His Vanderbilt record shows a compassionate doctor who routinely accepted patients without a prayer of ever receiving payment for his services. He actually negotiated the ability to perform those 'free' services into his contract before ever accepting the position at Vanderbilt. Furthermore, as a cardiothoracic surgeon engaged in the practice of transplantation, he was continually asked to play God, and yet he refused to do so. Often in his office, he would meet a man who had absolutely abused his first heart, crippling it through excessive drinking, smoking, lifestyle, the absence of exercise, without any regard whatsoever for the precious life-giving pump inside him, and yet Bill Frist would find a heart, fly all hours of the night to retrieve it, then return and selflessly place it into the chest of a man who may very well abuse it in the same manner that he had abused the first. Not a judge, he's a physician, one who took an oath to help heal the sick. Bill Frist is a tireless believer in the idea that at every turn, you affirm life. Just ask Jim Hayes.

Before his death from cancer in 1994, Jim Hayes may well have been the poster child for effective heart transplantation in the United States. From Dr. Norman Shumway, Jim received his first transplant in the '70s, and later made a cross-country bike trip documented on the television show *That's Incredible* en route to his five-year checkup. A decade later, atherosclerosis, set in and brought him to Vanderbilt to see a young apprentice of Dr. Shumway named Bill Frist. Bill found Jim a heart and transplanted it, but not long after, Jim Hayes's body rejected it as it had never before rejected anything. For months, Jim and his wife rode the roller coaster of an extreme regimen of antibiotics, but Jim continued to worsen. Jim's fever elevated to 105, he lost his memory, suffered a stroke, and eventually fell into a coma. He had to be intubated and placed on a ventilator, and talk around the hospital was, "For God's sake, Bill, just let the man die."

In order to fight the infection that was ravaging his body, Bill was intravenously giving Jim a regimen of radical new antibiotics, seldom if ever before prescribed to a human being in the doses or frequency he was receiving. At one point, Jim's wife stood in the ICU, peering into the tent in which Jim slept while hooked up to every monitoring machine known to man, and met an intern who, without knowing she was Jim's wife, said, "Yeah, this guy's only got twenty-four hours."

Jim Hayes lay dying. The hospital had written him off, the staff had written him off, maybe even Jim had written himself off, but not Bill Frist. Bill, the eternal optimist who has never given up on a patient his entire life, sat in his office, racked his brain, and then called a colleague named Ed Stinson back at Stanford. The two formulated a risky and seldom-attempted treatment once advocated by his mentor, Shumway, involving radiation. Immediately, Bill began radiating Jim Hayes as if he were a cancer patient. The hospital staff was once again dubious. A few days later, Jim opened his eyes, glanced at the machinery and tubes invading his body, and then slowly gave a thumbs-up to his wife. It took awhile for his strength and memory to return, but eventually Jim, the fighter, walked out of that hospital and returned home. And as he left, the voices of Bill Frist's critics faded into the Tennessee hills.

Long before he ran for politics, Bill Frist was flying around the South in rented, two-engine planes, educating people at small town sit-ins and late-night diners, telling anyone who would listen about the dire need for organ donation. Why? Because he was tired of seeing people die when all across the country good organs were never donated-organs that could have saved lives. Due to that shortage, he was often put in the unenviable position of playing God. Given only one organ, he was asked to decide between two people. Thankfully, a national computer now takes much of that agonizing decision out of his hands, but it's not perfect. He'll be the first to tell you that he hated being given one good heart and then having to choose between two equally deserving patients. More often than not, the other patient died before an organ was found.

Eating dinner with transplant recipient and Clemson University police officer Jimmy Moore in the late '80s, then transplant surgeon Bill Frist received a phone call. Moore remembers that the once-joking Bill Frist sat up from the table and grew immediately serious. "He put his game face on quick." Bill listened to the caller, pulled a three-by-five-inch index card from the shirt pocket on his scrubs and began reading its contents. He nodded, read back two names to the caller and said, "I agree. Give me a few minutes and I'll call you back." He hung up the phone, closed his eyes, unconsciously tapped his forehead with the index card and "mouthed a few words that looked like he was praying." Jimmy asked, "Bill, you okay?" Bill looked up, the agony written across his face, and said, "I can get in the trenches, operate for hours, and live for days with little or no sleep, but right now I've got two people and one heart. Chances are that whoever doesn't get it won't live long enough for us to find another. Somebody will live and somebody won't."[7] Bill made a return phone call, paid the bill and then moments later they were pulling into the hospital where Bill was immediately slated to hop on a chartered Leer jet.

Despite his accomplishments and the letters positioned both before and after his name, Bill Frist remains down-to-earth. Throughout the course of each term, he has traveled Tennessee's ninety-five counties and held "Listening Town Meetings" just to keep his hand on the pulse of his constituents. Prior to being elected majority leader, he routinely gave up part of a day to see patients, many of whom were indigent, at a free clinic in D.C. or school clinic or a rural hospital in Tennessee. He loves history, is never far from a medical bag, writes regularly, runs religiously, and as a multiengine-rated pilot who also holds a commercial and instructor's license, he flies a plane because he loves the feeling of escape.

Those who complain that Bill—a graduate of Montgomery Bell Academy, Princeton, and Harvard—is a silver-spoon child, born to privilege, who's spent his life propelled by ambition and greed, don't know the rest of the story. Bill admits he came from a privileged background, but what made it privileged were two parents who loved him and encouraged him to chase his dreams. Which he did. As for padding his personal fortune, if Bill Frist had been interested in amassing a fortune, he'd have tied his wagon to his brother Tommy's star and ridden it out on his coattails. If Bill were only interested in money, he'd have foregone a heart surgeon's long hours and a senator's salary and taken a job in the family business down the hall from his brother. Anyone who knew Tommy, knew he was destined to do well, and it didn't take a genius to see the writing on the wall that was HCA. Tommy was a born entrepreneur, and whatever he touched turned to gold. Today, he's one of Forbes 350 richest men in America whose net worth is reported somewhere above a billion. Bill's is about 5 percent of that. Granted, both are large sums, but the point is this: Bill knew what he was missing and yet—like his brother Tommy—chose the desire of his heart and not the promise of riches. And while it is true that the Frist family has been prosperous, they started with rags.

Bill Frist chose a path less traveled. Instead of living off his father's reputation, concentrating on how many rounds of golf he could play in one week or attaching his wagon rope to his brother's star, Bill Frist chose cardiothoracic surgery. And as if that weren't difficult enough, he upped it a notch and chose transplantation. After training under Norman Shumway, Bill chose Vanderbilt—where he was tasked not with building *a* transplant center to serve the Southeast, but *the* transplant center in the East. And after twenty years, having succeeded at his task and ascending to the top of his game, and despite the countless voices saying, "You're crazy," he requested a voluntary leave of absence and decided to run for the U.S. Senate. But before he could get there he had to defeat an unbeatable incumbent who was slated to become majority leader, given a Republican president. Once he defeated the undefeatable, he joined the Senate and, as the twenty-fourth man to take the seat once held by Andrew Jackson, was ranked dead last in Senate seniority, which is ironic given his current position. When asked why he left medicine to join the Senate, he responded, "I never really left. . . . By day, I'm a U.S. Senator, by life I'm a physician."[8] And now, when he finds time for two weeks' vacation, he doesn't book a villa on an exclusive beach in the Pacific Islands or ski resort in Switzerland to bask in how great he is or what he's accomplished.

Whether his schedule allows or not, he carves out two weeks and flies into war-torn Sudan, making sure to keep the plane at an altitude of less than 400 feet, because otherwise he might draw attention to himself and get shot down. Once there, he operates under the worst possible conditions, often operating by flashlight, because when the sun goes down it gets dark in a world with no electricity. And at night, when the day is done, he walks out of the hospital, past the ditches which serve as bunkers in the event the hospital is bombed, and returns to his tent where he showers beneath a bucket hung from a tree and swats mosquitoes and tsetse flies by lantern light. In a world of Washington insiders and political skeptics who suggest "no one is truly that sincere," Bill Frist is just that. He's an anomaly and a breath of fresh air.

If Bill Frist has a weakness, it's that he doesn't relax very well. Former chief of staff Mark Tipps says, "He'll never, ever, go to the beach and sit beneath an umbrella. No way. He'll dig a sand castle with his boys, go for a walk with Karyn, or go for a long run. . . . He is a driven person." Upon reflection, Mark states that "Bill admits his one glaring weakness is an inability to let-down completely. He doesn't vacate well, and he recognizes this. He has trouble putting aside big issues, going to do something to clear his mind and then coming back to it when he's fresh. He worries intently about big issues like Iraq, and he never quite gets away from them. Whether it's at his kids' lacrosse game, fishing or whatever, he doesn't escape those pressures very well. They're always just underneath the skin, always sort of pecking at him. I think he wishes he had the ability to have some free moments that are completely unburdened by the problems of the day."[9]

Maybe it has something to do with his training in transplantation, or maybe it has something to do with the genes given to him by his father, but whatever the source, when the pace grows too hectic or too pressured for most, Bill Frist is at his best. He flourishes under the worst of conditions. When most are looking for an easy or silent exit, Bill Frist is looking for a solution. Bill is an absolute, outright optimist, who looks beyond potential problems and "why something can't," to possibilities and "why something can." To his staff, he is clear in what he expects, but as Mark Tipps remembers, "I've never seen him lose his cool. He might let you know where you didn't measure up, but he never berates you."[10]

On a personal level, Bill Frist does not wear his emotions on his sleeve, seems constantly prepared for the unexpected, and is not seen as a backslapper or one who chums it up with everyone in the room. Friends say it might take longer to get to know him, but when you do, you find a warm, caring, loving father who is committed to his family, his country, and to what is good and right. He is also seen as a great listener who values everyone from the janitor sweeping the floors, to the nurse in the operating room, to the low-level staffer writing a legislative report, to fellow senators and George W. Bush. Across the board, people who meet

Bill Frist describe a man who listens, who is interested in them and their lives: "The last person he'll talk about is himself. He'd much rather talk about you."[11]

When asked about what some consider overconfidence or arrogance, Mark Tipps responds, "How could you not become confident when you are accustomed to reaching into another human being's chest, cutting out their old heart, and putting in someone else's. Bill understands he doesn't do that without God's help and blessing, but I think that characteristic just comes with the nature of the job, with doing 150 transplants. He is measured, in control, and the kind of guy you want driving the ship when the ship hits rough waters. Yes, he has emotions, he gets down, he's human like the rest of us, but he also has a lot of discipline. If that's mistaken for aloofness, so be it. I wish I was more aloof at times."[12]

Trying to manufacture skeletons, Bill's critics are quick to rummage through the newspapers and pull out some vague reference to HCA and a federal government investigation. When HCA merged with Columbia Healthcare, the two became Columbia HCA. A young executive by the name of Rick Scott became CEO and steered the company in a new direction. Sometime in 1997, the Federal government announced it was investigating Columbia HCA for "upcoding"—the systematic overcharging of Medicare. Some well-publicized raids were performed on hospitals in San Antonio, the company was fined, and Rick Scott and his executive team were eventually let go. The board of directors asked Tommy Frist to return, grab the rudder, and set the company straight. Tommy returned, cleaned house, righted the ship, and told everyone to cooperate with the government.

> If anybody was wearing a white hat in that whole deal, it was Tommy Frist. He told everyone to cooperate with the government. Furthermore, Bill Frist never worked at HCA, never operated at HCA hospitals, never served on the board of directors, and even though no federal law requires him to do so, he placed all of his assets in a blind trust over which he has absolutely no control. To suggest that there is a conflict of interest between Bill Frist's

> relationship with HCA and his work on making policy in healthcare is nothing short of ridiculous. Bill Frist is qualified to make decisions that affect healthcare policy because he studied it at the Woodrow Wilson School of Public Policy and then lived and breathed it for twenty years. If his critics believe that Bill Frist should, for some reason, recuse himself as would a judge for fear of conflict of interest, then there can be no such thing as a citizen-legislator. If that's true, then a senator who comes from a family of farmers can have nothing to do with agriculture policy and a lawyer now serving in the Senate can have nothing to do with judicial policy or judicial nominations. To follow that line of thinking suggests that the least knowledgeable, least experienced senators in a given area are the most qualified to serve in that area. That is not what the founders intended.[13]

Bill Frist's story is wrought with other such paradoxes, making him difficult to put under one's thumb. David Brooks, editor of the *Weekly Standard*, says,

> He is relentlessly ambitious, yet he is also a sincere do-gooder. He is a meritocratic striver, yet he also has a service mentality that transcends narrow self-interest. He has an ego, but he also performs unpublicized acts of charity. He is a member of genteel society, but he is not cowardly—or obsessed with the opinions of the parlor set. . . . He is political, but for much of his life had no interest in anything but medicine and still defines himself as a doctor first.[14]

Given his upbringing, his education, and his God-given talents, Bill Frist has always believed, in the recesses of his mind, that he was born to lead. As a result, he does. And evidently he does so effectively, which explains his rapid ascension to the top of the Republican ranks. If there is a bioterrorism crisis on the Hill, everybody wants Bill Frist in charge. This includes his critics across the aisle. During the anthrax attacks on Senators Daschle and Leahy's offices, they and their staff members continually called Bill's office looking for updated information, because having transplanted so many hearts had by default made him an expert on infectious diseases.

A believer in term limits, Bill has said he will leave the Senate after this present term (his second), but few think he'll leave politics. When speaking of Bill Frist's political career, most Republicans and Democrats alike use the terms *White House* and '08. But Bill Frist is less concerned with future titles and positions than what he can accomplish at present, because at his heart the senator is focused on one thing: diagnosing individual and corporate need, prescribing a remedy, and then leading a team of gifted personnel through the operation intended to jumpstart the healing. Today, his operating room is the United States and his patient the American people. Most call him Senator or Mr. Leader—deep down he would prefer Doctor. The president calls him Fristy, and yet to his friends, he has been, is, and always will be, Billy.

Bill Frist is not entirely unlike another Tennessee hero. From a mountaintop in Tennessee, Davy Crocket established a reputation for living by a moral code causing him to do something valiant and daring like fighting Indians and protecting others with his faithful musket, Betsy. Having made friends with the Indians and most everybody else in Tennessee, Davy became exposed to greater need, so he packed his saddle bags, saddled his horse, traveled to Washington, retired Betsy until a later day, and began fighting the evil he saw there. Operating from that same ethical code and desire to help those who couldn't help themselves, Davy Crocket soon became a national hero—one now permanently written into the fabric and song that is America.

Across both sides of the aisle, Bill Frist is seen as one who can build consensus and lead. His leadership style, by his own admission, is pretty simple: "Define a mission, and be able to write it on a single card in a single sentence."[15] First as a heart transplant surgeon and now as majority leader of the Senate, he's supremely focused, disciplined, and no nonsense, and he has never lacked the temerity to lead. Frist says, "The timid people in medicine don't go into the field of cutting hearts out and putting them in."[16]

This is the story of his life, his upbringing, and his decision to enter medicine and that most skilled of roles, the cardiothoracic transplant surgeon. The story follows his decision to enter politics, his quick rise through the ranks, his ascension to majority leader, and now as the darling of both the Republican Party and the White House, it discusses his faith and the challenges that lie ahead—which are many. Not the least of which is the fact that the fifty-one Republican senators are "about as unified as a Balkan parliament."[17] Further, what are his future plans? Many of his friends believe that the presidential election of 2008 will best answer the last question.

# 2

TENNESSEE PRODUCED PRESIDENTS Jackson, Polk, and Johnson, two senators by the name of Al Gore, governor Nelson Rockefeller, writer Alex Haley, Olympic Gold Medalist Wilma Rudolph, and most recently, a football team called the Tennessee Titans—the winningest team in the NFL from 1998–2002. Due to its inhabitants' overwhelming response to the governor's call to arms and the War of 1812, the state became known as the Volunteer State. It's home to a couple of colleges—UT and Vandy, the largest publisher of Bibles in the world, and a high-banked oval place called the Bristol Motor Speedway, where an aggressive fender-bender named Dale Earnhardt won nine times. It's native to the passion flower, the mockingbird, the Tennessee walking horse and over 2,300 Civil War engagement sites, which might help explain why she contributed more troops than any other state to the Confederacy. It's home to the nation's oldest distillery, started by a fellow named Jack Daniels, which oddly enough sits in a dry county. It's home to Beale Street, the unofficial home of the blues; the Cherokee leader, Sequoyah; an Indian fighter and later congressman, and Alamo hero, Davy Crocket; frontiersman Daniel

Boone; governor Sam Houston. It's where a legal argument became known as the Scopes Monkey Trial of 1925; a "secret city" called Oak Ridge built an explosive weapon that ended World War II. It's home to the most decorated war hero of World War I, Alvin York, and the quiet little daughter of a coal miner named Loretta Lynn. It's home to the Country Music Hall of Fame, the Grand Ole Opry, the "Tennessee Waltz," "Rocky Top," Graceland, and a hip-shaking country boy named Elvis.

It is also home to a reserved doctor named William H. Frist.

Tennessee is somewhat of an anomaly to other states. While most states chose one particular side on which to fight in the Civil War, Tennessee fought on both with equal conviction. That fact alone makes it tricky for the politicians she elects. The 300-mile walk from East to West Tennessee is an education in differing geographies. Mountainous East Tennessee was home to the state's earliest settlement with small yeoman farms. Middle Tennessee rolls with hills and fertile farming land. And West Tennessee is a rich delta fed by the Mississippi River. That same walk is also an education in the history of differing political opinions. More Civil War battles were fought in Tennessee than any other state except Virginia, and upon the war's end, 275,000 slaves had been set free.

Divided in the Civil War, they suffered a rough decade in the sixties, with lunch counter sit-ins and race riots, and the entire country heard the shot that rang out across the balcony at the Lorraine Hotel in Memphis where a giant of a man named Martin Luther King, Jr. was shot on April 4, 1968.

While Nashville may be called Music City—and yes the music industry does bring in about two billion dollars a year across the country—Music Row takes up a few square blocks while the healthcare industry takes up entire square miles. Senator Lamar Alexander points out that "country music still sits uncomfortably in Nashville, like McDonald's in Japan."[1] Known as the Silicon Valley of healthcare, Nashville is home to 450 healthcare companies and industry support firms.[2]

Nashville is home to Vanderbilt's sprawling, clean, brick campus, manicured athletic fields, and world-class hospital that, like Rome's, covers several hills. The students here seem serious, some even anxious. Most carry laptops and have long-term career plans and high school transcripts that record near 4.0 GPAs and near-insane SATs. The competition here is stiff, and these are some of the brightest, but they're too busy to brag about it. The football team is a perennial loser, but the basketball team is not—an item of contention, to say the least, especially when that orange-and-white team is always so good. But while the Volunteers may own the state's bragging rights and the Tennessee Titans may be the sleek new team in town, the locals don their black and gold and fill their season-ticket seats in Commodore stadium, because they can always hope and because most graduated from there and are now sitting in the seats once held by their parents.

Nashville is also home to Belle Meade, the fifth richest town in the U.S., complete with its own police department and extremely strict speed limits. Speeding tickets have been given to drivers traveling a half a mile an hour over the speed limit. And the police are no respecter of persons—they don't care who you are. They'll pull anybody over, even pedestrians such as His Highness Prince Edward. In February of 2004, the police scolded the Earl of Wessex for ignoring the strict pedestrian code on Belle Meade Boulevard. Quite disconcerting to newcomers, local decree states that the only place to walk on the boulevard is on the inside lanes, facing the oncoming traffic. When traffic approaches, pedestrians must move to the grassy median.

Some have called Belle Meade the old-money suburb of Nashville, and while that may be true, don't equate that with being ostentatious or showy. It's not Las Vegas. It's far more dressed-down and conservative. American flags flap on every street.

Certainly there's the occasional new-money house, but on the whole, it's rather subdued and reserved. Even colonial. The streets are lined with old magnolias, tall oaks, Leland cypress and brick and wrought-iron fences that outline winding driveways. The large, mostly two-story, stone and brick houses, many with columns and white trim, have driveways longer than the sideline at Commodore stadium. And the yards, many of which have that criss-crossed look like the outfield at Turner Field, are maintained by professionals who know what they're doing. People here seem careful and protective with what they have. Maybe that's why they still have it. Many of the cars are expensive, but many are also old, well-maintained and well outside the three-year, thirty-six thousand mile warranty. Churches don't dot every street corner, but certainly most, and come Sunday, most are full.

The Belle Meade Country Club is a one-hundred-year-old country club possessing a membership roster filled with some of the most powerful and established families in Nashville. Critics have suggested that the club carries with it elitist connotations and that politicians are wise to resign their memberships prior to running for office. Regardless, a walk through its simple front door exposes the fact that it's no showier than its members. To be truthful, it's in need of renovation. Even the members think so. The ceilings aren't overly tall, artwork seems faded, and floors are covered by worn carpet, so it's difficult to tell if there's hardwood underneath. The furniture has been sat in long enough and frequently enough to cause the seat cushions to take on the shape of the last ten thousand occupants. But that's just it. The members don't seem driven by vanity or the need to show you what they have. They know what they have, and they know what they value.

At one time, the Belle Meade Country Club and the Vanderbilt University board of trust were the city's power centers. There was even a secret society called Watauga that made many of the important decisions about the city life. Nashville journalist Bruce Dobie described the society as one comprised of the CEOs of the town's banks and businesses and a few select others such as Jack Massey, who built Kentucky Fried Chicken. They recruited mayoral candidates, gave money where they saw fit, and organized the business communities' efforts to recruit for the city and shape growth. If Watauga still exists, it is far less powerful, a shadow of its former self, because all of the city's institutions have been bought by larger out-of-Nashville firms. Now healthcare is the city's rising star, along with private prisons and music.

The Swan Ball is the highlight of the social season—even meetings to plan the event are listed in the local paper. Both of Tennessee's senators attend the neighborhood Presbyterian church, and every night there are charity balls, fundraisers, events for the homeless and those suffering from AIDS, and the like. In the last two elections, more money has been donated to campaigns from Belle Meade and its adjoining zip code than in any other area of the country.[3]

Nashville is also home to Montgomery Bell Academy, the 137-year-old, local college-preparatory boys' school where the motto is Gentleman, Scholar, Athlete. A list of alumni reads like a Who's Who of America. The portrait hanging outside the headmaster's office is of Confederate hero Sam Davis, who gave his life rather than betray his friends. On the wall of the school's weight room, a quote from JFK reads, "From those to whom much is given, much is required" (a paraphrase of Luke 12:48). Around there, the words *lady* and *gentleman* still mean something. These kids are raised not only to be one, but to respect them on their way up. They stand up when an adult enters the room, forcing their eyes to meet yours and "yes, sir" and "yes, ma'am" are spoken with regularity and sincerity in that somewhat-Virginian accent that is characteristically Nashvillian.

The campus looks a lot like a small Ivy League college crawling with clean-cut kids wearing khakis and button-downs. Athletes on game day will often wear a tie. And while the academics may be rigorous—the kids work their tails off—the athletic teams are perennial powerhouses and the debate team has a national reputation. The weight room looks like a downtown athletic club, and the track is covered with a red padded surface to decrease shin splints and other constant-impact injuries. Kids in after-school programs wear matching red-and-black sweats, and when traveling across campus they march in double time like polished platoons.

Despite its upscale presentation, the parking lot is relatively down-to-earth. While there is the occasional Porsche, Cadillac Escalade and new-model Mercedes, there are far more Toyota Forerunners, Ford and Chevrolet trucks, older Volvos, and passed-down midsize Buicks and Oldsmobiles.

Headmaster Bradford Gioia says they attempt "to imbue the students with a sense of humility . . . so they don't get too carried away with their own accomplishments and that integrity and true civility are the highest virtues."[4] As a result, MBA produces gentlemen with manners, who strive to lead. Gentlemen like Bill Frist.

---

THE FRIST FAMILY arrived in America carrying Scottish and German genes sometime after 1600. Many arrived on ships such as the *Saint Andrew Galley* and the *Glasgow* via Rotterdam. Oral family legend holds that two brothers jumped ship in port of the Chesapeake Bay, but if so, records of their passage would obviously not exist. William Penn, after having been given Delaware in 1682, divided the land into townships to be occupied by one hundred families giving the areas its name—the Hundreds. The Frist family grew out of the Hundreds of Delaware and would later be one of the original fifty-three families that founded Chattanooga. The patriotism that Bill Frist feels in serving his country must have originated from ancestors that lived over two hundred years ago, because family records show that two descendants fought in the Revolutionary War; one was found missing in action in 1776, while the other was discharged in 1781.

Bill Frist's father, Thomas Fearn Frist, was born in Mississippi in 1910, and he is the quintessential American success story. He is also the undisputed primary influence in the life of Bill Frist, followed closely by Bill's mother. Thomas's father, Jacob "Jake" Frist, was the stationmaster in Meridian, Mississippi, and died when his son Tommy was just eight years old. A woman and her young son were crossing the railroad tracks when someone flipped the wrong switch, sending a train on a collision course with the mother and her young son. Paralyzed with fear at the sight of an oncoming train, the woman and her son froze, seconds from death. Jake Frist sprinted across the tracks, knocked them to safety, heroically saving the pair while taking the blow himself. He would die five years later of injuries sustained in that event. For his valor, Jake Frist was awarded the Andrew Carnegie Medal of Bravery from the railroad and the Medal of Honor by President Woodrow Wilson in 1915 through the Interstate Commerce Commission. In his March 26, 1915, letter, thanking the ICC, Jake Frist wrote, "I shall hand them down to my children and hope my boys do the same thing when they grow to be men. . . . I think the duty of every man, when women and children are in danger of being killed, is to try to save them."[5] Tommy felt the loss of his father deeply and looked to his older brother Chet as a surrogate father.

Widowed, Jennie Jones Frist opened their house to boarders to support herself, her four children and the mortgages Jake Frist had left. One such boarder was Dr. S. H. Hairston, a surgeon. Dr. Hairston employed then twelve-year-old Tommy as an orderly at the town hospital, inspiring young Tommy to consider a career in medicine. In between mowing lawns, Tommy worked in the hospital, where he swept the wards, made beds, gave enemas, and emptied bedpans. Tommy worked for Dr. Hairston every year during the summer, long before rules governed who did what in a hospital environment. Gaining both experience and Dr. Hairston's trust, Tommy soon began sewing wounds and helping in the operating room. Seeing Tommy's interest, Dr. Hairston furthered the boy's practical education by showing him the business end of medicine. He sent him to collect accounts "door to door, face to face." At the age of sixteen, Tommy Frist followed his older brother Chet, then a senior, to Southwestern University (now Rhodes College) at Memphis and later the University of Mississippi.[6] Tommy Frist had skipped a couple of grades when he was younger so while he was four years younger, than his classmates, he was only two grades behind his brother.

Due to the early death of his father and his mother's exhausting task of attempting to make ends meet, Tommy worked his way through both schools. At Ole Miss, he piloted a mule-driven wagon and carted students and their trunks from the train station in Oxford to their dorms. Following college, he attended Vanderbilt Medical School, where the young entrepreneur once again supported himself, this time through publishing football schedules on desk blotters and earning a profit through the sale of advertising for local shops. Friends tell the story that Tommy sold his first advertisement to a local Chevrolet dealership. When the dealer paid him for the ad, he swore he'd never drive anything but a Chevrolet—and he never did. He also laundered hospital uniforms, installed and filled vending machines, announced in the local gym via a telephone the "away" athletic events, and ran a boarding house called Pauper's Paradise.[7] He was described as a straight arrow: He didn't smoke, drink, or use the Lord's name in vain. He wrote his mother nearly every day and sent her a portion of everything he made. Every month, this package home totaled over thirty dollars—this during the Depression. By the time he graduated from the university, his entrepreneurial endeavors had grown so large that he had seventeen people working for him.

Following Vanderbilt, he traveled to the University of Iowa for his advanced surgical training. While there, he suffered a collapsed lung forcing him to recuperate in Meridian, Mississippi, and Florida. Upon recovery he returned to Iowa, but his money ran out so he returned to Nashville in 1933 where he soon met Dorothy Harrison Cate, an elementary schoolteacher. Dorothy was born in Hopkinsville, Kentucky, in 1910 and graduated from both the George Peabody School for Teachers in 1932 and Ward Belmont Finishing School for Girls. She introduced him to her brother, internist Dr. William Robert Cate. Both relationships turned out to be winners because he entered practice with William Robert and married Dorothy in 1936. The couple married in Wightman Chapel at Scarritt College in Nashville with the Reverend John Chester ("Chet") Frist performing the ceremony.

With business slowly picking up, Tommy Frist once again supported his family's income with that entrepreneurial spirit that would radically change the family's fortune in the years ahead. Former Tennessee governor Winfield Dunn said Frist's early medical career included after-hours physical examinations at a dollar per person for the Interstate Insurance Company, work at the state penitentiary where he later started a hospital to treat inmates with tuberculosis, and an occasional private patient.[8]

Being the local neighborhood doctor, he was often absent from home seven nights a week, leaving much of the child rearing up to his wife. Bill's mother was one of fourteen children raised at Cate's Mill in Hopkinsville, Kentucky. Bill described her as selfless, never satisfied unless she was helping others, and often working behind the scenes. She was outspoken, vigorous, and enjoyed intellectual daring. She read constantly, and encouraged the same of her children, planting the seeds of inquisitive habits. She seemed at odds with many of the "hidebound" opinions of her acquaintances and often provoked them with her well-thought-out and well-spoken views. (The influence of her love for reading was so deep and engrained into her children that upon graduation from Princeton, Bill Frist would establish a book fund in perpetuity in her name.) As mother of five and surrogate mother to half the neighborhood, she never tired of welcoming kids for a meal, a sleepover, or just a chat. Even construction workers around the house were treated to a daily bucket of fried chicken at lunchtime. She was always busy, and she loved providing the attention and care that demanded of her. Bill admits, "She was always there, and we, of course, took her for granted."[9] While her political views might have been a bit more liberal than Dr. Frist, her support for her children was unquestionable. Just prior to Election Day in 1994, when her son Bill was first running for senator, Dorothy Frist said to Karl VanDevender, "Karl, I've been a lifelong Democrat. I've never voted for a Republican, but I'm about to."[10]

Their first two children were born in Nashville—Thomas Fearn Frist Jr. in August 1938, and Dorothy Cate Frist in 1941. When World War II arrived, Dr. Frist served in the United States Air Force from 1942–1946 as a major in the Medical Corps, later assuming the position of medical chief of staff at Maxwell Field in Alabama. Their third child, Robert "Bobby" Armistead Frist, was born in Montgomery, Alabama, in 1942.

After the war, the Frist family returned to Nashville where Mary Louise Frist was born in 1946. Living first on Sterling Road, then on Fairfax Avenue, they eventually moved in 1951 to 703 Bowling Avenue where they would live the remainder of their lives. The Frist home on

Bowling Avenue sits just down the street from Elmington Park and West End High School. Local Civil War historians point out that the ground on which Bill Frist grew up (Bowling Avenue) may very well have been trod by soldiers during the bloody Battle of Nashville.[11] Dr. Frist stretched well beyond his means to buy the Bowling house because he hoped it would serve as a haven during their children's childhood and as a retreat as they grew older. Previous publications have mistakenly reported that Bill Frist grew up as a member of the Belle Meade elite, but Bowling Avenue was not "Belle Meade." It's West End mixed with a little Green Hills—characterized at the time by hard-working middle-class folks chasing the American dream.

Dr. Frist was a devoted family man who made it home for dinner most every night before venturing out again with his black bag to make his rounds at the hospital. He was home late and away early—a picture and an ethic engrained in the minds of his children. Dinnertime conversation was remembered as a sharing, both of the events of his day and theirs. Topics also revolved around private enterprise: how to best serve people, patient care, the entrepreneurial spirit, the role of private enterprise, the power of a visionary idea, and the American dream.[12] Dr. Frist used the dinner table to water the roots of his children's dreams, enabling them to one day sprout and become oaks. Bill Frist's earliest memories are of his father leaving the house after dinner carrying a worn doctor's bag, loading into an old Chevrolet (never new), and driving off into the night for his rounds at the hospital, returning long after the kids had gone to bed.

One evening at dinner in 1951, Dorothy announced with a smile that she had bad news for him. At forty-one, she said she was expecting another child. This was big news to Dr. Frist, who dropped his knife onto the butter dish, sending it flipping upward to the ceiling where it left a grease smear "to the utter delight of the children." The baby of the family, William Harrison Frist was born February 22, 1952—the same birthday as George Washington.[13] Based upon the observation that his parents were older, as were his brothers and sisters, friend and colleague John Morris says with a smile, "Bill was an 'oops.'"[14]

Throughout his career, Dr. Frist developed a thriving and highly respected medical practice. The Frist Clinic was the first in Tennessee to offer both an EKG and new medicine called "insulin" for diabetics. People from all over flocked to his door, and soon Dr. Frist was serving people throughout middle Tennessee. In the early years of his career, recognizing the need of both citizens and doctors for access to better medical facilities, he routinely traveled to smaller, rural regions away from home, furthering his reputation as a warm and caring physician and heart specialist.

People who had only met Dr. Frist once often marveled at his ability to remember not only their name but their spouse's and children's names as well. Those who knew him best knew it was a skill he had acquired over time and something at which he constantly worked. To aid his memory, Dr. Frist carried a small black notebook in his shirt pocket. When he met someone new, he'd write down their name, his notes regarding the specifics of their conversation, and include a picture if he had one and any comments he had. It was not unusual for Dr. Frist to use the pages and notes in that book to refresh his memory sometimes two to three years from the first conversation. Several contemporaries of Dr. Frist remember, "If he was real impressed with you, he'd put stars next to your name. As a result, very few people didn't feel as though they had a real special relationship with Dr. Tommy. That was the magic of the man." While friends are quick to praise Dr. Tommy, they are vehement in their praise of Dorothy Frist, "She was the power behind the throne."[15]

In the developing years at HCA, Dr. Frist hung eight-by-ten-inch pictures of his executive team and board members across the wall in his office. On the back of the pictures, he'd write their spouse's and children's names along with their interests and the highlights of previous conversations. Before he phoned any of those people, he'd pull their photo off the wall and refresh his memory. While he talked he'd study the picture and make more notes.

Alongside his medical career, Dr. Frist joined in founding the Cumberland Heights Foundation for the rehabilitation of alcoholics, the Medical Benevolent Association to help medical missionaries deliver healthcare around the world, and the Park Manor Presbyterian Apartments for the elderly in Nashville.

In 1960, Dr. Frist founded Parkview Hospital and Park Vista Nursing Home in Nashville where he would serve as chief executive. In 1968, this commitment to both Nashville and Middle Tennessee, along with an entrepreneurial spirit, the business acumen of his oldest son, Tommy Jr., and the financial backing of friend and patient Jack Massey (founder of Kentucky Fried Chicken), would lead to the development of Hospital Corporation of America. (When Dr. Frist first came to Nashville, he received his first stethoscope from Massey, then chairman of the board of the largest hospital in Nashville.)

The concept of investor-owned hospitals funded by marketplace capital to build new facilities and modernize outdated facilities had not been invented. As a result, no bank would loan them the money. So Dr. Frist, Tommy Jr., Jack Massey, and sixty-two friends put up their personal assets (including the house at 703 Bowling) to start the facility. The initial HCA facility was Parkview Hospital, and while father Dr. Tommy concentrated his attention on patient care and quality assurance, son Tommy Jr. focused his resources on marketing, finance, and business development. Because Parkview had been the initial facility of the HCA empire, folks naturally thought the idea had been his. They were wrong. The stimulus to apply successful fast-food chain principles to hospital development came from Tommy Jr.

Having completed a year of surgical training at Vanderbilt, Tommy Jr. had been called into the Air Force during the Vietnam War and was serving as a flight surgeon at Warner Robbins Air Force Base in Macon, Georgia. In the scarce down time of his intern schedule, he began wondering how hospitals could act autonomously in what until then had been a cottage industry. As the idea developed, he began asking how market capital and public financing might be used to build new, clean, well-equipped and state-of-the art facilities. But he didn't stop there. He also asked how those same facilities might join together for mass purchasing, creating better economies of scale.

Initially, no one took him seriously. Not even his dad, who tried to talk his son out of his far-fetched scheme. So, being an entrepreneur himself and quite literally a chip off the old block, he approached Jack Massey who immediately took to the idea. He believed in the idea so strongly that he wrote Tommy Jr. a now-famous letter that forced young Tommy to decide forever between two very different paths: "Chicken, beef or medicine. Make your decision soon."[16] Given Jack's enthusiasm and Tommy's argument that he wanted to make healthcare more accessible, especially in the rural communities, it didn't take Dr. Frist long to give up his idea that his son would follow him in medicine. He packed his black bag and jumped in with both feet, wanting to make certain that providing high-quality, humanitarian care would become and remain the guiding ethos of HCA. To his credit, it did. The men met in April 1968 at the Augusta National Golf Course during the Masters Tournament for two days of planning. When they emerged after two secluded days, they carried with them the mission statement and business plan of HCA.

Revolutionizing the way both for-profit and not-for-profit hospitals operated, HCA grew rapidly through explosive growth and maintained a twenty-year reign as the largest and most-productive hospital chain in the country. In 1970, HCA was listed on the New York Stock Exchange and became the first exchange corporation in history to achieve one billion dollars in sales in the first ten years of operation, growing to 460 hospitals with 69,000 beds around the world. In a speech made that same year, Tommy Frist said, "It's not mortar and brick that makes a hospital. It is the warmth, compassion and the attitude of good employees that leads to quality care."[17] In 1989, a leveraged buyout forced the sale at 5.5 billion dollars. Like a lot of Nashville families, the Frist family acquired their prosperity the old-fashioned way: they chased the American dream and earned it.

Patients and employees alike remember Dr. Tommy, in his seventies, nearing the height of his and HCA's rise to the top, routinely eating lunch in the employee cafeteria. What made it more amazing was the fact that he knew each and every employee by name. At the age of seventy-eight, he continued to put in ten-hour days as the ceremonial figurehead of HCA. Nothing slowed him: not the fractured neck that occurred in a car wreck a decade before, not the colon cancer five years later, and not the heart attack or stroke. He regularly accepted speaking engagements and with his thinning reddish-white hair, he bespoke trustworthiness, sincerity, and hope.

Despite the success that would come in later years, the experiences of those early times embedded in him a disposition which he carried into both his business and professional life. Bill Frist said that medicine offered his father the two things he needed most—the opportunity to provide for his family and to "validate the selfless generosity that lay behind his father's impulsive sacrifice. Dad fell absolutely in love with the notion of family. And he became a creature so rare I doubt we'll see his likes again—an honestly humble physician."[18]

For fifty-five years as a traveling doctor, "Dr. Tommy," as his patients affectionately called him, developed a practice that that included Minnie Pearl and eight governors of Tennessee. His influence upon his own boys is evident: each holds a medical degree. Bill remembers, "I'm not sure whether Dad or Mother hoped that all their sons would become doctors, although I'm pretty sure they did not expect us to do so. I know they never asked any of us to study medicine."[19] They may have never asked, but they set the bar rather high. Tommy earned a medical degree and then became what Bill calls a "super administrator," Bobby became a well-established heart surgeon, cousin Johnny became a popular and successful plastic surgeon, and Bill entered transplantation.

Dr. Karl VanDevender—the man handpicked by Dr. Tommy Frist to replace him at the Frist Clinic—states, "Dr. Tommy was like Erasmus of Rotterdam in the fifteenth century. Erasmus was the power behind many thrones. He gave council to five different kings at once, many of whom were at war with each other. Dr. Tommy was like that—they [governors and celebrities alike] all sought his counsel."[20]

Bill Frist swears his parents never said an unkind word to him, backing him up no matter what he did. In medical school, they would later write letters that encouraged him, praised him, and reminded him that he could excel at most anything. As a result, he began signing up for classes that weren't required or that he'd avoided, taking on a project he previously thought he might not pull off, and making choices that once frightened him. This enabled him to take risks that he wouldn't have otherwise, because in the back of his mind, he knew that even in the face of failure, he always had his parents. He is quick to point out that this kind of love is what made his background privileged.

Because of his father's influence and soft-spoken bedside manner, Bill would grow to detest the domineering, dismissive doctors with strong egos, longing for a sense of control. For Bill, a doctor was someone who traveled about at all hours of the night, carrying his black bag, sitting by bedsides, listening, and treating people as equals.

The influence of Dr. Frist extended from the Governor's Mansion to the Grand Ole Opry to the corner gas station. Gordan Inman, whose father had been a barber in Nashville for forty-five years, was a young boy working for his brother at the Shell gas station at the corner of West End and Natchez Trace. As an admitted "grease monkey," he was responsible for Frist's two Chevrolet vehicles. From pumping the gas, to changing the oil, to replacing batteries, tires, and windshield wipers, Gordon became responsible for maintaining the Frist's cars. Several mornings a week at 5:30 a.m., Dr. Frist would pull into the gas station where Gordon, a young teenager, would greet him and fill up his car. It didn't take Dr. Frist long to notice young Gordon.

In the summer of 1956, following Gordon's graduation from high school, Dr. Frist's secretary called Gordon and told him Dr. Frist wanted to see him in his office. Gordon immediately thought, *Oh no, what'd I do? Leave the gas cap off? Dipstick out? Oil plug out of his tank?* Gordon arrived at his office wearing his greasy uniform with his name printed on his shirt.

"Yes sir, Dr. Frist."

"Gordon, I've watched you grow up. You've always taken good care of us and our cars and you've got a great work ethic for a young man." Gordon listened trying to figure out where this was leading. "I'd like to send you to college and then med school. I think you'd make a great doctor."

"Dr. Frist I'm really honored, but I don't want to go to medical school and I don't want to be a doctor. I want to make a lot of money."

Dr. Frist didn't give up on Gordon and continued to foster the relationship. As his medical practice flourished, Dr. Frist began buying and selling real estate. On Sunday afternoons, he'd drive by the gas station, pick up Gordon and the two would drive around Nashville and surrounding counties while Dr. Frist told Gordon how to buy and sell real estate.

Gordon remembers, "He had a foresight that was unbelievable. One Sunday afternoon, he took me up to a hill outside of town to show me three hundred to four hundred acres that he owned. He asked me, 'Gordon, you like that piece of property?' I said, 'Yes sir, Dr. Frist, it's real nice.' Dr. Frist told me, 'Well I own that; just wanted to see if you like it, because I own it.' Today, one of the largest shopping malls in Tennessee sits on that property."

Sometime in early 1968, Dr. Frist stopped by the station and said, "Gordon I want to tell you about something. Jack Massey, Tommy Jr., and I, along with some other friends, are going to start this little company. We're going to buy Parkview Hospital, and you need to invest in it with us. You need to put in ten thousand dollars." Gordon remembers, "I could see Parkview Hospital from my gas station. I'd look across Centennial Park and there it was so I could relate to what he was talking about, but at the time I didn't have ten thousand dollars. Sure wish I did. It'd be worth a good bit more today. Dr. Frist had a very strong entrepreneurial sense. He was half doctor, half entrepreneur and I loved the Frist family very much. Mrs. Frist was one of the most giving people I've ever met. At least two to three times a month, she'd send someone to the station and tell me to fill up their tank, change their oil, put on a new set of tires, or change the battery, and then put the charge on her house account. She'd never let them pay her for it. That happened routinely."[21]

Following two years fighting in Korea, Gordon returned home in his twenties and bought the gas station from his brother. After twenty-two years working as a gas station attendant and later, manager and owner, he sold the station to his cousin in 1975, got his real estate license, and opened an office.

Gordon grew the real estate office through the early eighties, and in the late eighties began raising funds to start a private bank with a few other friends. The group was attempting to raise 6.5 million dollars but when they could only come up with 3.5 million dollars, Gordon mortgaged and leveraged everything he owned to put every penny he had—three million dollars—into the bank.

Within a decade, the bank grew into the most profitable privately-owned bank in the United States and in May of 2004, merged with Fifth-Third for the highest multiple stock swap ever paid for a private bank—somewhere around 314 million dollars. Today, Gordon lives in a home in Franklin, Tennessee, along the Harpeth River and to his credit, he still owns and can still wear that Shell station shirt with his name printed on it.

# 3

WHILE A STUDENT at Woodmont Grammar School, Bill Frist operated on his first patient at the age of seven. Knowing Bill's dad was a doctor, neighbor Jimmy Shapiro brought over his injured dog, Scratchy. Scratchy's neck had a deep gash in it— ugly, open, three inches and oozing—and the dog was whimpering and in a good bit of pain. Bill ran into the family den where his father kept his black bag, dug around and pulled out a small, flat jar with a screw-top lid. Inside, the jar held a brown powder, the nature of which to this day is still a mystery. Like it was something he did every day, he confidently sprinkled the dog's neck, knowingly patted him on the head, and then sent him and Jimmy home. The next afternoon, Jimmy reappeared with a miraculously revived Scratchy. When the young Dr. Frist examined the dog, the wound had almost healed. Bill's first thought was, *How'd I do that?* Jimmy, on the other hand, was certain that Bill was a certifiable genius. Bill remembers, "I knew I was no such thing. Mother Nature had done all the work. But the wound looked good, the dog was cured, and Jimmy was thankful. I will always remember the look on Jimmy's face. It was one of the reasons

I went into medicine. Every time I remembered that look, I knew how my father felt, knew why he became a doctor. I wanted to feel that way, too. I wanted to be a doctor, too to be just like my dad."[1] Bill was not alone, childhood friend John Gibson remembers, "I also became a doctor because of Dr. Frist."[2]

The big, white house on Bowling where time stood still and the imaginary was possible had become an enchanted kingdom for Bill and his siblings. There were horses, a pool, and an immense backyard. In truth, it was the house on the block where all the neighborhood kids would come to play. With such a warm and enchanting home environment, Bill hated kindergarten. Seeing his displeasure, his mother pulled him out and took him home.

It was his mother that protected his sense of self-worth, spoiled him even, but Bill learned to be thankful and never to apologize for that. "If Woodmont Grammar School conducted a paper drive, she motored me about afternoon after afternoon, making sure I collected more papers than anyone else. She helped me sell our raffle tickets to her friends, always buying a few extra herself to give away. When I innocently misled my second grade teacher about my ability to play the banjo in the upcoming talent show, Mom not only bought me my first banjo, but also taught me to play "Home on the Range" respectfully enough to get through the show. She wanted me never to know humiliation, never to suffer defeat, never to feel self-doubt. She felt that if she could protect me in that way, I would grow up confident and eventually become independent, strong-willed, *a Frist*. . . . Not surprisingly, with the family emphasis on self-worth, I longed to be first in everything, to be king of the hill, the grammar school *capo di capo*. I imagine I was quite insufferable."[3]

For years, Bill had flown with his brother Tommy, obtaining his pilot's license before his driver's license and eventually soloing himself at the age of sixteen. Bill was on top of the world. Then came the accident.

Bill was riding his older brother Bobby's Vespa motor scooter when the car in front of him stopped. Bill had taken his eyes off the car to wave to a neighbor. He slammed into the rear of the car and flew through the rear windshield, slicing himself to pieces and coming to rest atop the groceries. Had he not been wearing a helmet and had a doctor not seen the accident, chances are quite good that Bill Frist would have bled to death. He shattered his kneecap, which was surgically removed—ending any thoughts of athletic heroism—suffered a concussion, multiple facial and extremity fractures, and a fourteen-inch leg laceration. "On a magic carpet ride until then, I suddenly found out I was mortal. The brush with death punctured my sense of self-importance."[4] Bill's priorities changed; things that were once important now seemed superficial and he began to question many of his prior achievements. John Gibson went to see him once in the hospital, which was enough. "On the ride home," Gibson said, "I told my mom that I wanted to sell my motorcycle. We all did."[5]

The accident did not stop him from wanting to be successful and maybe more importantly, not wanting to fail. "Local rich kids, scions of socially prominent families, have few crosses to bear in life, but one of them is that they can never fail, not really, not the way others can."[6] To channel his physical activity, Bill took up karate and eventually advanced to a brown belt. At Montgomery Bell Academy, Bill was elected president of his class five out of six years. He was editor of the yearbook, played football and was voted most likely to succeed during his senior year. He was selected as a member of Totomoi—the elite honor society, was active in the Fellowship of Christian Athletes, the Forensic Club, the Service Club, and the Photography Club. He won the math medal, was named Outstanding Sophomore and Junior Awards, received a National Merit Letter of Commendation, was elected to the National Honor Society his junior and senior year. His nicknames there were "Mr. President," "Precious," "Wilbur," "Willie Joe," "Carrots," and under his school picture in the yearbook, he was quoted as saying "Can I borrow your motor?" and "But I don't like to rest."

One of his teachers remembered him as a "bright, good-hearted kid with a touch of the devil in him." In the introduction to his senior yearbook, he wrote:

> In three weeks I graduate. I've eagerly awaited commencement since I first entered MBA. But now I have mixed emotions. "I went to MBA," instead of "I go to MBA." Somehow it doesn't sound right. My attitudes have changed. I have changed. Sometimes it scares me to think how much I've changed. In three weeks I will be out of high school; in three months, in college. I used to wonder if I would not be better prepared for college life, independent as it is, if I had been allowed to make more of my own decisions while at MBA—athletics or not, long hair or short. You know, my friends at other schools are never reminded to get their hair cut. But now it strikes me that MBA is not like other schools; it doesn't want to be. MBA is on a hill. Its ideals are to produce the combined gentleman, scholar, athlete. And it does just that. MBA is a preparatory school. It directs us through some of the most formative years of our lives. Some people say it molds us. Maybe. But nevertheless, we leave MBA better-equipped to cope with the decisions of tomorrow. And to think, some of us complain because we can't wear jeans to school. MBA is on a hill."[7]

John Eason remembers: "MBA had three classes: the honors class, the middle class and the last class. Billy was always in the honors class and I wasn't."[8] Not surprisingly and given his many achievements, Bill was voted, Most Likely to Succeed by his classmates.

It is also during this time that he began dating Katie, a cheerleader at the nearby girls' school. Katie, too, desired a career in medicine. When Bill expressed his desire to attend Princeton, Katie chose Hollins. The two planned to delay getting married until after medical school. Everything had a place and seemed to be in its place, which, at the time, seemed fine.

Princeton was not what the family had anticipated, and he didn't know how to tell his dad he wasn't planning to attend Vanderbilt. Looking for help, he sought Tommy's advice, "his guiding light in matters Fristian,"[9] and Tommy told him to explore the world; go it alone. Bill chose Princeton primarily because he wanted to get out of Nashville and go someplace where the name Frist might as well have been Smith, to find out once and for all if he could succeed on his own merits and not those passed down to him.

After their high school graduation, Bill suggested to John Gibson, "Let's drive out west. Go to California." John knew his parents would never let him go if it were his idea, "but they saw Billy as different. They saw him as responsible and because it was his idea, they let us go." The two drove Bill's Chevrolet Chevelle 396 SS—his first car which his parents had given him for his eighteenth birthday-all the way to California and back. They walked to the bottom of the Grand Canyon, stayed with a friend in Palo Alto, and drove the Pacific coastline in California. The two were gone three and a half weeks, "just 'cause Billy thought it was a good idea."[10]

Bill would later write that in the high school years following his motor scooter accident, he began to build what he called *the "Great Wall"* between himself and his peers—an emotional barrier between himself and those who would wish to become close. Careful to pick his friends, he said he built, brick by emotional brick, a wall that kept him from emotionally engaging his peers. Other than Katie and a few close friends, few people were able to scale the wall. This does not suggest that he was mistrusting of others; it simply means that he was careful in whom he chose to trust.

At Princeton, he discovered his Great Wall was portable. Except for Katie, he found himself admittedly lonely in the barricade he had built. Letters from home cheered him up, but in that first year he threw himself into his studies, student government and extracurricular life. The busier he remained, the more in control he felt and the more he liked himself. He became resident advisor in the dorms, ran the Big Brother program, and was elected president of the Princeton Flying Club. Sometime later he would worry that he had spread himself too thin, "cheating himself of a more emotionally fulfilling college career. At the time, only the ticking off of accomplishments seemed to matter."[11]

With few friends, a girlfriend in Virginia, and his family in Nashville, Bill's first year at Princeton was a lonely one. His mother realized this and softened the distance by sending both frequent letters and almost monthly "care packages" filled with Goo-goo Clusters and sometimes a Smithfield ham. His friends remember anticipating Bill's mail as much as their own.

Gilchrist "Gick" Berg met Bill their freshman year at Princeton. Gick's girlfriend also attended Hollins, so he and Bill often flew to Virginia—about a two-and-a-half-hour flight—in the plane owned by the Princeton Flying Club. Remembering his ability as a pilot, Gick states, "I never doubted him. He inspired total confidence."[12]

At nineteen, Bill told Gick that he wanted to write a book. "Actually, several," Berg says, "which stuck with me at the time because I was struggling so much with just keeping my head above water."[13] Then before spring break, Bill told Gick that he was going to go to a camp where he could learn to fly a plane aerobatically. And he did.

Later that year, Bill was returning to his dorm from class late one night, when three men attempted to mug him. The muggers however, didn't anticipate the brown belt in karate held by their prey. The student paper claimed that the unnamed student kept them at bay until the police arrived. Gick states, "I read about it in the school paper and it didn't surprise me. I knew it was him. He was always practicing his forms. We'd be standing in the line at the movies and there was Bill, doing his karate."[14]

During his first year at Princeton, Gick told Bill about a professor named Uwe Reinhardt who taught economics. Reinhardt is, in fact, a world-renowned economics professor who taught, among other things, classes in healthcare policy. Gick remembers: "My fifteen seconds of fame are going to be that I introduced Bill to Reinhardt. I told him that Reinhardt was a wonderful, fabulous guy with a health care focus. For all I know, Bill may have been going the health care route and would have found Uwe anyway, but he hadn't found him yet. So, I'd like to think I had something to do with steering him toward public policy, but I doubt it, Bill was always thinking ahead."[15] Years later, when asked about Bill Frist's entrance into politics, Reinhardt would remark that, "Bill's always had such a policy brain, I was surprised he went into medicine."[16]

In his sophomore year, Bill joined Cottage Club on Prospect Street—the Princeton version of a fraternity. Former members were F. Scott Fitzgerald and Bill Bradley. "Prospect Street was like an eating club row and Cottage Club may have been one of the more Southern clubs. You joined in your sophomore year and began taking meals in your junior and senior years." On initiation night, Gick—then a junior—remembers worrying for Bill. "Bill didn't drink anything alcoholic, but during our initiation, the candidate had to stand atop this great stairwell in front of all the members like something out of *Gone with the Wind* and then drink this chalice filled with what looked like five or six beers. I knew he wouldn't do it, so I filled the thing full of ginger ale."[17]

From July to August of 1972, Bill worked as a twenty-year-old intern in the congressional office of Joe L. Evins in D.C. All summer he'd been waiting for an opportunity to thank the congressman for allowing him this opportunity and, maybe more importantly, pose the one question he had waited all summer to ask. Finally, on a hot and muggy morning, the day before his return to Princeton, he left the Georgetown basement apartment he was renting with four friends hoping that today he'd get his chance. That afternoon, it came. Joe Evins sat in a worn leather chair behind an imposing and expansive desk framed by a dark red rug. Bill stepped onto the carpet, the nervousness cracking his voice, "Excuse me, sir, if someone my age wanted to serve in the U.S. Congress someday, what advice would you give them?"

"Bill," Congressman Evins responded in a fatherly tone, "Washington is full of career politicians. If you really want to serve your country well, go do something else—and it doesn't matter exactly what you do—but do it outside Washington and do it successfully. After that twenty years of something else, come back to Washington, and use what you've learned to dedicate a part of your life to the greatest of all careers, public service."[18]

Bill returned to Princeton and split his academic schedule between two types of classes—the required pre-med classes and those in the school of public and international affairs. The seeds of the *citizen legislator* had been birthed, although it would be more than twenty years before Bill would return to D.C. to serve in public office.

By his senior year, he had been elected vice-president of his class, admitted to the Woodrow Wilson School of Public and International Affairs, and had taken his medical admissions boards, scoring well enough to gain acceptance into Harvard Medical School. During the summers he had worked for Congressman Evins in Washington and as an intern for the *Nashville Banner*, mainly writing obituaries. During his senior year, in order to provide accuracy and integrity to a paper he was finishing regarding the rights of the mentally handicapped, he checked himself into a psychiatric hospital to write about the civil rights of the patients (with the knowledge of both his professors and the administrators of the ward). He graduated with a degree in healthcare policy and, following graduation, was elected to the board of trustees of Princeton.

In the end, he came to love Princeton, and quite possibly for the first time in his life he felt as if he were in his own element. As a Woodrow Wilson scholar he was free to formalize his own study and allowed to explore issues at his own pace with all the resources of the university at his disposal.

Katie and Bill had continued to date throughout college but somewhere during that time, he became involved with a woman who had recently graduated from Princeton. She was an actress in a local theater and she, too, was dating another whom she intended to marry. He should have seen this relationship as a warning sign, but admittedly, he did not. Instead, he convinced himself that the separation and distance from Katie was the problem. "We needed to be together."[19]

But Bill had other nagging doubts. Katie had said she wanted a career after their children were grown, "a way to feel good about herself apart from the family." Bill realized that while that sounded attractive in high school, he began to realize that it was not what he hoped for his family. Away from home, the memories of his mother and her selfless devotion returned. The impact of her life on him became apparent; he idolized her. And like his father, he began to value the traditional family above all else. He believed his mother's selfless devotion to her children and husband was one of the highest goals to which a man or woman could aspire. "I imagined myself as a leader, a Ulysses out on his travels to conquer the world; I possibly wanted a Penelope back home waiting for me and managing the home I so treasured."[20]

Despite these doubts, there was something else beneath the surface that caused him to further question his relationship with Katie. In truth, he didn't know what he wanted and tradition became the convenient mask behind which he hid. He wrote her what he admits was a caddish letter, explaining his wishes for a more traditional family and how her time spent in medical school in Texas would be difficult, to say the least. He argued that he needed someone to raise his children and provide him the support his mother had provided his dad. Katie changed her plans. She moved to Boston, attended Boston College and they saw each other every weekend. "Our relationship survived."[21]

---

THE FIRST HEART Bill Frist ever saw or held belonged to a dog. During his second year at Harvard Medical, the curriculum in Dr. Barger's physiology class required the students to perform surgery on animals. For most of the students it was a highlight, because up until that time all the organs, tissues and systems had been diagrams, pictures and theories in a textbook. During one class, they had removed the dog's spleen, and at the end of the operation they sacrificed the animal by cutting out its heart. Another student removed it from the chest cavity of the dog and handed it to Bill, in whose hand it continued to beat for over a minute. "I was hooked." While the other students returned to their desks to review data, Bill could not put the heart down. He stared at it, cradled it; he was "spellbound, amazed that it could still beat outside the body." He then took a scalpel, cut into the heart's thick muscular wall and stared wide-eyed at the delicateness, "the narrow, glistening, sculptured cords that pumped over two thousand gallons of blood a day through more than one hundred thousand beats a day." Leaving the lab that afternoon, he had fallen under a spell and knew he would devote his career to the study of the heart. While his fascination was both scientific and medical, he, too, attached sentimental value to the heart—"the sanctuary of our emotions . . . I never lost my feeling of awe." [22]

Bill had always loved animals, but he realized that he could not practice medicine on humans without first mastering it on animals. He realized that without the use of animals in laboratory research, such as rats, cats, dogs and sheep, most of the miraculous surgeries performed today on the human heart would be mere theory and not practice. "People walking around today leading full, healthy lives would be dead. It was that simple. Humane societies might object, and I would agree if the issue were the humane treatment of animals. But the issue was human lives."[23]

Having come from Princeton and the department of public and international affairs, Bill felt he lacked sufficient scientific background in both knowledge and research. To curb this inadequacy, he took six months out of the regular course of study to work in the lab of a cardiac physiologist. His work would include investigating the effects of hypoxia, or low oxygen tension, on how well the heart relaxes after each squeezing action. He lived in the lab around the clock, taking out the hearts of cats, dissecting each, "suspending a tiny strip of muscle that attaches the mitral valve to the inner wall of the cat heart, and recording the effects of various medicines I added to the bath surrounding the muscle." For the first time in his life he was making original discoveries, performing science that had never before been performed in the history of man.

Watching that strip of muscle beat inside that chemical bath for hour after hour in the basement of that hospital, he began to believe that his project was truly a grand enterprise and that he was on the edge of some grand truth. But his experiment came to an abrupt halt when he lost his supply of cats. With only six weeks remaining before he was to resume his clinical rotations, he began visiting various animal shelters in the Boston suburbs, "collecting cats, taking them home, treating them as pets for a few days, them carting them off to the lab to die in the interest of science.

And medicine. And healthcare. And treatment of disease. And my project. It was of course, a heinous and dishonest thing to do, and I was totally schizoid about the entire matter. By day I was little Billy Frist, the boy who lived on Bowling Avenue in Nashville and had decided to become a doctor because of his gentle father and a dog named Scratchy. By night, I was Dr. William Harrison Frist, future cardiothoracic surgeon, who was not going to let a few sentiments about cute, furry little creatures stand in the way of his career. In short, I was going a little crazy."[24]

Critics have noted that the concept of the "Great Wall" and Bill's work with cats as disturbing flaws in his character. In truth, if they are honest—as Bill Frist has been—every leader at some point erects some type of barrier between himself and those who would throw fiery darts. It is the nature of leadership to develop tough skin. And while the work with cats seems ghoulish, it is arguable that time in the lab formed the critical process that became the bedrock of his later surgical career. In short, it was instrumental in making him the doctor he would later become and more than one hundred fifty heart and heart/lung transplant recipients would agree. (For those still worried about Bill's thinking regarding animals, in June of 2001, having been made aware of the illegal poaching of some forty thousand black bears each year in Tennessee and Kentucky, Bill joined Senator Mitch McConnell in introducing the Bear Protection Act.)

Amidst the personal turmoil in his relationship with Katie, Bill also found himself contending with an animal he could not tame—medical school. No matter how many hours he studied, he knew he could never digest the mountains of facts and information, all regarded as essential. If he didn't memorize everything in every book, he feared, he might not become a good doctor, might not have the information needed to take care of patients. He remembers that he gamely tried to master it all, but that became impossible. From the laboratory exercises to the introductory clinical rotations to the independent studies, "piled on in a conspicuous attempt to guarantee that you don't have time to do things right, that you have to think on your feet, that you have to function well in ever more dire situations when you're ever more tired. It is intentionally rigorous, intentionally threatening, and intentionally destructive to your ego and your self-esteem."[25]

Bill Frist arrived at Harvard Medical School "starry eyed," amazed at the ancient and tradition-laden halls. He naively believed they took the best of the crop, poured them into a certain type of mold and produced the best doctors in the country. But somewhere in the middle of that tradition and mystique, the starry eyes were replaced by glassy ones staring out of a body exhausted from years with no sleep and high anxiety. He began to drink coffee by the pot, doubt every opinion he ever had, and question notions about himself that had once kept him going. He soon realized "that medical school was in the business of stripping human beings of everything but the raw, almost insane, ambition that you must have simply to get through. That may be good training for long-distance runners, but I'm not sure it makes for great physicians." If a good doctor was to respond to his patients with compassion and understanding, Bill Frist did not experience that training in medical school. He later wrote that his diary in those years was filled *not* with high ideals and high aspirations, but rather the "nutty calculations" of how much time he could afford to spend studying or working in the lab versus time to spend sleeping, exercising or eating. "They were the worries of a young man who had no time to think, who had lost sight of the big picture, who could only concentrate on small things."[26]

During his second year at Harvard, Bill published his first scholarly article based on research he had performed at Princeton. Working with several other researchers, he evaluated the efficiency of a VD hotline in New Jersey County. He and his colleagues determined that the costs per call were a bit high but that the presence of the hotline had moved the principal source of VD treatment from the emergency rooms to clinics. While seemingly insignificant on the surface, the study reveals that even at a young age, Bill Frist was already considering the needs of patients balanced with the public policy aspects of cost and benefit.

Somewhere in his first year at Harvard, Bill and the Princeton woman parted ways. Now, he had developed a close friendship with a fellow medical student who was liberal and Jewish. She tried to scale his "Great Wall" but he added more bricks, knowing that the pressures of medical school and the strain in his relationship with Katie only threatened its very structure. He knew something was wrong in his relationship with Katie, but he was unwilling to admit that it was them.

Bill Frist may have thought he was going crazy, but it is far more likely that, unbeknownst to himself, he was laying the foundation that he would build upon in the years ahead. If he thought life was difficult and rigorous at Harvard, he'd soon discover it waned in comparison to the schedule kept at Mass General. At Harvard, he had spent most of his entire third year in the cardiac physiology laboratory learning the skills of the scientific method: hypothesis and testing, the compilation of accurate and complete data, the formulation of specific questions.

Graduating Harvard with honors, he applied to Massachusetts General—the most sought-after general-surgery residency program in the country. Annually, Mass General selected candidates from the best medical schools in the country to fill twelve slots in their five-year surgical rotation. Beginning with a written exam, followed by a two-part oral exam in front of two different boards comprised of six surgeons each, Mass General selected from the pick of the litter, the best of the best, and Bill was accepted.

With little warning, the residents were thrown into the cauldron and placed on a "seven out of fourteen" call schedule. Being on call every other night, meant that every other day, he'd make rounds at 6 a.m., work all day, serve on-call duty that night, immediately roll into rounds and work all the next day making it home sometime after seven or eight in the evening. A night slept at home was always followed by a night in the hospital seeing patients and forcing enough caffeine into the system to pry the eyelids open. To say it was rigorous is an understatement. It was beyond boot camp. The regimen of the work schedule plus sleep deprivation produced doctors who could think on their feet, focus when tired and perform under pressure. Dr. Kim Jett remembers: "We became like brothers. We hung blood, we started IVs, and we were the backbone of the hospital."[27] It worked, because today, the graduates comprise a *Who's Who* of the best surgeons in the country. But that prestige and training came with a price, and the negative effect exacted its toll with his relationship with Katie, although Bill was too tired to notice and too occupied and excited to become depressed.

One night during his first year, a seventy-year-old patient developed abdominal pains after a fairly routine chest operation. Bill was one of two interns in the surgical service team of five residents supervising the ward care of nonpaying patients. Bill performed a physical exam and ordered the standard regimen of tests: a urinalysis, blood tests, abdominal X-ray. Bill had been working for twenty-four hours, and it was now late. Compounding his exhaustion, Bill had six other patients on his watch that night, each with a different set of problems. The blood and urine tests returned "normal" so Bill called radiology for the X-ray report and interpretation. Also normal. So, Bill did not look at the abdominal picture himself—a mistake.

The night passed, morning came and the team began making rounds at 5 a.m. The chief resident, seven years ahead of Bill asked about the X-ray. Bill, who had seen night come twice without any sleep, muttered it was normal. "Can I see it?" The chief resident looked at the film and there, plain as day, was a pocket of free air in the abdominal cavity—Bill knew immediately what it was: a perforated ulcer. The chief resident wasted no time in humiliating Bill in front of his peers. The patient lived, as did Bill, but the lesson learned was painful and poignant.

Soon after, again during rounds, a patient checked in complaining of "excruciating flank pain," typical of someone passing a kidney stone. Bill ordered a urinalysis, but the results showed only three or four red blood cells in the urine. Bill decided that it was not a significant finding and did not report it. Again, wasting no time, the chief resident lit into him, once again shaming him in front of the other junior doctors. "I remember vividly the expression on his scolding face and my own sense of shame and ignorance. That was the way we learned to be doctors . . . I have since come to despise it." Bill's time at Mass General convinced him that arrogant, demanding and insensitive surgeons create a tense, uptight atmosphere where people feel as though they are walking on eggshells, "worrying more about the temperament of the surgeon rather than the welfare of the patient. Efficiency, perfection and order were musts, but throwing instruments and humiliating others never made much sense to me."[28]

The idea of training doctors through the motivation of fear, shame, guilt and rejection never resonated with Bill. Silently, he vowed, if given the opportunity in the future, to buck the "dictatorial tradition" inherent in most hospital surgical programs and train doctors through a team approach because doctors need to learn to be quarterbacks, not tyrants. The training would be no less rigorous, no less bent on success and healing, but much more constructed around the idea of a team—and possibly a bit more sleep. His vow would be affirmed and encouraged in the very near future when he met a man named Norman Shumway and it would come to fruition later, when he started his own world-class transplant program at Vanderbilt.

But the worst was not over yet. Nearing the end of his first year, Bill would encounter a patient and situation that would cause him to question his desire to be a doctor.

Bill was working in the burn unit, supervised by a senior resident two years older, when paramedics brought in an eight-year-old girl from another city. Burns covered sixty-five percent of her body and she was having trouble breathing. The senior resident quickly admitted her while the anesthesiologist tried to get a breathing tube down her throat.

Over the next five hours, the girl stabilized. The resident left her, and the rest of the patients, in Bill's hands and returned home for some much-needed sleep. Nearing midnight, the girl took a turn for the worse, evidently having more trouble breathing. Bill ordered another chest X-ray and blood-gas analysis—standard tests to measure ventilation. The extent of her burns made it difficult to find an artery to draw blood. The X-ray returned clear but the blood-gas test told another story. The child was extremely hypoxic—her body was starving for oxygen. With her oxygen readings deathly low, Bill analyzed the situation and assumed, incorrectly, that he had drawn blood out of a vein by mistake. Certainly understandable given the condition of the patient. Right? Wrong.

Bill repeated the test four times, even using a different type of needle called a butterfly, to draw blood. Each test returned the same results. Bill read the results and shook his head—the little girl had almost no oxygen in her blood.

He didn't know what to do.

He ran each course of action through his head and checked them off one by one. She was intubated, the ventilator was working and her chest X-ray was clear; nothing seemed amiss. Yes, he'd done everything he should have. He'd left no stone unturned. Bill remembers it was hot that night. He was in charge and the halls were empty. No one else was around, and he was ultimately alone. Bill called the medical chief resident in pediatrics and picked his brain. He encouraged Bill and dismissed the problem: "Don't be alarmed. Occasionally, young kids have low blood gases."

Bill hung up the phone feeling no better. The little girl was still having trouble breathing and her blood gas was nearing zero. Again, Bill racked his brain but nothing explained his patient's situation. Over the next three hours, he took three more chest X-rays. Each was normal. Not a sign of trouble anywhere. The girl continued to worsen. Finally, at three in the morning, Bill called his chief resident at home who rushed to the hospital. An hour later, the girl's heart stopped.

The resident frantically attempted to put an arterial line in both her wrist and ankle but the burns did not allow him to find an artery. Bill assisted, the two now working in tandem, but in the back of his mind he couldn't quit asking, *What'd I do wrong? What'd I overlook? Why hadn't I called earlier?*

Tirelessly they worked to revive the child, but nothing worked. She died there, on Bill's watch, while he was in charge. "I felt as if I'd killed her."[29]

The guilt set in, occupying his every thought, and Bill wanted to quit. "I did not know then that the guilt would never leave me, that years later I would look at my own children and see the face of a little girl. That I would picture her in my dreams at night to this day. All I knew then was that I felt useless, burned out."[30]

Bill flew home for Christmas and sought his father's calming voice, his reassurance. Dr. Tommy told him stories of his own—stories with faces that came back at night. "Gently . . . lovingly," his dad encouraged him to "go back, stick it out . . . and become the best surgeon possible." Bill spoke with his brother Bobby, by then an accomplished cardiac surgeon, who reminded him "that death, nature's course, was not always within our control."[31] Despite their support, Bill could not erase her gentle face and he could not hide from his own sense of helplessness and deep guilt.

Later that week, Bill and Katie announced their plans for a wedding. The Nashville papers carried the announcement and the June date. Bill returned to school, threw himself headlong into his work and tried not to think about the fact that he didn't want to marry Katie. When he asked for a week off to get married, he was told to wait a year, that no time was available. They continued with their plans, delaying the honeymoon but not the wedding. They appeared at parties, received presents, reserved a church, bought a dress, and sent invitations.

But none of these events changed his mind or helped allay the uncertainty that nagged him. Was it the pressures of medical school? The loss of an eight-year-old girl? Or was it that he didn't actually love his bride-to-be?

The answer came in a late-night walk along the Charles River. With only a few weeks remaining before the wedding, Bill met a Lubbock, Texas girl named Karyn Jean McLaughlin. Born to William Eddie and Kathryn Louise McLaughlin in 1954, she inherited her parents' Texas ethic, which valued personal responsibility, self-reliance and hard work. She had earned a bachelors degree in elementary education and special education from Texas Christian University in Fort Worth, was a member and rush chairman of Kappa Kappa Gamma sorority and served as president of the Pan Hellenic Council. Prior to moving to Boston, she had taught children with physical and mental disabilities in Dallas public schools.[32]

Karyn was teaching part-time in Boston while also working as a flight attendant. One night while Bill was working the emergency room, Karyn arrived with a sprained wrist. It was love at first sight, and Bill felt as if he'd known her his whole life. He doctored her wrist, probably taking more time than the injury required, and sent her home. A few days later, he phoned to check on her and ask if he might come to see her. Bill remembers vividly the day and the way she met him at her one-room flat on Columbus Avenue in a not-so-good part of Boston: the white dress, sunburned face, big wide eyes, her laugh and the lilt in her West Texas voice. She melted him.

He suggested that they walk or even hitchhike to Charlestown and she kidded him for being so cheap. They ate dinner at Warren Tavern, where Bill remembers the chemistry and not the food. Late that evening, the two strolled along the Charles River. While Bill Frist's "Great Wall" may have been portable and had made the trip to Princeton, Harvard and now Mass General, keeping most everyone at a safe distance from the carefully guarded emotions of a cardiothoracic surgeon in training, Karyn walked right through it and made her home on the inside. Maybe it was along that river stroll that Bill Frist, the burgeoning heart doctor, gave his own heart away.

But what about Katie? The wedding? And his parents?

Two days prior to the wedding, following a forty-eight hour shift at Mass General, Bill flew to Nashville. "I was still dressed in my white hospital pants, tired and stretched to the limit, blunted emotionally, staring blankly into the long, dark tunnel of the wrong future. It would be years before I could fully assess the trauma medical school was doing to my soul, but it would be even longer before I could face the memory of what I did that day, like fingering a long, hard surgical scar and wondering how much had been cut out inside. I had come home to call off the wedding."[33]

His mom picked him up at the airport and took him to see his dad.

Surprisingly, they took the news rather well. Even to Bill, the excuses sounded hollow and lame. He drove to Katie's house: tables covered in white tablecloths, gifts piled high atop every one, plates, silverware, a large silver bowl. Bill sat with Katie in the living room on a long sofa, "its soft pattern of flowers familiar to me from a thousand other nights we'd spent sharing our feelings."[34] Bill explained that nothing was right in his life, with him, with the two of them. He cried; she cried. Bill remained an hour and then flew back to Boston, numb and alone. Still wearing his hospital whites, he drove to the hospital because his shift was starting. He had not missed a minute of work. And he had not mentioned Karyn.

During his second year at Harvard, while getting his bearings in his first clinical rotation, his father suffered a heart attack and underwent emergency coronary bypass surgery—something Bill, by this time, knew a good bit about. Knowing his father could die, Bill was frightened enough to take the first flight home he could find. Gick Berg remembers, "Billy was real close to his dad and the heart attack scared him."[35]

Bill tried to remind himself that it was a fairly routine operation, but he felt better only when he found his dad sitting upright in bed and resting peacefully. When Dr. Tommy gently ordered his son back to school, Bill knew he'd recover. For a week, his father progressed nicely, then developed chest pain and coughed up blood. He had developed pulmonary emboli—or blood clots in the lungs. Not routine, it complicated his father's recovery. Bill boarded the next flight and returned to Nashville. His family assured him there was nothing he could do. "Return to school," they told him, "it's what Dad would want." They were right and he knew it but it didn't make leaving any easier. He returned to Boston, to Mass General and the routine daily grind. Five days later, his brother Bobby called and said, "Dad's had a stroke."

Bill flew all night to join his family alongside his father's bed. Tired from the stress of work, the countless hours without sleep and the emotional drain of watching his father's decline, Bill bordered on despair. His father's 6'3" frame lay in bed. The stroke had crippled his speech, something Bill knew frustrated the man known for his warm and charismatic voice. When his father did speak, a mere garbled whisper, the despair grew deeper because Bill could not understand what he had said. The whisper "betrayed him, carrying with it hints of his mortality."[36] Fifteen years later, Bill would remark that it was that whisper that haunted him every time he left Nashville and it was that whisper that urged him home. When Dr. Tommy was finally able to stand and walk, his movements had been reduced to the shuffle of an uncertain old man.

While intimacy had admittedly not come easy for Bill with Katie, he found himself swirling as he and Karyn continued to date. In 1981, while he was still at Mass General, they married and moved to a small house on Beacon Hill. John Eason says, "Billy wouldn't be Senator Bill Frist, MD without Karyn. She's a rock and he knows it."[37] While time off was rare, they took what time they had, boarded Bill's vintage 1954 airplane and soared above Boston for a few hours of scarce and blessed freedom.

In the remaining years at Mass General, the training intensified. More was demanded of him by others and thus, he demanded more of himself. He rotated through the various surgical specialties, took on more patients, learned to live with stress unlike he'd ever known, and one thing became clear; he was instinctively drawn to the most challenging, most demanding, most risky and most stressful of all specialties—cardiac surgery.

He had also learned how to deal with loss—a must if he were to continue down his chosen path. He knew that he either had to learn to deal with failure, with death, or get out. Medical school had not provided Bill with ready-made psychological tools with which to face the inevitable, so he had learned this on his own as an apprentice, observing and assimilating the behavior of those around him in the hard knock school of experience.

Due to its very nature, a surgeon's job dulled his sentiments. Even routine and mundane surgeries required him to make quick decisions with limited information under less-than-perfect circumstances. He had to make those decisions without reservation or fear of mistake, knowing well that the wrong move or wrong decision could mean death to the patient who had placed his or her life in Bill's hands. Bill learned to live with his decisions—whatever the outcome—and sometimes that was not easy.

The field of transplantation was new, growing and quite risky, but the front edge of medicine began to intrigue Bill and he kept its developments on his radar screen. Bill found the nature of the patient-doctor relationship in transplant surgery particularly attractive. Most surgeons operate on a patient, meet with them a time or two following the procedure, and move on to the next case. But not transplant doctors. When Bill accepted a patient, he accepted them for life, knowing full well that he'd develop a long-term relationship with each one. While the transplant surgery itself remains, in the grand scheme of things, relatively simple, the postoperative care remains a tenuous balancing act requiring the surgeon to closely and routinely monitor the patient's health. Following transplant surgery, the surgeon needs to prescribe enough immunosuppressants to force the patient's body to accept the new organ but not so many that he cripples the immune system making it a target for every germ or bacterium the patient encounters. That balancing act demands a lifelong commitment from both doctor and patient. An equal if not greater commitment and investment comes from the nurses who spend an exponentially greater amount of time with the patients, entrusted with implementing the decisions made by the physician. For this, Bill came to appreciate, admire and trust them implicitly.

Having succeeded at Mass General as he had at both Princeton and Harvard, Bill earned the prestigious opportunity to study thoracic surgery in England for six months. The newlyweds jumped at the chance, even planning to fly across the Atlantic together in their old twin-engine plane—the adventure of their life. Their daring plans were changed though, when Karyn became pregnant with first son Harrison. Instead, they flew "commercial," arriving safely in England where Bill spent a year as a surgical house officer at the Southhampton General Hospital as a senior registrar in thoracic surgery.

Bill loved the British no-frills approach to surgery, but had a difficult time accepting the socialized medicine that rationed health service. The differences between British and American medicine were striking: the amount of time post-op patients spent in bed, the methods and frequency used to treat various ailments or conditions, the resources made available to patients in need. The experience was a true eye-opener for the young doctor.

Bill returned to the U.S. more aware than ever how high-tech American medicine had become. He refused to say which system was better, both have their merits, but the time in England served its purpose well—it reminded Bill why he had become a doctor. He realized that "he was a high-tech surgeon who wanted a family doctor's practice."[38]

Bill and Karyn returned to Boston where he accepted the Chief Residency position at Mass General in cardiothoracic surgery. Though Bill had become increasingly interested in heart transplantation, about this time MGH made a policy decision not to begin such a program. Consequently, Bill began exploring his options, specifically on the west coast at a place called Stanford, otherwise known as, "Transplant Mecca."[39]

In the early 1980s, Norman Shumway, the father of transplantation, had become so well respected in the cardiothoracic medical community that he had his pick of the best students in the best programs in the country. Thus, the legendary Shumway reached into Mass General and handpicked Bill Frist, inviting him to interview at Stanford. He wanted to see for himself if what he had heard about Bill was true and whether the East Coast boy would fit into the West Coast world of medicine.

Shumway immediately liked young Frist, and offered him an eighteen-month fellowship in transplantation—the most sought-after and elite assignment in all of cardiac medicine. Shumway furthered the possibility of transplantation by developing the techniques and methods used to monitor the heart and detect early signs of rejection. Few, if any, assignments for a heart surgeon carried the promise of more excitement. After four years of college, four of medical school, at least five of general surgery, a year or two of research, and three of cardiothoracic surgery, Bill jumped at the chance. In 1985, Bill joined the Stanford team, moving with Karyn and baby Harrison to a rented clay-colored stucco house, complete with a pool and flower garden, set in the Palo Alto hills behind main campus.

At Stanford, Bill Frist enjoyed his first taste of true fulfillment—the kind that comes when gifting, desire and opportunity line up.

The facilities at the Stanford Hospital were calm and beautiful. Palm trees lined the grounds, a fountain sprayed over the ducks who frolicked all summer, and next door sat a tennis court where hospital staff played more months of the year than not. Bill, found himself in a "medical Eden."

Bill made his office in a free-standing structure adjacent to the hospital called the Cardiovascular Research Building—fondly known as the 'CRB.' The building was split down the middle much the way cardiac care is today. The non-surgical heart specialists (cardiologists) seeking to cure heart disease non-invasively with medication, occupied one half the building, and while they succeeded much of the time, when they reached the limits of their capabilities they sent the patient to Bill's side of the building—the side occupied by the surgeons.

The CRB, a West Coast style building with skylights, two-story atrium, manicured gardens and a laid-back atmosphere starkly contrasted the historic Harvard buildings. Perched next door, The Stanford Hospital—twenty-eight years old, three stories high, equipped with escalators rather than elevators—was, at the time, attempting to raise one hundred million dollars for renovations. The idea that the facility was somehow outdated amused Bill, having come from Mass General where little had been updated in over in sixty years.

Shumway, "the old man" inspired Frist. He painted a vision and then followed it, encouraging others to join him, while he perfected the now standard transplant technique. He held everyone to high standards but amidst his call for perfection, he was playful and patient. His teaching culture was the antithesis to the rapid-fire training Bill had witnessed back East, at both Harvard and Mass General. Shumway motivated through encouragement, not fear. His fellows strove for excellence, not out of fear of failure but out of respect for their mentor. His gentleness and creativity produced the most talented group of surgeons in the world, most of whom are now leading transplant centers around the country. Because complexity increased the chance for error, he encouraged simplicity. "If it looks complex, it's not right." He routinely asked nurses and assistants, those closest to the patient, their opinions prior to beginning a surgery. The doctor made those around the operating table feel as equals, colleagues in the true sense of the word. "In a profession filled with cutthroat ambitions and big egos, he knew how to be a father."[40]

This modus operandi at Stanford cultivated Bill's desire to emulate a good quarterback rather than a great surgeon. Shumway "valued teamwork, the calling of the plays, the attention to details, the timing and execution of a master plan that made for a successful operation."[41] And, he had a "pathological love" for one-liners. Whether it was a nurse, patient or fellow doctor, Shumway always carried a new joke. Bill remembers that "the old man" got away with jokes and quirks because he had a feel for transplantation, "a sixth sense for making good decisions and finding the right answers."[42] Shumway's most valuable asset was the ability to size up individuals, even before they became doctors, and know who could make the important contributions to cardiac surgery.

Calling himself "the world's greatest first assistant," Shumway tutored and led residents painlessly through the most challenging cases. He strove to make those around him look good, including the green and fumbling residents he was attempting to teach. "Never be afraid to double-dribble," he'd say with affirmation.[43] In short, Shumway taught Bill to perform cardiac surgery in a manner and fashion that reminded him of his father.

At Stanford, in sharp contrast to the instrument-throwing tantrums of his Harvard or Mass General predecessors, Bill saw what a calm, efficient and congenial operating room looked like. Shumway stressed that the skill of the surgeon was a minor part of a successful transplant. He encouraged his colleagues to remember that they were able to do what they did because years before someone had discovered cyclosporine; because a family, amidst great personal grief, had the strength to donate organs;

because a nurse had the temerity to ask them amidst that grief, for that donation; because the recipient patient had the courage and stamina to take some fourteen pills a day that would convince his or her body not to reject the alien heart, and countless other discoveries that made their job possible. Each transplant was truly a corporate undertaking and Shumway reminded them, "Cardiac surgery is not hard to do. It's just hard to get to do."[44]

Most every night after dinner, on his way back to work, Bill would celebrate his newfound exuberance by satisfying his sweet tooth with a chocolate milkshake from Bud's Ice Cream and he put on weight—a first in the lean Frist family. Soon, Karyn, too, was putting on weight as she was now pregnant with Jonathan. Bill remembers, "In California . . . I felt all my abilities and talents coming together, the disparate strands of my past and my training and my personality suddenly coalescing."[45] Up to that point in Bill's life, the first six months running the transplant center at Stanford alongside Shumway were the most powerful and fulfilling of his life.

Upon Bill's shoulders, Shumway placed tremendous responsibility along with a healthy dose of stress. He was "under fire" and he learned not to miss details and to "settle for nothing less than perfection."[46] Bill had to quickly diagnose infection and rejection, because if he hesitated, if he didn't work proactively, the patient would die.

Shumway's methods were so alien, so different from what he'd been taught elsewhere that he felt he was learning heart surgery all over again. He still worked too much, but for the first time since medical school, he spent five nights a week sleeping in his own bed. The hours at home seemed like a vacation. His job at Stanford was a dream come true, a once-in-a-lifetime opportunity. He devoured it and he loved the people with whom he worked.

As an outsider who had trained on the East Coast, Bill never understood one peculiar aspect of life at Stanford: everyone, except Shumway, wore cowboy boots. He didn't know if it was some tradition he'd never accepted or some mark of toughness. The staff was also filled with some bizarre personalities, from a hobbyist who collected machine guns, to a crude-speaking monosyllabic rider of powerful motorcycles and fast airplanes who had single-handedly compiled the world's largest transplant database to Shumway's right-hand man, Ed Stinson, the backbone and guts of the Stanford transplant program. Behind them all, was Shumway—the determined, committed, dedicated, unrelenting, inspirational leader.

True to his team approach, Shumway encouraged each of his protégés, giving them room to grow and expand their creativity. When people made mistakes, they knew it but never resented Shumway for telling them. He had a way of communicating mistakes that didn't imply some defect in their character. He also leaned heavily on his nurses, even referring to them as "colleagues" in a scientific paper—a habit Bill admired and would take with him to Vanderbilt. Along with learning how to doctor, Bill grew fascinated with the ethical and social issues associated with transplantation—the core of which was the paradox of waiting for someone to die so that someone else might live.

Bill transitioned to senior fellow in transplantation—a path that led straight to the heart of his brave new world. Elsewhere when he had served as chief resident, he was assisted by a team of junior residents who worked under his command, but at Stanford, Shumway had set up a different structure. His design was purposeful. Shumway believed a doctor could only truly learn the art of transplantation through total and complete immersion.

Now, as senior fellow, Bill was responsible for everything including all the "scut" jobs that interns often seven years his junior performed in other places. Bill performed diagnostic lumbar punctures (inserting needles into the spinal columns of fever-ridden patients), drew blood, changed central venous lines and arterial catheters, and changed dressings. No job was too mundane and in short, Bill was reminded that in order to heal, he must first learn to serve.

Bill emerged from Stanford knowing "how to care for the sick, how to assess difficult clinical situations, how to move quickly and efficiently, how to work with all support people, including—and especially—nurses. I learned how to make the people around me trust me and have faith in me, to feel good about the work they did, to open up, to give me the right information unhesitatingly when I needed it. In short, I think, I hope, I learned how to be a leader."[47]

Bill had found his calling and he left the Stanford experience so deeply involved in the world of transplantation that he knew he'd never shake free. His specialty brought "hope to the hopeless, and life to the doomed . . . It challenged me at every level. And I loved it, day in and day out, for its endless complexity."[48]

During this time, Bill missed his kids' first steps, their discovery of the spoken word, an inch grown here and a pound added there, and much of their early lives. Though Stanford was less rigorous than Mass General, he still spent two, sometimes three, days in a row at the hospital—napping when time would allow. The adage that behind every good man is a better woman certainly applied in Bill's case, and he is the first to admit it. His rock during these times was Karyn. She kept them all together. Bill took refuge in his respect for Karyn, the sacrifices she made, and as a result, he knew his marriage would not crack as other doctors' had. This said, it did not reduce the guilt he felt for his all-too-often absence. It never has.

Following his time at Stanford, Bill began looking for transplantation opportunities across the country. Shumway had filled that need on the West Coast and Boston had already made their decision not to pursue transplantation so Bill listened to the whisper that urged him home. In 1986, he returned to Nashville at the invitation of Dr. Harvey Bender to join the Vanderbilt transplant team with whom Dr. Walter Merrill, had already performed three heart transplants. Seeing the possibilities, Bender recruited Bill to create a world class interdisciplinary program that brought all of Vanderbilt's transplant programs, including kidney, bone marrow and heart, under one roof. The challenge excited Bill, as did the thought of returning home. This time, however, he returned not as student but as teacher and director of the Multidisciplinary Transplant Center.

# 4

THE CALL CAME as he was reading a bedtime story to his boys. Long past bedtime, little brother Jonathan had already crashed, but Harrison had stayed awake enjoying the rare evening with dad. Mom was tired and so was Bill, but nonetheless, he, too, relished the rare time with his sons. Then the phone rang. As the director of Vanderbilt's prestigious transplant center, Bill was literally on-call 24/7, married as much to his beeper as his wife and family. The caller told Bill that a man in Tampa had not been wearing his seat belt in a car crash two days ago, allowing his head to plow through the windshield. Unresponsive from the moment the paramedics arrived, he clung to life only with the help of a ventilator. Declared brain dead, his family had agreed to donate his organs.

Karyn eyed the phone warily because she knew that late-night calls usually meant someone across the country had died suddenly and violently. Before Bill could save a life, someone had to die. The awful flip side to Bill's lifesaving work was knowing that next to the bed of that someone, a family was grieving. Bill listened intently, formulating the specifics in his mind. The doctors in Tampa had posted the organs on the nationwide computer network that matched organs and recipients, and the computer had come up with a match—a patient of Bill's. Actually, it had matched the heart with two patients under Bill's care.

While he was grateful for the computer matching system, its current selection placed Bill in a predicament he wished on no human alive—having two patients and only one heart. His decision could mean the other recipient would die before another heart became available. Bill made his decision based on a mountain of scientific evidence and also the knowledge that one of the men was nearer death than the other. Somewhere across the state, the beeper on Jim Hayes bedside table began to vibrate, flash and rattle.

Twenty minutes and fifteen phone calls later, Bill Frist grabbed his keys, kissed Karyn and then decided to make one more phone call. He called Jim Hayes himself, knowing the patient would appreciate hearing his voice. "Jim, we won't know for sure until I get a good look at that heart, but I think you'd better get to the hospital." Jim Hayes had been here before. This would be his second transplant.

As one of the longest-living transplant recipients, Jim Hayes had received his first transplant at Stanford in 1976 under Shumway, when half of the patients died soon after transplantation. On the fifth anniversary of his transplant, Jim rode his bicycle cross-country from Knoxville to Palo Alto for his annual checkup. The television show *That's Incredible!* covered the ride, and the mayor had declared Jim's day of departure as "Jim Hayes Day." But, like his first heart, atherosclerosis—the hardening of the arteries—had infected his second heart. With arteries as hard as rocks, he needed yet a third heart or he'd be dead in six months.

Leaving his driveway, Bill glanced in his rearview mirror and marveled at his wife's strength. Bill hadn't seen the house before they moved—he couldn't get away from Stanford. Karyn met with the Realtor, negotiated the contract, packed the kids and moved the contents while Bill designed and organized the burgeoning transplant program.

By the time he returned to his office at Vanderbilt's Transplant

Center, his own handpicked team was assembling. Among the best in their field, their success percentages routinely bettered the national averages. People all across the country were standing in line to ask Bill Frist to place his stethoscope on their chests and listen to their hearts.

Final preparations were made, orders given, operating rooms assigned and scrubbed, creating a sterile field. Bill synchronized his watch with his right-hand man Walter Merrill, and, on his pant leg, wrote the estimated time they would begin the operation. He and Walter agreed to communicate every thirty minutes over the next six hours, and while Walter oversaw preparations at Vanderbilt, Bill, carrying the signature red Igloo cooler, boarded a Leer jet en route to a small hospital in Tampa.

Bill and Walter made an effective duo. Walter remembers that he and Bill never established a formal arrangement as to who flew and who prepared the recipient. "Wasn't any particular rhyme or reason to it. It had more to do with me asking Bill, 'Oh, what do you want to do tonight?' Bill would say, 'Oh, I don't care.' We sort of just decided at the time and nobody ever kept count as to who flew and who didn't. We'd go as far as Denver. Even went to Puerto Rico one time. It wasn't unusual for us to fly five hundred to eight hundred miles. Most transplant activity is a nocturnal sport so Bill and I used to joke that we spent more nights together than we did with our spouses."[1]

Absolute precision and perfection were paramount. Once he had extracted the heart, he only had four hours to re-establish it in Jim Hayes chest. Upon brain death, the body suffers a gradual deterioration in organ function. Furthermore, ischemic time—when the heart has been stopped and no blood flows through the chambers—starts as soon as the heart is taken from the body. After that, every second counts. After four hours of ischemic time, Jim's chances of survival fell precipitously. Walter Merrill remembers: "The consequences of even one slight mistake could be quite grave. A lot of what we do is working on a pretty thin margin between success and disaster."[2] Vanderbilt colleague John Morris continues, "Often times, we're just five minutes ahead or behind the reaper."[3]

Bill arrived in Tampa and waited while the other doctors, who had come to harvest organs, prepped the donor for their own procedures. Everyone knew though, that Dr. Frist would make the first incision. The heart went first, then the liver and kidneys followed by bone and other tissues.

The donor ready for harvesting, Bill called Walter, established the timeframe and then headed to the sink to scrub. Eight minutes later, he walked into the OR, hands held at heart level, asked a nurse to wrap him in sterile clothing and gloves, then leaned over the man on the table.

Bill asked for a scalpel, cut the skin vertically from throat to belly button and then asked the nurse for an electric sternal saw.

"We don't have one," she responded.

"What about a sternal knife?"

She shook her head.

Bill improvised, "Okay, how about a pair of heavy scissors?"

The nurse handed him the scissors. Fifteen minutes later, Bill placed the near-perfect heart into two sealed Ziploc bags, placed it in the cooler, surrounded it with ice, broke scrub, and handed the cooler to his assistant Rusty. With Rusty carrying the cooler like the secret service agent who carries the "football" never more than a few feet from the president, Bill and his team sprinted from the hospital where a helicopter waited to take them back to the jet. Once airborne, he called Walter, "It looks good. We're in route." He checked his pants leg, noticed that they were two minutes behind schedule, but didn't worry because he knew they would make up some time in the air.

Back in Nashville, Jim Hayes kissed his wife and told her he'd see her in a few hours. The nurse then began the drip of medicine through his arterial catheter. Once settled into a deep and peaceful sleep, the nurses scrubbed him, shaved his chest and created their own sterile field in anticipation of Bill's arrival.

On final approach to the airport, air traffic control informed Bill's pilot that another aircraft had priority due to an instrument malfunction. Left with instructions to circle for five minutes, Bill realized that neither the heart nor Jim had an additional five minutes to spare. Immediately, he stood from his seat and keyed the mike to speak with the controller, "Approach, this is LifeFlight. Four Kilo Bravo. We have a live organ aboard. Request immediate clearance to the run-up area, runway fifteen."

The controller responded, "Four Kilo Bravo you are cleared for immediate run-up to runway fifteen." The helicopter landed, the team jogged across the tarmac, loaded the helicopter, buckled in and Bill eyed Rusty and the cooler. Because Igloo coolers were common, especially among pilots who filled them with soft drinks and stored them behind the jumpseat, Rusty would not let it out of his hand. It had happened before: other doctors had exited the plane, arrived at the hospital and opened the patient only to reach into the cooler bringing out a Pepsi. As long as Rusty kept that cooler on his lap, there was no room for such error.

They landed in Nashville, tumbled into an ambulance, and sped their way, lights flashing, back to Vanderbilt. Spotting the team's arrival with the cooler, the receptionist immediately phoned the OR where Walter would sever the connection to Jim Hayes' heart and place him on bypass. There was no turning back now. Jim Hayes lay on the table, supported entirely by a machine that both breathed for him and pumped blood through his body. His life lay entirely in the hands of those who stood over him.

The team skipped the elevator, climbing three flights instead—a small price to pay to eliminate another variable—and changed into clean scrubs. Moving quickly but under control and without signs of panic, Bill and his team entered the operating room where Walter, waiting patiently, stood next to Jim Hayes. The room was bright, calm, efficient, congenial—a Shumway influence. Every type of the most highly technical machines known to man lined the walls, flashing, beeping and monitoring Jim Hayes's biological activity.

Bill removed Jim's still-beating heart and placed it in a pan at the end of the operating table. In the ever-progressing science of transplantation, scientists would study every square molecule of that heart over the next several days. The transplanted heart now being removed to make way for a second transplanted heart, contained invaluable information for scientists, doctors and future transplant patients.

Walter began stitching in Jim's new heart. Bill turned to a nearby nurse, knowing Jim's needed an update. "Tell Shirley, we'll come off bypass in an hour. Everything's going along just fine."

Walter and Bill trimmed the heart, stitched in the arteries, and then Bill said to the perfusionist behind the heart-lung machine, "Let's warm him up."

They'd reached the moment of truth. When warm blood hit the heart, Jim Hayes would either live or die. And nobody, not even Bill, could convince that heart to begin beating again if it decided not to. Every time Bill did this he knew the heart would come alive, that's what God had made it to do, but because he had absolutely no control over it, he always had a healthy fear that it wouldn't. There was still so much they didn't know about transplantation.

The warm blood filled the heart turning it a rich red, filling every cavity and artery. The heart quivered, jumped, and beat—powerfully and regular. Bill breathed deeply "sure that God was in heaven and all was well down below . . . Jim Hayes was alive again."[4] Bill broke scrub again, pulled off his mask and headlight and walked briskly to the waiting room. He needed to tell Shirley.

Bill had come to Vanderbilt to build one of the nation's leading interdisciplinary transplant centers. And he had done just that. But he had not limited his vision solely to hearts. Because the need was so great, he knew that he and his team needed to venture into the ultra-risky world of heart-lung transplantation and they did.

Due to the shortage of available organs, Bill was constantly fighting an uphill battle. His list of patients in need of transplants was growing and he was tired of seeing good people die when good organs were available but simply never offered.

Two patients in particular offered unique challenges. Little Jonathan Jones was barely a year old when his mother brought him to see Bill. The son of a single mother, he had five other brothers and sisters living in crowded conditions in East Nashville.

The hurdles were multiple. At the time, only fifteen babies in the world had ever been given heart transplants. Jonathan's mother did not own a car, so weekly checkups to Bill's office were problematic. Nor did she have a phone in her home, so contacting emergency services also posed a problem. Additionally, because the nerves of transplanted hearts are not reattached, transplant patients often don't know if they're having trouble, and baby Jonathan was at an age where communication of any sort was guesswork at best. Furthermore, should his mother ever cut back on his medication for any reason whatsoever, Jonathan's body would reject his heart. And lastly, because so much was unknown about pediatric transplantation, it seemed likely that Jonathan would need a second and possibly third heart as he grew older. But because Bill strongly believed that transplantation was not solely for the privileged few, he elected to accept Jonathan Jones as a recipient. Two months following the operation, Jonathan was improving daily and doing great. His mother, completely dedicated to his future, never missed an appointment. Those weekly visits by the smiling Jonathan often provided the highlight to the week for Bill and his staff.

When Vanderbilt hired Bill Frist, they agreed to allow him a few patients with little or no ability to pay for their transplant. Like Stanford in the early years, they were hoping to select patients based on need and financial ability to pay. At some point, that honeymoon would end but it had not yet, when Jean Lefkowitz called. What made her case special is that Jean not only needed a new heart, but a new pair of lungs as well. If Bill transplanted Jean, she would be Vanderbilt's first multiple-organ transplant.

After hearing a brief medical history over the phone, Bill agreed to meet her in his office. Her mom rolled her wheelchair into his office, and Jean, looking directly into Bill's eyes, wasted little time: "Dr. Frist I am very ill. I have two children I want to see grow. I have been considered by Pittsburgh and they think I am a good candidate. But I can't come up with the kind of money they want, not in the time I've got left anyway. I have raised some money from bake sales. I've appealed to the newspapers. I've written to hundreds of businesses asking for money. I've asked everyone to help. I've looked into other programs, like the one in

Arizona, but they've done so few. Stanford is just too far away for me, and the waiting list is too long. I'll die before they get to me. You were at Stanford. You know how to do the operation. You don't have a waiting list. You're not asking for cash up front. I want to come to Vanderbilt. I want you to do the operation."[5]

Bill arranged for her to meet with the rest of the team to get their impressions. They all had to agree, and they did. The chemistry seemed to fit. She was young, strong-willed, determined to live; she understood the risks and was gifted with both optimism and faith—all of which she would need to survive the grueling weeks in postoperative care. Bill agreed to list Jean but not until his team was ready—which might take six months. Bill was eager to help her but not before his team performed a successful "dry run."

Bill hung up the phone and did two things: he arranged for a company in Florida to fly Jean to Nashville in a private jet at a moment's notice and he sent Bob Lee, a surgical resident, in search of a couple of sheep that Bill could use to demonstrate the operation to the rest of the team.

Christmas came and Bill walked the team through the dry run using the two sheep as patients. The success of the procedure encouraged them and on New Year's Eve, Bill officially listed Jean on the national computer network. He called her to tell her that he'd just listed her and heard, in return, the palpable relief in her voice.

Twenty-four days later, a teenage girl in Nashville shot herself in the head. She arrived at Vanderbilt where doctors pronounced her brain dead. That night, the phone rang late again in the Frist household. She was a near perfect match for Jean Lefkowitz. With the green light on, Bill and his team were set to perform the country's one-hundredth heart-lung transplant and Vanderbilt's first.

Jean flew to Nashville, and within hours, the operation began. It took a long time, about eight to ten hours longer than a heart transplant, but it occurred without incident. Everything went perfectly. The next morning, Jean lay in bed recuperating in the ICU, breathing peacefully and facing a new future.

Jimmy Moore, a twenty-eight-year old healthy husband and father of two, jogged regularly, was an avid rock climber, scuba dived and coached his kids' t-ball and baseball teams. He volunteered with the local fire and rescue squad, didn't smoke, didn't drink and, by all accounts, lived a relatively healthy lifestyle. Then he caught the flu and the virus attacked his heart. Within days, he could barely climb out of bed.

Following a full physical including chest x-ray, his doctor sent him to a nearby hospital to see a heart specialist. The report was not good: "Jimmy you have cardiomyopathy—you're heart is growing and we don't know why."

At first, the doctors believed they could control the growth, but Jimmy continued to decline as his heart continued to enlarge. Finally, he was recommended for a transplant and on March 22, 1986—just a month prior to Bill Frist's arrival—Walter Merrill put a new heart in Jimmy.

Jimmy recovered and was sent home but the once active father had a difficult time obeying the doctor's orders to "be careful, and not get too excited." Jimmy remembers, "they put so many restrictions on me, they were treating me like a China doll, afraid I'd break."[6]

Jimmy wanted to enjoy life and he wanted to return to work, but everybody continued to treat him differently. In secret, he started doing what he called 'girl pushups.' He went to some old climbing places with friends, lied and told them his doctors had given him the okay, and then videotaped his slow ascent. His doctors were furious, as was Robyn his wife. Then, during his second monthly checkup at Vanderbilt, Jimmy met the new director of the transplant program, Bill Frist.

Jimmy was noticeably frustrated and depressed at the restrictions placed on his life. He felt good, better than he had in a year, yet he was still so limited. Jimmy shared with Bill his desire to get out and be active, to rock climb, ride bikes with his kids, coach again. When Bill asked, "Well, why don't you?" Jimmy's eyes widened.

The doctor continued, "Do you wear safety ropes when you climb?"

Jimmy responded, "Of course."

Bill nodded, "I think it's great."

Jimmy asked, "So I can mow my lawn now?"

Bill asked him, "Why'd you have the surgery?"

Jimmy responded, "So I could be a father, a husband, be active . . . to live life."

Bill said, "Sounds like a good thing to me. But," he cautioned, "We're not going to Mount Everest are we?" Jimmy laughed. From then on, every time he went to Vanderbilt, he saw Bill.

Soon, Bill began calling Jimmy asking him speak to a group about organ donation. It started off at hospital then spread to PTO meetings and school functions. Jimmy remembers Bill telling him, "We've got to do something to promote organ donations. We're losing too may patients. I can deal with it if we lost a patient to an infection or something else but to lose patients just because we don't have enough organs out there is unacceptable." Jimmy returned to Vanderbilt a few weeks later and suggested to Bill that he and some other transplant recipients participate in a bicycle trip across Tennessee to promote awareness. Jimmy suggested that they attempt to cover the entire state during national organ awareness week. Bill stepped into the elevator, and punched the button for the 7th floor. When the doors opened, rather than turn left toward his office, Bill turned right. Jimmy scratched his head. "Bill, where you going?"

Bill pointed toward the psychiatric ward ahead of him.

Jimmy said, "But Bill, that's the psych ward."

Bill nodded, "That's right, and that's exactly where you're going if you think I'm letting you ride across the state on your bicycle!"

Eventually, Jimmy and a few other transplant recipients prevailed on Bill to let them undertake the trip. With conditions, he relented. The trip made national headlines, and for several months following, organ donation actually spiked and Bill began thinking of organ donation awareness on a more national scale.

As for the indomitable Jimmy Moore, he was the first transplant patient in the history of transplantation to graduate the police academy. He's now a member of the Clemson University Police Department, umpires Little League baseball games in his spare time, and is considering a run for Mayor of Easley, South Carolina. "Bill has encouraged me to do it. He's told me, 'You'll never know until you try.'" Jimmy pauses to make a point, one that's important to him: "A big part of what I am today, I owe that to Bill Frist."[7]

Bill arrived most days at Vanderbilt before the sun rose and left long after it had set. Some days, he didn't make it home at all. Every day at Vanderbilt, he faced new challenges and opportunities. As the patient list grew, so did the need to get the word out that there was a shortage of organs in this country. He took the education process upon himself, often flying himself to and from his destination, to educate the people of Tennessee about the dire need for organ donation.

Sometimes he would drive fifty miles, sometimes fly hundreds of miles to small communities, schools, civic groups and women's clubs, to give a presentation on the need for organ donors and the need for doctors to ask grieving families for those donations. Bill would rather have spent his time with patients, but potential donors needed to hear the request from a surgeon—one who was watching people die.

He'd show a videotape of the transplant operation itself, sometimes a slide show, giving a brief history of transplantation, the legal and political history of the field, the development of the criteria for brain death, donor cards, living wills and the right of next of kin to make decisions and the National Organ Transplant Act of 1984, which established the nationwide computer network that lists both patients and recipients. He ended his talks with a plea to doctors to have the courage to ask grieving families about donation.

One night at a particularly hostile reception before a community of doctors, an elderly doctor stood up and challenged Bill. He cut Bill off in mid-sentence, "You miss my point doctor. I don't like the government telling me how to practice medicine. It is none of their business how I interact with my patients. I mean, I know these people, I've known them all my life. Been their doctor for twenty years. Their son dies, I'd feel like a vulture, some kind of ghoul asking to mutilate his body. I'm a physician. They expect me to console them at that a time like that. Not badger them."

Bill responded, "Exactly, you're a physician, licensed by the state, certified by a legal medical board, and charged with a certain responsibility to the welfare of society. That includes your patients' feelings, but it also includes the health and life of the fifteen people who could use that son's tissues and organs. We, as physicians, are ghouls indeed if we don't let the family know it has an opportunity at that point in time—"

He broke in again, "You're talking socialized medicine. I mean, I sit here, and I listen to you, and I can't believe you are Dr. Tommy Frist's son. You let people die, for God's sake, because they don't fit on some computer. How can you play God like that?"

"That's why I need you to help me find more donors. So no one is asked to make those types of decisions. No one has to play God."[8] In 1989, primarily to further awareness for the need of organ donation, Bill wrote and published *Transplant*, his compelling first-person account of his work prior to and with the Vanderbilt Transplant Center.

One evening, some months later, the phone rang again, although this call was not the usual summons. Bill answered, and the caller asked, "Dr. Bill Frist?"

"Yes."

"This is Barbara Mandrell. I'm interested in organ donation. I've heard of your work, and I'd like to help you raise money through a celebrity charity event that I'll organize. Maybe a softball game. What do you say?"

Bill arranged for her to visit the transplant center, meet with patients, and get an overview of the program. She was immediately taken in, especially by the young and charming Jonathan who was now crawling and walking his way down the halls to his weekly checkup.

Having heard about her work with Bill, Bryant Gumbel invited both Barbara and Bill to be his guest on the *Today* show. The show was hosted by guest personality, Phil Donahue and by the time the show was over, Bill had communicated his message to millions of people, more than he could ever have reached in his short drives and flights around the southeast.

Following their appearance on *Today*, Larry King invited the duo to appear with him on *Larry King Live*. With Barbara prompting Larry to talk more about the need for organ transplants and less about her career and music, Bill once again communicated his message. True to her fiery determination, when Larry tried to steer the questions back to Barbara, she immediately redirected the questions to Bill. Throughout these experiences, Bill witnessed the exponential power of the media to broadcast a message.

On the day of the charity game, 25,000 people filled the stands at Vanderbilt Stadium. Barbara had obviously spent a lot of time organizing and calling her friends. Bill was amazed at the number of high-profile celebrities that had come to participate: Chuck Norris, Bob Hope, Lynn Swann, L.L. Cool J, Herschel Walker, Sheena Easton, Dick Clark, John Stamos, Meat Loaf, Ralph Emery, Frank Gifford, Walter Payton, Minnie Pearl, Ahmad Rashad, Phylicia Rashad, Danny White, Erma Bombeck, the Statler Brothers, and Oprah Winfrey, to name a few. But beyond all the names, photo shots and media cameras, the highlight for Bill came when Barbara escorted a tiny two-year-old boy, little Jonathan Jones, onto the pitcher's mound to throw out the first pitch.

At the end of the day, Barbara had shown Bill how to accomplish on a macro scale what he had been attempting to do on a micro scale. He thought long and hard about the lesson. He began thinking back to his summer internship in the congressional office of Joe Evins and more specifically, the question he had asked him, "If someone my age wanted to serve in the U.S. Congress someday, what advice would you give them?"

Through the years, Bill had felt increasingly confined by the "suffocating hand" of excessive managed care and government bureaucracies. Medicine, as a practice, had begun to abandon the doctor-patient relationship his father had so amiably modeled in favor of a "cookie-cutter, one-size-fits-all, Washington-knows-best" approach. Bill began asking himself if his energies would be better spent impacting people's lives through the legislative process. Should he consider public service and if so, where and at what level?

On March 6, 1990, Bill met with Senator Howard Baker—former

Majority and Minority Leader, Watergate Committee Vice Chairman and Chief of Staff to President Reagan. Between the years 1980 and 1984, whenever senators, senators' aides or the press were polled to determine the best, most influential, most effective and most persuasive, Howard Baker routinely finished first. During Watergate, Baker hit national headlines with the now-famous question, "What did the President know and when did he know it?"

Baker candidly apprised Bill of the rewards and pitfalls of politics. He warned from the beginning that Bill needed to develop a thick hide because as soon as he threw his hat in the ring, the attacks would come, and from every direction. He also told him that the rewards were worth the risk and, when considering whether to run for a local or statewide or national office, he said, "Washington is where the action is."[9]

Bill continued his work at Vanderbilt while considering his options. His choices had become easier because his team at Vanderbilt, though they would miss him, had become self-supporting. He had successfully passed the baton and they could make it without him—a sign that he had learned to lead.

In 1992, Bill met twice more with Howard Baker and set the stage for a 1994 run against incumbent Tennessee Senator Jim Sasser—Chairman of the Senate Budget Committee, who five years earlier had lost only one county in all of Tennessee. As one article stated, "At first it looked like Rocky Balboa planning to fight Apollo Creed."[10] Bill's friends were incredulous, "Against Sasser? You've got to be kidding. You'll just be one more sacrificial lamb just like all the others."[11]

Longtime friend, Barry Banker remembers, "Many people thought he'd lost his mind. We went to Houston's over on West End and he said, 'Barry I'm going to run for Senate.' So I asked him, 'Has Karyn blessed it?' He said, 'Yes.' I asked him, 'Has the family blessed it?' He nodded again. So, I said, 'Okay, I'll do whatever you need. To tell you the truth, I wasn't surprised. I've never seen him lose at anything, except those MBA football games as a senior. I thought he could beat Sasser. We knew it wasn't going to be easy, but he's got an uncanny ability to handle all the irons in the fire."[12]

Later that spring, on April 6, 1992, Bill had just been called out of the operating room at Vanderbilt Hospital, by an urgent page calling him to the bedside of a seventy-four-year-old male who was acutely short of breath. Bill diagnosed the problem and quickly explained what he needed to do. Working quickly, he anesthetized the chest wall, made an incision and inserted a large tube to drain two quarts of malignant pleural fluid from the chest. The procedure lasted only thirty minutes, but the conversation with the grateful patient lasted more than three hours. The man was Ross Bass, Tennessee Senator and the person responsible for the exact wording of the Surgeon General's label on cigarettes, "Smoking may be hazardous to your health." Ross Bass died nine months later, but his late-night advice had been invaluable to Bill. On New Year's Day 1994, Bill took a leave of absence from Vanderbilt to organize his campaign.

Wanting to stretch his political wings, and maybe test the waters a bit, Bill wrote four op-ed pieces for the *Tennessean* that demonstrated his knowledge of and opinion on healthcare policy. Writing comfortably as a doctor, he was characteristically analytical and diagnostic rather than partisan and prescriptive, chastising both President Bush and then-Governor Clinton for various aspects of their plans. He identified the issues as universal access to healthcare, portability, cost containment, and the need to reduce bureaucratic red tape. Only in his conclusion did he indicate a preference for primary, preventative, long-term care and the desire to preserve freedom of patients to choose their own physician.

Late November 1992, recognizing Bill's abilities, Tennessee's Democratic Governor Ned Ray McWherter appointed Bill to his only political office prior to his election to the Senate. The governor asked him to chair his taskforce on Medicaid reform, a program with a 2.8 billion dollar a year budget—equal to one-quarter the budget of the entire state of Tennessee. Bill's leadership on the task force was soon rewarded as Tennessee was able to opt out of the traditional Medicaid program—only the third state to do so. The experience showed Bill first-hand how public policy directly affected an individual's care, exposing the invisible link between an individual's health and government policy.[13] Bill moved one step closer to affecting patient care through serving the nation.

Trying to make sure that time spent with his boys didn't get lost in the shuffle, Bill called Barry Banker, who had three children roughly the same ages as his own, and said he wanted them to plan a father-son trip to spend some time with their boys. They planned an end-of-March train trip, starting in Chicago to see the aquarium and then heading to a resort in the Wisconsin Dells. They arrived in Wisconsin to six inches of snow and almost every hotel full of snowed-in guests. Barry got on the phone and found one room at a theme resort. "But Bill, it's like a hundred and fifty a night and it's a cowboy and Indian theme room. Stuffed animals, and full size cowboys and Indians all over the place."

Bill's eyes grew wide, the smile from ear to ear, "Oh, we've got to do that!"

Barry recalled, "At this point I'm wondering, who are the kids here."

Just prior to the launch of his campaign, Dr. Tommy—worried that Howard Baker had pushed his son into politics—called the senator and said, "Senator Baker, don't talk my son into running for the United States Senate. He's spent nineteen years becoming a great heart transplant surgeon and is doing great service here."

Senator Baker responded, "Dr. Frist, I'm not about to tell your son not to run . . . I'm not going to encourage him too much, but I'm not about to tell him not to run."[14]

On March 1, 1994, surrounded by his family and many of his patients, Bill announced his candidacy for the Senate of the United States—a forty-two-year-old heart surgeon running against an eighteen-year veteran of the Senate. In a proactive effort to educate himself about his candidate, Bill's campaign manager Tom Perdue, pulled Barry Banker aside one night and whispered, "Barry, you've been a friend of his a long time. Just between us, tell me about the skeletons in his closet." Barry shook his head, "He doesn't have any." Barry remembers: "If the 'cats' thing from *Transplant* is the worst thing somebody can dig up on somebody else, then he's pretty squeaky clean."

Despite one of his opponents criticizing Bill's failure to vote during his surgical training, Bill defeated five opponents in the GOP primary through educating Tennesseans on Sasser's increasingly liberal voting record and by establishing solid organizations in eighty of the ninety-five counties.

He ran on a conservative platform, endorsing welfare reform, voluntary school prayer, spending and tax cuts, term limits and espousing a fundamental belief in individual responsibility. Bill loved the campaign trail and Mark Tipps remembers that time never seemed to matter to Bill. From town hall meetings with several hundred to shaking hands in a late-night diner with only two or three people, Bill never tired. He would shake every last hand and sit and listen to people from late at night until early in the morning.

In the final weeks of the campaigning, Bill Frist and Jim Sasser scheduled three debates. As preparation, Bill met with two trusted men in the conference room of the Vanderbilt Plaza Hotel and spent hours examining issues. They studied issues raised by other candidates across the country, watched C-SPAN, and filled in the gaps with research while trying to formulate both an opinion and an answer.

Jim Sasser articulated that he'd been in Washington eighteen years and could do more for Tennessee than a freshman senator who hadn't voted until his thirties could ever accomplish. Furthermore, the news reported that Sasser and Tom Daschle were both vying for the position of majority leader—depending upon the outcome of the Dole and Clinton Presidential election. Jim Sasser was a heavyweight, a political force to be reckoned with and Bill Frist had his work cut out for him.

At the time, in Washington, the Democrats controlled the presidency, the House and the Senate. Bill Clinton had been elected in 1992 and immediately encountered troubles. By many accounts, his wife, Hillary Rodham Clinton, had not handled the healthcare issue well and to make matters worse, Jocelyn Elders had made some controversial statements about masturbation, much to the chagrin of the White House. The electorate had seemingly become disenchanted with the administration, tired of seeing nothing accomplished. Issues of tort reform, a balanced budget, term limits, welfare reform, moved to the forefront. These questions later became several of the planks in the "Contract with America" and this created a ripe environment for the Gingrich revolution that would soon sweep across America. (This environment would also bring with it a negative side. After so many promises, and what some would say was an overconfident and less than gracious victory lap, the Republicans quickly passed a litany of laws in the House which came to a screeching halt in the Senate where a minority of Democratic Senators were able to stall the momentum that then Majority Leader Bob Dole wished to see continue. The electorate once again had become disenchanted as witnessed in the fact that, despite his growing list of troubles, Clinton defeated Dole in 1996 and held onto the White House. Some would say that Clinton never ran against Bob Dole, but rather against Newt Gingrich.)

Bill Frist and his team responded with, "Eighteen years is long enough." They used Sasser's incumbency against him in a time when people were tired of incumbents. Sasser "accused Bill of being a Belle Meade doctor out of touch with America who doesn't know what the average person wants or needs." Bill responded by saying, "I've seen more real people and touched more real humanity in one night in an emergency room ward than you've seen in eighteen years walking the marbled halls of Washington."[15]

Bill communicated his belief in the idea of a citizen-legislator. He had done exactly what Congressman Joe Evins had suggested years ago. He had served in some other capacity for twenty years and now he intended to bring that experience, expertise and vision to Washington. He had no intention of becoming a professional politician or a Washington insider. He stated that if he were fortunate enough to be elected, he'd serve six years. If again he were fortunate enough to be re-elected he'd serve a second term but no more. Bill Frist sought to accomplish his goal and then return to live in Nashville under the laws he helped enact. He had no intention of going to Washington and never returning, a politician whose perspective was forever limited to the view within the beltway and who had lost touch with the rest of America. Bill approached politics not with the immediate thought of re-election but rather with the long-term perspective of what was good and right for Tennessee and America. Bill remarked that Washington had become a "two-year town when it should be a twenty-year town,"[16] meaning that it needed longer-term thinking among its leaders. Bill reminded voters that career politicians were not what the Founding Fathers had intended for government by and of the people; that those career politicians had become so enamored with re-election, so wedded to their jobs, that their careers interfered with the decision making part of their jobs. The soil of Tennessee voters must have been tilled with discontent because Bill Frist's words and ideas began to take root.

Surprisingly, the press reported that the first Frist-Sasser debate ended in a draw. In the eyes of Bill and his team, they won big. He'd evidently held his own against the current Chairman of the Budget Committee. The press declared the second debate, held in Memphis, a draw as well. This time, Bill appeared visibly more comfortable and substantially more detailed in his answers. As always, he learned quickly and the polls showed he was gaining points on Sasser. The third debate, staged in a Nashville town hall, featured questions from the audience. By all accounts, Bill walked smoothly and confidently away with the debate amidst a surge of support. Sasser, it seems, lost his momentum that night and never regained it.

Three weeks prior to the election, Bill donned an American-flag necktie and, along with his team, boarded a bus and began traveling Tennessee. His message was rather simple: most politicians were too busy talking while what America needed was politicians who would listen. And as a good doctor, Bill had become pretty good at listening to his patients. He was ready to advocate for them: "We need people to take some scalpels into Washington, listen, diagnose and fix the problem."[17] Bill and his team stayed on the road for three weeks and stopping in every town hall, corner café and radio booth that would give him five minutes of time.

Back home in Nashville, Dr. Karl VanDevender, the man handling the reins of the Frist Clinic, was on call at Centennial Hospital. Late in the day found Karl closely monitoring an old family friend. The elderly man dying of kidney failure had served the Frist family for much of his life as yardman, housekeeper and Mr.-Fix-it. The family affectionately knew him as "Mr. John." The end was inevitable. Karl and Mr. John both knew he'd die that night. It was only a matter of hours.

While monitoring Mr. John, Karl kept an eye on the election returns and in order to pass the time and talk about something other than the discomfort, he asked Mr. John, "Who do you think will win?"

"Dr. Karl," Mr. John said assuredly, "I know who's gonna win."

"How do you know?" asked Karl.

Mr. John shook his head, "Don't make me tell you that." Karl pried and Mr. John repeated, "Don't make me tell you that. Let me die in peace." Mr. John waved him off with a hand, "Don't make me tell you that."

Something in Mr. John's voice told Karl that his patient was beyond humor and these might be his last words. His tone was serious, solemn and there was no doubt that Mr. John believed every word he was about to say. Mr. John whispered, "Dr. Karl, since the day this happened, more than forty-four years ago, I've only told two people—my pastor and my wife." Dr. Karl pulled up a chair, sat down and leaned in close. "The day after Mrs. Frist brought that boy home from the hospital, she walked out on the front porch carrying a baby basket. That boy was wrapped up inside, sleeping. I remember it was unusually warm for February and he wasn't but a few days old. Mrs. Frist put him on the porch, pointed down the street to her sister's house and asked me not to move. She asked me to watch that boy and wait right there until she got back. She said, 'I'll be back in five minutes.' So I sat down on the porch next to the boy and no sooner had she left than a bright light came down from heaven. An angel wrapped his golden wings around the baby and said, 'John, don't worry about this baby. He's going to be fine.'" Mr. John paused and caught his breath, "'One day, he's going to be president of the United States.'" Mr.

John took a deep breath and motioned to the world outside, "That Senate race? That ain't nothing. He's got that in the bag."

Karl remembers the night and shrugs his shoulders, "Do I believe it? I wrestle with it just like you do, but those are the words of a dying man. Who am I to argue with him and why would he lie."[18]

Mr. John died that night but not before hearing that Bill Frist had defeated Jim Sasser in a landslide—by more than two hundred thousand votes, almost two to one. Bill was the only challenger to defeat a full-term incumbent in the 1994 elections.

On election night, after he'd been declared the winner, Bill's dad joined him on the stage where Bill placed that American tie around his dad's neck. The picture of the two, arm-in-arm, made the front cover of the next morning's paper.

Bill would later write in his book *Tennessee Senators*, "I salute Jim Sasser as a devoted public servant and a strong family man who raised two outstanding children and fought hard for the Populist principles he learned as a youth. In times when people wanted their government to take more of a role in their daily lives and were not so concerned about the level of spending, Jim Sasser was the ideal servant of his constituents." Jim Sasser accepted defeat gracefully and would later serve as President Clinton's U.S. Ambassador to China.

Bill moved to D.C. and took with him a young attorney from Nashville named Mark Tipps to serve as his chief of staff. Years later, Bill would write, "There was no one whom I trusted more, who displayed more integrity, who worked harder than Mark Tipps." Leaving their families with children in school in Nashville, they shared a D.C. house. Mark remembers, "Bill slept almost never. I'd get e-mail at one, two, three o'clock in the morning. I don't know when he slept."[19] They'd share a taxi to and from work and maybe a late-night pizza when the eighteen- and twenty-hour days forced them to skip several meals.

From his transition office, a cubbyhole in the basement with a phone, a desk and a few folding chairs, Bill began the process of hiring staff and setting up his Senate office. He also took time out to attend the freshmen senator meetings where he learned such mundane details as how he was to be paid, what type of healthcare he had, where to park and to what committees he was assigned. Finding themselves in a whirlwind of information and schedules, Mark remembers, "It was like putting your mouth around a fire hose."[20]

On their first day in Washington, Bill Frist, Mark Tipps, and Tom Perdue walked out of the Hyatt Hotel on New Jersey Avenue and up to the Capitol. Today was an orientation of sorts, and they were slated to meet with the other Senators, the first being Senator Paul Coverdell of Georgia. It was not entirely unlike the freshman recruits walking into the locker room and meeting the veteran players. They walked up to Constitution Avenue and stood at the intersection next to the Taft Memorial across from the Capitol. Bill looked at the agenda and stated to Mark and Tom, "Okay, we need to go to the Russell Building and see Paul Coverdell." The three men looked at each other but nobody moved. Soon, smirks broke into smiles. Admittedly, no one knew where to find the Russell Building. Bill, Mark, and Tom laughed and finally turned to a young lady walking the sidewalk carrying a stack of papers—a staffer who obviously knew where she was going. "Excuse me. Do you know where the Russell Building is located?" The lady pointed to the closest building, about seventy yards away. Welcome to Washington, Dr. Frist.

Bill was sworn in January 5, 1995. Following the swearing in ceremony, Bill gave his mother and father a tour of the Capitol, the Senate Office Building and his temporary office. When Bill's father saw Bill's name, "William H. Frist," printed on the door, he put his arm around him and pointed at the nameplate, "Something's missing, isn't it?" Bill looked, immediately understood what his father was implying and nodded. His father continued, "Don't forget who you are . . . and what you are." Within the week, Bill's staff had requested that "MD" be added to his nameplate—both on his door and his desk on the Senate floor. He was the first Senator in the history of the United States Senate to do so.

Given the fact that he had no real political experience and had held no political office prior to his election, he was tied for dead last in Senate seniority—99th and 100th out of 100—with Senator Spence Abraham from Michigan. This meant that when it came to office and committee assignments, Bill Frist got the dregs of the barrel—which is ironic given his current position.

To complete his immersion by fire, on his first day in office—as a newly elected member of the Banking Committee—he attended hearings on Orange County's municipal finance disaster involving defaulted derivatives. Speaking to the committee that day were such authorities as Alan Greenspan and Arthur Levitt. In one day, Bill Frist went from transplant surgeon in Nashville to a mere face behind a microphone at a Senate hearing, staring into C-SPAN and CNN television cameras.

Having term-limited himself to only two terms, Bill wasted no time in making an immediate contribution. On January 11, 1995, after just six days in office, Bill spoke on the floor of the Senate:

> Mr. President, I rise to address two matters. First, Mr. President, to let you and my other colleagues in the U.S. Senate know how honored I am to be part of this noble institution and how much I look forward to working with each of you in conducting what Senator Howard Baker called, "the business of the people." As I look around this great body I realize that I am one of the very few members who has come directly to the Senate from the private sector with no previous ties to Washington, D.C., or, for that matter, politics. The people of Tennessee elected me as a true citizen-legislator—to come to Washington for a period of time with a mission to accomplish and then return to Tennessee to live under the laws I helped pass. As a recently elected citizen-legislator, I carry a very distinct advantage: a closeness to the people with real jobs, and an immediate understanding of the message of November 8. During the last year, I have traveled to most all of the ninety-five counties in my home state of Tennessee—from Memphis to Mountain City—listening to the thoughts and concerns of private citizens and local officials. Coming directly from the private sector, I heard their message in the clearest possible terms, unfettered by the preconceived notions and prejudices of Washington.

> And their message was, "Change the direction of the country. Get the Federal Government off our backs, out of our pockets, and off our land. The arrogance of Washington is stifling us, and we are capable of making our own decisions." A simple, crystal-clear message. Mr. President, this is the message I bring to Washington. And there is no better example of the Federal Government's arrogance and unwanted meddling than the unfunded Federal mandates. [21]

Bill's first legislative proposal before the Senate was a term limits bill—something of a cattle prod in Washington. Quoting Harry Truman he said that term limits, "cure both senility and seniority, both terrible legislative diseases."[22] He supported a constitutional amendment requiring a balanced budget, extending a line-item veto to the president, and he was one of eleven freshman Senators who supported Trent Lott's ascension to Minority Whip. His first committee assignments were to Banking, Budget, Small Business, and Labor and Human Resources.

He also wasted no time in joining the Senators' weekly Wednesday morning prayer breakfast and the Senators' Thursday afternoon Bible study. Chaplain Dr. Lloyd Ogilvie remembers his dedication: "It was there that I first saw his great openness to reach across party lines. Unless he was required to attend a vote on the floor of the Senate, he never missed."[23]

For ninety days, Bill and his skeleton staff operated out of the basement until they finally moved into their permanent office. By this time, Bill had hired a full complement of staff, was routinely making speeches on the Senate floor, attending committee meetings and speaking with constituents. Mark Tipps recalls, "That's when he got his sea legs. The rest is history."[24]

In early 1995, Bill was sitting in a meeting with player representatives from major league baseball when his assistant, Ramona Lessen, handed him a message—President Clinton had nominated Dr. Henry W. Foster, the Chairman of Obstetrics and Gynecology at Nashville's Meharry Medical School, to serve as Surgeon General. After serving only six weeks in the Senate, Bill Frist stood at the brink of the first political test of his career—a test that would do much to define him in the years to come.

The nomination had thrown conservatives into a frenzy because of Foster's suspected support of abortion and his veracity pertaining to the number of abortions he had performed.[25] Opinions on Foster differed greatly. To some he embodied "the quintessential people's doctor of Nashville," and to others, a man who misestimated the number of abortions and been associated with a somewhat questionable birth control study by the Tuskegee Institute.[26] (Foster had performed or was listed as "physician of record" for thirty-nine abortions. When asked to explain, he stated that he abhorred abortion and supported abstinence first.) Clinton's team had failed to accurately vet Dr. Foster. The average American—still reeling in the wake of the Oklahoma City bombing, bored with the O.J. Simpson trial, and cringing at Dr. Jocelyn Elders' comments about kids' personal sexual activities—could see that the battle lines were drawn. On one side sat Planned Parenthood and the National Abortion Rights and Reproduction Action League, and on the other sat the Christian Coalition and several Republican presidential hopefuls like Bob Dole and Phil Graham.

Bill had served with Foster on an ethics board for area doctors in Nashville and knew him to be both a good man and a good doctor. He focused on Foster's credentials and his record, which included having founded and run the successful I Have a Future Program (one of George Bush's Thousand Points of Light) in Nashville. Bill personally read Foster's medical papers rather than rely on an assistant's summary, and invited Foster to his office to explain what he believed to be the role of the Surgeon General. Based upon his own investigation, he made his decision—one that was not popular with members of his own party.

Bill reasoned that when the Senate had confirmed C. Everett Koop as Surgeon General, an abortion opponent, his nomination had not outlawed abortion. Therefore, voting for Foster would not condone abortion. While Foster had in fact performed abortions, Bill knew he had spent his life providing care and hope for at-risk teens in a prescriptive program of what he liked to call "preventative medicine" countering teen alcohol and drug abuse, poverty, violent crime, low self-esteem, and other problems that plague children's lives.

Bill didn't want to upset his own party, but he was torn between the party line and what he felt was morally right. He also knew this would constitute Bob Dole's first major battle against Bill Clinton, one that would no doubt return in the upcoming election. In the days before the committee vote, several prominent Republicans cautioned Mark Tipps that this decision would bring a sure end to a short career in politics for Bill Frist. Additionally, the pro-life groups at home were angry because they felt betrayed—Bill had campaigned as a pro-life candidate.

Bill went to see Dole in his office, laying all of his cards on the table. He explained his reasoning, and, despite the difficulty of his decision, he admitted his intent to support Foster out of the committee. To his credit, Bob Dole understood Bill's position, thanked him for his candor and told him that while he'd like to have his vote, he appreciated him voting his conscience. Bill then returned to his office where he began phoning the pro-life groups back in Tennessee. Again, he explained his position, his reasoning and his belief that supporting Foster was not condoning abortion. In the months ahead, given the fury over partial birth abortion, Bill would get the chance to prove his pro-life stance.

Swimming against the current of his own caucus, Bill supported Foster's nomination out of the committee (a nine-seven vote) where it went to the floor and immediately met resistance and a Phil Gramm filibuster. Though, Henry Foster did not receive confirmation as the Surgeon General, the experience put Bill Frist on the political map, establishing him as an independent thinker—a true statesman not easily pigeonholed—admired by senators on both sides of the aisle. In the weeks, months and years that followed, even if they did not agree with him, Democrats began approaching him privately with questions regarding various medical practices and proposed healthcare policies.

A few of the pro-life groups that had supported Bill during his campaign had questioned their support of him following the Foster experience, but in September of 1996, Bill was given a chance to redeem himself on national prime time television. He was invited to participate in a *Crossfire* discussion hosted by Geraldine Ferraro and John Sunnunu regarding the partial birth abortion ban passed by the Senate. The Senate had passed the ban eleven months prior to the election and sent it to President Clinton who sat on the bill, only to veto it two months prior to the election. Sitting opposite Kate Michelman, Bill articulated the procedure as a form of barbaric infanticide and reinforced his pro-life position among viewers and potential voters. In an argument that grew heated, Bill returned time and again to the description of the procedure and the fact that alternatives existed. The horrific procedure simply served no medical necessity. He came across as calm, thoughtful, articulate physician who spoke with authority. If pro-life groups questioned his position prior to that night, they did not thereafter.

Later in the year, Bill once again swam against the tide of proposed legislation mandating helmet use by motorcyclists in all fifty states. The Republicans cited the Tenth Amendment and made a clear, and some would argue compelling, case for keeping that authority in the hands of each individual state. Though an ardent states rights proponent—as evidenced by his very first statement made on the floor of the Senate January 11, 1995—Bill uncharacteristically disagreed in this case. Because most of his transplant donors were motorcycle crash victims, and because he himself had survived a motorcycle crash, he knew from experience that federally mandated helmet use would save lives. When Bill Frist said he was pro-life, he meant it. Despite his support, the legislation did not pass, but Bill once again gained notice for his statesmanship and independent thinking.

Later in 1995, Dole appointed Bill chairman of the Medicare Working Group, a task force empowered to develop policies that would strengthen Medicare. The Democrats had charged the Republicans with cutting

Medicare, so Bill's job was to prove otherwise. In fact, Republicans were cutting expenditures in order to save and strengthen Medicare.

On September 14, 1995, Graeme Sieber, the director of a home for troubled boys in Cleveland, Tennessee, was lobbying Senators to limit cuts in facilities like his. Standing outside Senator John Chaffee's office in the Dirksen Building, his heart stopped. Literally. The director clutched his chest, gasped and collapsed sending aids and assistants into a frenzy. One Chaffee aid ran to Bill's office and screamed that a man in the hall was having heart attack. Bill grabbed his black bag from atop his closet and rushed down the hall. Upon reaching Sieber, he dropped to his knees and began immediate chest compressions and mouth-to-mouth cardiopulmonary resuscitation. He intubated him by inserting a plastic tube down Sieber's windpipe directly into his lungs, injected drugs directly into his veins and with a defibrillator (brought by the Capitol physician's office), shocked Sieber back to life. A few days later, Bill visited Sieber in the hospital, who gratefully thanked him and then reminded him, "Remember, Doc, I want you to help my boys back home."

Toward the end of that first year, Mark Tipps found Bill sitting in his office one day, staring at a patient picture and tapping his palm with a reflex hammer. For a man that had logged more than eighty thousand hours in hospitals, Bill simply missed medicine. He asked Mark if he knew of anyplace nearby that might let him spend an hour or so treating patients. Mark's staff found a local clinic and while Bill listened to people's hearts Mark checked to make sure his malpractice insurance was still effective. Bill continued "working" once a month at the clinic for months before the press ever caught wind of it.

In just six months as a senator, Bill began to gain the attention of those inside the beltway, and in July of 1996 was voted a "Freshman All-Star" along with Fred Thompson and Olympia Snowe in the July issue of *The Washingtonian*. As early as August, only eight months into his first term, *The Hill* printed its guide to some of the fast-rising stars of the GOP with input from pundits, pollsters, and political scientists around the country. Along with others such as Fred Thompson, Steve Largent, J.C.

Watts and Trent Lott, Bill was selected as one of the eight up-and-comers in D.C. out of all members in both the House and the Senate. Washington lobbyist Tom Korologos remarked that Bill "would be someone who I would think is looking at some point to run for President."

Staffers remember freshman Bill Frist as an approachable, likeable senator, never afraid of rolling up his sleeves. They also remember him outside the Senate Office Building standing in line at the corner hotdog stand at lunchtime with a handwritten list—there to buy lunch for his staff as well as himself.

In 1996, as the presidential showdown between Clinton and Dole neared, the Republican heavyweights from Bob Dole to Fred Thompson to the six Republican members of the House planned a rally in Bill Frist's backyard—Knoxville. Mark Tipps received a phone call from Dole's people asking Bill to speak. Mark hung up the phone, walked into Bill's office and reported the good news. Bill looked at his calendar and began thinking intently, tapping his palm again with the reflex hammer. When first elected, Bill asked his assistant, Ramona, to meet with his wife Karyn and merge both the family's schedule, i.e. baseball games, birthday parties and Cub Scouts, with the Senate schedule. That way, any time Bill had an afternoon in which no votes required his presence on the Hill, he could check his schedule and attempt to make one of his three boys' afternoon events in D.C. Somewhere in the past months, Bill had helped his youngest son Bryan, a Cub Scout, whittle, saw and drill holes into the wooden block that would soon become his Pinewood Derby car. Mark remembers: "It was something they had spent a good bit of time on." After finishing the small car, Bill's Senate schedule forced him to miss the inaugural race. Bill promised his disappointed son, that he'd make the next race. It just so happened that that race coincided with a visit from the Republican presidential hopeful, Bob Dole. Bill looked at Mark, shook his head and said, "I can't do that."

Mark was incredulous. Finally, he asked, "What do you mean you can't do that?"

Bill pointed to his schedule, "Bryan's Pinewood Derby race. I promised him I'd be there and I've got to keep it."

Mark was puzzled but knew better than to argue with his boss. If Bill said he either could or could not do something, Mark knew he had good reason. Mark nodded, walked back to his office and tried to think of a way to convince his boss to change his mind. After about ten seconds of thinking, he saw the clarity of Bill's position. "That was exactly what Bill Frist should have done. In a time when the country was talking about 'family values,' Bill Frist wasn't just talking about them, he was living them." Bill wrote a letter to Bob Dole welcoming him to Tennessee, apologizing for his absence and candidly admitting the reason. The letter was read at the rally and Bill's stock rose once more among his fellow Republicans.[27]

Given Bill's commitment to and knowledge of healthcare, the Republican Party, gearing up for the election, asked Bill to speak at the 1996 Republican National Convention in San Diego. During the 105th Congress, he joined the Foreign Relations Committee and was appointed to the National Bipartisan Commission on the Future of Medicare. Armed with his extensive history with medical research and the fact that he had treated tens of thousands of patients, Bill was chosen to head a public-health subcommittee that wrote bills to authorize the National Institutes of Health and eight other health agencies. Well suited to the role, he would quickly emerge as a thoughtful leader in the areas of science, technology and education.

By 1997, he had formed the Senate's first bipartisan Science and Technology Caucus, sponsored a resolution to double the NIH's budget over five years, and soon after, chaired the Subcommittee on Science, Technology and Space. As chair, he brought the multibillion dollar Spallation Neutron Source to Oak Ridge.

That same year, the aging and ailing Dr. Tommy Frist sent a letter to Bill and his siblings. Dated 15 December, it was addressed "For my family and future generations with great love." Much of the ethos and many of the tenets guiding Bill become evident upon reading the words of the senior Dr. Frist:

Dear Great-Grandchild,

My children have asked me to write down what I believe. They want their children and their children's children to know about some of the things that are important in life. That is why I have written you this letter. I am writing it to you, even though I cannot know you. I hope, as you read it, you will know me, and know your parents and grandparents, a little better.

I am now 87 years old, and so happy to be alive. I have had so many blessings and such a full life. Every day of my life has been happy. I hope what I have to tell you will help you know the happiness in life I have known.

I believe in a few simple things. I learned about them a long time ago from my mother and my father, my sisters and my brother, my teachers and my friends. I learned a lot in life, but I never changed these beliefs all the way through. This is what I believe.

I believe that religion is so very important. I was raised in the Presbyterian Church in Meridian, Mississippi, and I never missed a Sunday from when I was three to when I was eighteen. I believe there is a God and in Jesus Christ. The only prayer I ever pray is thanking God for all the blessings I have.

I never pray when I'm in a tight spot because I think God in his wisdom, knows what you need. I believe in the morality of religion—the Golden Rule. I say something nice to people when they deserve it. When they don't deserve it, I say something nice about other people, so they know how to act and they always smile.

I believe that culture is so important. My mother was so kind, so giving, so unselfish. My wife, Dorothy, is the same. When you marry, marry someone who believes in the same things you do.

Be happy in your family life. Your family is the most important thing you can ever have. Love your wife or your husband. Tell your children how great they are. Encourage them in everything they do. I never punished my children, never raised my voice with them. If they know you expect them to do right, they will do right. If you praise them for the good things they do, the bad things will disappear.

Be happy in your career. I was a doctor. I loved being a doctor because it meant helping people, being with patients every minute. All my sons were doctors. It's a great thing to be a doctor. Whatever work you do, do it well. Remember any job worth doing is worth doing well. Always do a quality job.

Be happy in your community. Charity is so important. Be active. Don't be self satisfied. There's so much good to do in the world and so many different ways to do it.

In politics, I believe in voting for the man, not the party. I voted for President Reagan and President Bush because they were good leaders not because they were Republicans. I am conservative. I believe the free enterprise system can do a better job at most things than government can. People should learn to be self-reliant; when they are self-reliant, they will have self-respect.

I believe good people beget good people. If you marry the right person, then you will have good children. But everywhere else in life, too, good people beget good people. In your work, when you hire good people, they, in turn, will hire good people and right on down the line. That's how we built Hospital Corporation of America. From the board members right on down to the man in the boiler room and the woman who makes the beds, we wanted good people with integrity and high moral standards. We made such a difference in the world with HCA, and we did it because good people beget good people.

I believe life is made up of peaks and valleys. But the thing to remember is that the curve is always going up. The next peak is a little higher than the previous peak, the next valley isn't quite so low. The work gets better all the time. Think about wars and peacetime—that's the challenge for great leaders. Think about business—there are always recessions and good times, but the good times always get better. Think about politics—we'll get a bad president and then a great president who corrects the things the other one did; that's a great thing about the party system. Or think about medicine, which is how I spent my life. Right now medicine is really at a peak as far as technology and science are concerned, but we're always down in a valley with the cost. In time, we'll get this fixed too. I'm sure we will.

Finally, I believe it is so terribly important in life to stay humble. Use your talents wisely and use other people's talents to help other people.

Don't think about the reward; that will probably come along if you don't go looking for it. (I always said at HCA that if we just concentrated on doing the best job we could of giving quality care, then the bottom line would take care of itself. And it did.) Always be confident. But never be cocky. Always stay humble.

So, my great-grandchildren, I hope you will live happy and long lives like I have. I hope this letter will help you. Maybe you will give it to your children, and they will give it to their children right on down the line. The world is always changing, and that's a good thing. It's how you carry yourself in the world that doesn't change—morality, integrity, warmth, and kindness are the same things in 1910 when I was born or in 2010 or later when you will be reading this. And that's a good thing, too.

Love,
Granddaddy[28]

Twenty days later, on January 4, 1998, after surviving a heart attack, two by-pass operations, a broken neck, colon cancer and a stroke, Dr. Tommy Frist died. Two days later, Bill's mother, Dorothy Fearn Frist, died. A joint funeral was held at Westminster Presbyterian Church on January 7. During the eulogy, Dr. Karl VanDevender opined, "One death is the story of the end of a long and illustrious life. Two deaths is a love story." He went on to describe Dorothy: "She was a wonderful mother. Her family was the center of her world. She was exactly the kind of wife any doctor would want. She was interested in his patients, liked to ride along on house calls, and was known to prescribe her favorite antibiotic to people who called when he wasn't home. And when he wasn't home, she understood."[29] At the time of their deaths, they had fourteen grandchildren and five great-grandchildren. When the procession pulled out of the church in a pouring rain, it stretched bumper-to-bumper down West End Avenue to the Cumberland River—a distance of four miles.

---

Descriptions of Africa, more often than not, include the words war-torn. This certainly applies to Sudan. Throughout the decade of the '90s, a government of Arab-Muslims in the northern half of Sudan declared war on the black Christians in the south. By all accounts, it is definitional genocide. Samaritan's Purse, led by Franklin Graham, learned of the atrocities, the dire need for medical help and opened a hospital in southern Sudan in an abandoned school when the existing hospital had been mined. Staffed with a full-time doctor and nurse, the hospital remained a common bombing target.

Franklin had known the Frist family for most of his life. He had grown up with two of Chet Frist's sons, Tommy and Bobby. He'd become familiar with HCA through the corporation's habitual donations of old or used equipment to Samaritan's Purse. Oddly enough, Franklin and Bill didn't meet each other until 1994, when Bill's campaign brought him through the Nashville airport. Though the two were introduced in passing, as Franklin boarded the plane which Bill had just exited, a friendship developed.

Living in Boone, North Carolina, Franklin also knew Dr. Dick Furman, a sixty-three-year-old heart surgeon, who, along with his brother, had started World Medical Mission—an organization that sends doctors into third-world countries to offer free medical services and operations. In another coincidence, Dick had completed his cardiac surgical residency with Bill's brother, Bobby, so he too knew the Frist family and Bill's work and reputation as a transplant surgeon.

Dick and Franklin both knew Bill was a member of the Foreign Relations Committee, so Dick was not surprised when Bill called him in early 1998 and asked if he could be included on a medical mission trip to Sudan to see grass-roots African medicine.

Several months later, Bill sat at the controls of a single-engine plane across Sudan at less than four hundred feet hoping to avoid detection on enemy radar. They landed on a grass plain and spent two weeks touring Samaritan's Purse hospital facilities around the Sudan. A mission organization using a plane for African travel might seem like an unwise use of resources, but they had limited options. Transportation by jeep simply wasn't feasible—an hour's ride in a plane, might take three days in a jeep—and northern troops looking for southern rebels made it quite dangerous.

The first morning, Bill and his team landed in a grass strip hundreds of miles from the nearest light bulb or asphalt road. As soon as the plane came to stop, camouflaged and armed soldiers emerged from the grass and surrounded the plane. Bill eyes grew wide. He looked to Dick and asked, "Are we in the right place?"

Recognizing the Sudanese rebels who had come to protect the plane and its passengers, Dick Furman responded with a smile, "I sure hope so." The soldiers were needed as a precaution because in the previous five years, the hospital had been bombed nine times.

Awake long before dawn, Bill would go for a jog with Dick, then return to shower beneath a bucket tied to a tree, in the twilight. He'd dress, characteristically skip breakfast and then, walking past the bunkers or ditches used in the event of a bombing, join the local doctors for rounds. And he never forgot to encourage the staff, as Franklin Graham remembers: "He's a great encourager of people. He lifts people up and takes time to look at what they do."[30]

Realizing that he might have as much to learn as to teach in sub-Saharan Africa where he witnessed disease and ailment not common to American operating rooms, he was slow to speak and quick to listen when asked his opinion. Bill would ask questions, listening intently. He seemed to value the opinion of the doctor who'd been "on the front lines" more than his own opinion. When asked to join in an operation, he'd scrub, washing his hands in bottled water, and join the team in the OR, where he'd ask a nurse to wipe the sweat from his brow. Needless to say, conditions were somewhat more sparse than he'd experienced in the States or even in the British socialized healthcare system.

Converted classrooms serving as the operating rooms, offered no running water and no electricity, so creating a sterile field became a constant challenge. By day's end, Bill often found himself operating by flashlight. Despite the primitive conditions, Bill found the doctors nothing short of amazing in their ability to practice much-needed medicine with innovation, a smile and a quick sense of humor.

In 2000, Bill again called Dick Furman and said he'd like to see what could be done about the HIV/AIDS situation in Africa. "So," Dick says, "Franklin and I took him back in and I guarantee that Bill's seen AIDS on a different level than 99 percent of the people who go to Africa." A few days into their trip, they met a young, single mother about twenty-five-years old. She welcomed the group into her thatched hut where the "walls were papered with newspaper. It was sparse but everything was clean as a whistle." The girl sat quietly on her bed with Bill on her right side and his niece on her left, holding the young girl's hand. Through an interpreter, she explained to Bill, Dick and Franklin that she was leaving her home the next day to return to live with her mother while she waited to die. The girl pointed to her infant baby beside her on the bed and smiled, telling them that her mother had agreed to raise the baby. The AIDS worker who had accompanied the group told them that, in fact, the girl had less than three months to live. Dick remembers: "We talked for thirty minutes and, yes, we talked about buying antiretroviral medicines for her. We talked about getting the medicine just for her and then realized there were millions more just like her. When we finished talking, Bill asked his niece to pray."[31] Dick pauses at the memory,

> That was hard. I think it really broke Bill's heart to walk away from that hut that day. But you want to talk about one man having an impact on a country. Bill went home and the next thing I know the President has signed a 15 billion dollar AIDS package designated for Africa. Now when we go over there, we can get drugs. I mean it's a whole different ball game now. We went back to Tenwek Hospital and met a husband and wife who had tested positive. In fact, their whole family had tested positive. When the father found out, he was going to kill his family and then himself. His wife ran back to the hospital and they told her, "No, wait. We have these drugs and they can help you. You can live another ten to twenty years and watch your kids grow up so they won't be orphaned." We went from nothing medically to offer them the idea that they can live a healthy life and raise their kids.

It's made a dramatic change in Africa. The world doesn't realize what Bill Frist did in making that happen. One man with one idea went in there and said, "We got to find out what can be done." And he did.[32]

Senate Chaplain Lloyd Ogilvie believes that Bill "comes to mind as one who has answered the call of peacemaker—not only in the Senate, but in faraway lands where war has raged for decades. A noted physician and surgeon, Frist has earned the respect of senators on both sides of the aisle, partly because he always seems to be on call—to talk, to listen, and to bring people together. Perhaps it is his medical training and years as a physician that have caused him to accept this role as healer—that have made him willing to bridge the gap between opposing camps. But more likely it is his own faith in Jesus Christ that enables him to reach out to others with needs greater than his own. But the peace he gives away is not limited to Washington. Each year he travels to sub-Saharan Africa with the missionary organization Samaritan's Purse, bringing not just his surgical skills and services, but also food, medicine, and most importantly the truth about Jesus Christ. Their motto is, 'We treat, Jesus heals.'"[33]

In July of 2002, a unanimous Senate passed the United States Leadership Against HIV/AIDS, Tuberculosis, and Malaria Act of 2002, and the International AIDS Treatment and Prevention Act of 2002. The combined, comprehensive package provided one billion dollars in spending the first year and two billion dollars per each year thereafter, with a five-year plan to reduce AIDS worldwide. Designated for treatment, vaccines and education, the funds included the creation of a children's assistance program to provide care and treatment to parents and caregivers infected with HIV. The President signed the bill into law on May 27, 2003. Following the signing, Bill told an audience,

HIV/AIDS threatens the survival of countries and the stability of our world—it undermines the hope for a better future for untold millions of people. But today, under President Bush's leadership, our nation makes a promise to commit unprecedented new resources to fight the plague that is

> HIV/AIDS. This emergency HIV/AIDS initiative will save millions of lives around the world. The new law will elevate U.S. leadership in the fight against HIV/AIDS to new heights. It will bring medicine, care, and education on prevention to places where none exists today. It will challenge other wealthy nations to join us in committing more resources to the fight. Most of all it will bring hope to people now resigned to disease, despair and death.[34]

That same year, sitting in the surgical waiting room of the Arlington Hospital, Dr. Ogilvie, waited alone while his wife, Mary Jane, underwent bypass surgery to alleviate a clogged artery in her heart which was hindering blood-flow to her badly infected lung. Hospitalized since April 12, her condition had grown progressively worse, and eventually she needed emergency cardiac surgery. Dr. Ogilvie waited patiently during the operation, praying constantly, and tensed up when, halfway through the operation, the young doctor entered the room, shaking his head. He pulled off his mask. "Dr. Ogilvie, I'm sorry, I can't finish this operation. It's too delicate. There's only one man in D.C., a doctor at Georgetown University, who could perform this operation and, because it's late Friday afternoon, there's only one man in D.C. who could convince him to do it." The doctor paused, "Would you happen to know Bill Frist?"

Dr. Ogilvie nodded, "I know him well. He's one of my best friends. We're in Bible study together every Thursday afternoon."

The young doctor asked, "Would you call him?"

Dr. Ogilvie did, and Ramona patched him through to Bill. Bill listened quietly and without another word, promised his friend, "I'll be there in fifteen minutes."

The senator raced across town, walked into the room and gently assured Dr. Ogilvie, "This is my expertise, let me take a look at the X-rays."

Bill examined the X-rays and nodded, "There is only one person in Washington who can finish this operation, and I'll call him."

When he called the head of cardiac surgery at Georgetown University hospital the doctor on the other end responded, "I'll scrub and be waiting on you." True to his word, the surgeon stood waiting at the door when Mary Jane arrived at Georgetown Hospital. After consulting with Bill for a few minutes, the doctor and his team wheeled her into surgery. Then to Dr. Ogilvie's utter amazement, Bill sat down with him to wait.

Dr. Ogilvie asked, "Bill, don't you have anything else you need to be doing."

"No." Bill said simply. "I have nothing else to do today except be with you."

In a later conversation, Dr. Ogilvie would reflect, "Can you imagine? He cancelled everything for the rest of the day."

Bill sat in the waiting room all during that surgery, thumbing the keys on his Blackberry, handheld computer. Dr. Ogilvie later joked, "I guess life is just too exciting to limit yourself to one conversation at a time."

Watching his fingers skim across the keys, Dr. Ogilvie asked, "Bill what are you doing?"

"I'm talking to your son Scott."

"What'd you say?"

"I told him that his mom was in a critical operation, and that the two of us are sitting here, waiting."

Within a few seconds, the Blackberry rattled again. Bill passed the handheld to Dr. Ogilvie and he read Scott's answer quietly to himself. It read, "I would give everything I have or hope to earn to be sitting there with you two guys."

The operation lasted for hours, well into the evening. Finally, after it had grown dark outside, the doctor walked through the doors and nodded. "It went well. She's okay. You can see her shortly."

Bill immediately pulled out his Blackberry and started thumbing a message on the keys. Dr. Ogilvie asked, "What are you saying?"

"I'm telling Scott that his mom made it and everything's okay."

The two walked to the recovery room to see Mary Jane as the Blackberry rattled again. Scott's answer read, "The hand of God has been on this day. And the fingerprints are those of Bill Frist."[35]

# 5

FOLLOWING THE HORROR OF SEPTEMBER 11, 2001, Americans could barely catch their breath, and then on the morning of October 4 national news reported that a photo editor at a tabloid publisher had contracted inhalation anthrax—possible only when at least ten thousand spores are present. Local and federal authorities rushed in, evacuated and quarantined the American Media Inc. building in Boca Raton while national media raced to cover the story.

In Florida and elsewhere, Americans watched for the latest reports wondering who was responsible and if the deadly toxin would strike elsewhere. It did. While false alarms erupted in Ohio, Upstate New York and Hawaii, paranoid accusations flew aimlessly about: "If they can do that, they can get it anywhere." Just as video images of 9/11 rocked the world, the invisible spores known as "weapons-grade anthrax" paralyzed communities. On October 8, a second Florida case emerged. The man, a co-worker of the stricken photo-editor, showed symptoms. Unbeknownst to Bill Frist, fracases that would erupt over the next several days would test his leadership abilities in much the same way that September 11 had tested President Bush.

Days later, reports surfaced that a woman in Tom Brokaw's office at the NBC *Nightly News* studios in New York City had been infected with skin, or cutaneous anthrax. Later in the day, additional cases of each type were confirmed. FOX News in New York reported that a letter addressed to its president, Roger Ailes, and containing a mysterious white powder, had been opened by an assistant. In Reno, Nevada, officials reported that a letter returned to Microsoft from Malaysia had apparently been tampered with and contained the same suspicious powder. Overnight, lab tests returned three positive tests for the letters sent to Microsoft, NBC and American Media. Worse yet, the tests confirmed that someone had intentionally "weaponized" the bacterium. The two floors surrounding Brokaw's offices were evacuated and Brokaw delivered his broadcast that Friday evening from the *Today* show studios in the adjacent building.

Then on October 15, a clerk in the office of Senate Majority Leader Tom Daschle opened an oddly-worded letter containing a powdery white substance exposing an undetermined number of staffers to the potentially lethal biological agent. The letter, dated "09-11-01," read, "You can not stop us. We have this anthrax. You die now. Are you afraid? Death to America. Death to Israel. Allah is great."[1]

Bio-terrorism is a different type of warfare, but it is still war, albeit without the explosions or other visible signs of attack. The enemy and their weapon remain invisible while evidence of their attack may not surface for days. Regardless, they achieve the same results. People die and when they do, they are just as dead as if they'd been shot.

"Bioterrorism is the intentional release of potentially deadly bacteria, viruses or toxins into the air, food, or water supply. Ounce for ounce, biological agents such as anthrax or smallpox are among the most lethal weapons of mass destruction known. Inhalation of a millionth of a gram of anthrax may be deadly. Some estimated that as little as 220 pounds of anthrax spores released over Washington, D.C., given the right atmospheric conditions could cause three million deaths."[2] Bill knew that such aerosolized forms of anthrax were perfected by the Russians in the 1970s. He also knew that following the dismantling of the Soviet programs in the 1980s, some seven thousand of their biological weapons system scientists posted their resumes, seeking employment with the highest bidders.

Bill had known for some time that America was woefully underprepared for such an attack. Working in emergency rooms had showed him the importance of a systematic approach and careful preparation. "After the Capitol shootings and the Oklahoma City bombing, I got to thinking about our nation's vulnerability should we be hit with a larger catastrophe, such as a bioterrorist attack."[3] To some extent he had been expecting this, though he did not know when or in what form. As early as 1997, Bill had led a series of hearings on bioterrorism, public health preparedness and antimicrobial resistance in the Senate Public Health Committee, which he chaired. In March of 1999, before a hearing on the United States Subcommittee on Public Health, Bill warned, "As a nation we are currently more vulnerable to bio-weapons than any other traditional means of warfare . . ."[4] In July of the following year, at a speech before the Center for Disease Control and Prevention's International Conference on Emerging Infectious Diseases, Bill asked, "Is the threat of bioterrorism real? Most experts agree that it is no longer a question of 'if' but 'when.' Today most Americans remain complacent to the threat of infection and skeptical of bio-warfare. And therein lies the danger. This trusting facet of our nature opens us up to terrorist attack." In October of 2000, Bill gave an address before the American Association of Medical Colleges saying, "Our ability to track outbreaks of infectious disease, foodborne illness, antimicrobial resistance and potential bioterrorist attacks is vital to our nation's public health and that of our global neighbors."[5]

Following the 1998 hearings before his Public Health subcommittee, he co-sponsored and ultimately passed, the Frist-Kennedy (along with twenty-seven co-sponsors) Public Health Threats and Emergencies Act of 2000 (Public Law 106-505) which provided an emergency preparedness framework across the nation. The bill improved hospital response capabilities, upgraded early warning systems at the Center for Disease

Control (CDC), improved training, staffing, and consequently, care, for victims of bio-terrorism as well as expanded reserves of vaccines and antibiotics, and provided additional preventative measures. In short, the 540 million dollars in the bill filled many gaps in the current bio-defense and surveillance systems.

Following September 11, Bill once again sensed the need to place bioterrorism on the front burner. On September 20, 2001, nearly a month before the Daschle anthrax incident, Bill sent a letter to President Bush recommending a series of steps to enhance the government's preparedness against potential biological attacks. Those guidelines would later serve as the framework for a bill he and Senator Edward Kennedy would introduce following the anthrax letters to Daschle and Leahy.

Anthrax is a bacterium, a naturally occurring disease, which when exposed to air, produces spores resembling seeds. These odorless, tasteless seeds, invisible to the naked eye, become lethal when totaling somewhere between eight and ten thousand spores—a quantity still smaller than a speck of dust. Thus, when the Daschle and Leahy staffers opened the suspicious mail, fears emerged that the entire Hart Senate Office Building had been exposed via the air ducts through which the spores could have traveled, unseen. In the moments following, panicked federal employees inundated the Capitol Hill operator with thousands of phone calls, crippling the telecommunications system. Following an informal event at the White House, President Bush notified the nation confirming what everyone had feared—anthrax had reached the Capitol. It was only the second known biological attack on U.S. soil—the first involved a religious cult in Oregon who had poisoned salad bars with salmonella in hopes of swinging an election in 1984.

Fear rippled through D.C. and the shockwaves continued days later, when two postal workers died after having been exposed to the bacteria at a non-Capitol Hill facility. Ordinary citizens began wondering, "Who's responsible?" "How much do they have?" "Who's next?" "How do we protect ourselves from something we can't see?" Health officials, nurses and doctors began asking, "How do we diagnose it? Treat it?" "What proactive steps can we take to prevent infection and what do we do to protect those who have been exposed?" And maybe more importantly, "how do we communicate with the international community, looking to us for answers?" The questions ran rampant and no one had answers. Media reports conflicted, confusion fed panic, and it soon became apparent that the public health system was ill-equipped to handle a widespread epidemic.

Bill Frist sat stunned at a roundtable discussion on bioterrorism at the Tennessee Emergency Management Agency headquarters in Nashville. Guests included doctors, nurses, hospital administrators, firefighters, police and other law enforcement, public health and emergency personnel from across Tennessee. At the crux of their discussions lay the unfettered truth. Not one branch of the state's system had the adequate training or resources to respond to such an attack. Bill's work in transplant surgery had essentially made him a de facto expert in infectious diseases. Sitting among his colleagues and constituents with so few answers made Bill realize that he and his team needed to act quickly before panic paralyzed the nation. The need for accurate, timely dissemination of information from the Capitol headed the list of priorities. With that in mind, Bill returned to his D.C. office and began organizing resources.

Bill soon learned that front-line responders in D.C.—those answering the calls and treating the possibly infected—lacked sufficient training, information and protective equipment. State and county public health laboratories suffered from a shortage of trained epidemiologists—scientists who understood how the disease spread—state-of-the-art facilities and equipment. Community hospitals had no established system to share information either with each other or other public health facilities in a timely manner. Even Vanderbilt Hospital acknowledged to Bill that it had no bioterrorism preparedness plan nor had it trained personnel to deal with such emergencies. From rural doctors, to city police and firefighters, to state public health officials, even to the governor's office, no one was prepared to respond to what might happen. Immediately, people remembered the movie *Outbreak* with Dustin Hoffman and René Russo, and asked, "Can that really happen to us?"

When Bill first heard about the Daschle letter he quietly minimized it because three years before he'd received a similar letter claiming to have been carrying anthrax. Bill had fortuitously instituted mail-handling protocols for suspicious letters. Thankfully, the letter had not contained anthrax and was later confirmed as a hoax. Bill hoped Senator Daschle too, had received merely a hoax. Still, he reminded himself, if true, the reports would confirm the first witnessed exposure of multiple people to airborne anthrax.

In the fifty years prior to 1994, only 224 cases of cetaceous anthrax were reported in the United States, while in the last century only eighteen cases of inhalation anthrax were reported. Not a single one of those inhalation cases was linked to 9/11. For most of recorded history, the threat of anthrax existed primarily for farmworkers, woolsorters. More rarely those who ate tainted meat might fall prey to the bacteria. Because the spores can survive in a dormant state in the soil for decades, anthrax most often infects grass-eating animals such as cattle, goats, sheep and horses. Today, viable anthrax spores can still be found along the cattle trails of the Old West.

Bill's next scheduled stop was to speak with the Nashville Rotary Club at a downtown restaurant. Oddly enough, the topic—picked some three weeks earlier—was bioterrorism. By the time Bill arrived at the Rotary meeting, he learned that his own Public Health Subcommittee staff had been meeting on the same floor in the Hart Senate Building, just doors down the hall from where the Daschle letter had been opened. Further reports confirmed that the Daschle letter did in fact contain a large amount of white powdery substance. Nasal swab testing had begun and the Capitol physician had distributed a short course of antibiotics for those in the Daschle suite. Bill felt the issue escalating.

Despite the fact that the HVAC had remained on, circulating the air, and workers elsewhere in the Senate Building had been exposed, the building remained opened and staffers continued to work in their offices. Bill wondered, "Why isn't the building closed and everyone out?" Unfortunately, the building would remain open another day and a half.

Bill flew to Washington that afternoon where Senate Republican leader Trent Lott immediately asked him to act as the liaison between the Republican senators and the medical and law enforcement investigators at the Hart Building. Senator Daschle had, in the meantime, set up a public health command room in the Secretary of the Senate's office on the third floor of the Capitol. From this room, staffers shared data and made their first attempts at a strategy. Soon, the same space became the command post for virtually every agency on Capitol Hill—the CDC, the Capitol Physician's Office, the Defense Advanced Research Project Agency (DARPA), the Senate Sergeant At Arms, the Capitol Police, Senate leadership, the deputy surgeon general representing the Department of Health and Human Services, and the Director of the District of Columbia Health Department. These agencies would, together, determine the best strategy and then communicate their plans to their home agencies.

Despite these attempts at coordination, Bill's own Public Health subcommittee staff, just a few doors down from the Daschle Suite, was receiving conflicting and outdated information. They knew about the letter and had obtained much of their information from the media.

In order to provide better information to Senate staff and to the public, Bill and his team held two press conferences that first day. Thereafter, they held one scheduled press conference each day for the remainder of the week. Unfortunately, many staffers remained confused about their own health risks. Most wondered how close they had to have been to Daschle's office to consider themselves exposed, but those questions stopped when everyone learned that the HVAC had continued to circulate. That's when everyone began to wonder if the innocent opening of a letter had been the catalyst to a nationwide health crisis.

Late Monday evening, staffers from Senator Daschle's office asked Bill's health subcommittee what they knew about anthrax and, more specifically, about the severity of their own health risk. Everyone on Capitol Hill knew Bill to be the Senate's only doctor and knew also that his team had been researching issues surrounding bioterrorism for years.

Naturally, they began directing their questions at him: "Is anthrax contagious?" "If so, and I've been exposed, is my family at risk?" "Will antibiotics kill the infection?"

Not contagious, anthrax only infects through direct contact with the spores. Consequently, the first order of business, that night, was to close off a section of the Hart Building. A uniformed officer stood outside Bill's office door to make certain that his staff could continue to operate without media interruption. Staff members continued to enter and exit the building totally unaware of the potential health risk.

Everyone who had been in the building submitted nasal swabs but only those staff members present in the direct vicinity of the opened Daschle letter received preventative antibiotics. Others were told to wait until the results of the nasal swabs were confirmed and reported.

Late that night, nasal swab test results confirmed that twenty-eight people inside or adjacent to Daschle's office had been directly exposed. Anxiety blanketed Capitol Hill. Capitol employees were afraid to go to work. Though officials quarantined Congressional mail answers had yet to take shape. What about the people whose results returned negative? Why did they have to take the antibiotics? Confusion reigned, even among the media trying desperately to interpret the news.

On Tuesday morning, police barricaded the southeast corridor of the fifth- and sixth-floor Hart offices. The police instructed staff members not return to their offices and to sit for a nasal swab if they had not done so already. Several hundred people lined up inside the Hart Building but progressed slowly due to the uneven supply of cotton nasal swabs and of the antibiotic ciprofloxacin (Cipro). Though testing was voluntary, word spread and staff members from other buildings began joining the line. No one felt safe no matter how far they'd been from Daschle's mailroom. Many people who stood in line, did so out of both fear and confusion, but they took solace in knowing they'd been tested. Anyone waiting for nasal swab results received a three-day prescription of Cipro if they so desired. Prevention became the buzzword throughout Capitol Hill.

Because Republican and Democratic lawmakers across Capitol Hill began calling Bill's office for new information, his staff took to updating his website as new information became available. When the CDC's website crashed, Bill's site took the overflow traffic. Digging their own mail-handling protocols—now some three years old—out of their files, Frist staffers, posted them on the website. The website had been one of the first places, even before the postal service, to post pragmatic information on what to do and how to handle suspicious mail. In an attempt to arm themselves with some type of proactive plan, businesses and government agencies across the country began printing out and instituting his office's preventative measures.

Working with the Capitol physician in the command room on the third floor, his staff continued to update their site, including FAQs, as minute-by-minute postings became available. The questions mounted and grew more specific, "Were the twenty-eight people now infected with the most deadly form—inhalation anthrax?" (They were not. Tests confirmed they had merely been exposed to the spores, but little information existed that explained what that meant.) "How long would they be out of their offices? Should they attempt to go to work the next day?" Desperate for information, people grew frustrated, even angry. Few knew where to turn.

On Wednesday, forty-eight hours after the letter was opened, committed staff continued to show up for work because good information was scarce. However, by then officials had closed the entire Hart building and moved the testing site to the Russell Senate Office Building.

Thousands of Senate and House staff and guests who had visited the Hart Building Monday, lined up for a nasal swab and three-day supply of Cipro. Bill's staff printed out information bulletins and handed them to each person standing in line. They knew that if someone was infected, symptoms would present themselves in one to seven days. Ninety-five percent of all anthrax cases were cutaneous. In the case of inhalation anthrax, the deadliest form, they knew that if antibiotics hit the bloodstream before the anthrax released its deadly toxins, they had an excellent chance of recovery.

Early Wednesday morning, Senate and House leadership met to receive reports that environmental cultures from several locations had proved positive for anthrax—including the service elevator—the vehicle that carried the mail from floor to floor. This suggested an even greater area of contamination and widened the net for possible infection. Their worst fears seemed confirmed. Immediately, Senate and House leadership independently decided to close office buildings for more thorough testing.

Later that day, the full Senate met to discuss their options. Bill presented what he knew, reassured many, and at the end of the meeting, his colleagues voted to keep their offices open through Thursday's session. Several senators urged that Senate business continue. They argued that to do otherwise, would merely convince those responsible that they could shut down the government with a single letter. No one wanted to give in to the terrorists. Even with little to no information available, most lawmakers seemed to believe that the letter was somehow linked with the attacks of 9/11. A plane had struck the Pentagon and killed 189, another plane—most likely headed for the Capitol—had crashed in Pennsylvania killing forty-four, and now, a contaminated letter addressed to the highest ranking member of the U.S. Senate threatened to shut down the U.S. government. The incidents, many logically concluded, must be related. The Senate compromised by closing their office buildings but remained in session in the Capitol Building on Thursday—as much a show of resolve to the terrorists as it was a necessity to remain attentive to the needs of the nation. In a separate meeting, House members closed their office building and adjourned. The media caught wind of the dichotomous decisions, fueling a volley of accusations. In fact, the miscommunication between House and Senate leadership resulted from conflicting interpretations of the environmental cultures taken from contaminated buildings. Few if any left the morning meetings with a true sense of the best course of action.

Acknowledging Bill's growing role in the crisis, Senate leadership asked that the Tennessee senator brief the chiefs of staff of all the senators, in the basement of the Capitol at 1 p.m. Bill remembers "it was a tense meeting."[6] By all accounts, the staffers were angry, frustrated and resentful. Though responsible for their offices, they had yet found a way to obtain accurate information. Questions flew: "Were they safe?" "Why the lag time between when the senators and their chiefs of staff were briefed?" "Were they in danger of real harm?" "Were the clothes they were wearing still carrying the spores and, if so, could they infect their children at home?" "How long would their offices remain closed?" "And with many working from home, how would they get information without access to their office computer?" Bill listened, gauged the level of stress rising in the room and saw the critical need for correct and effective information.

With offices closed, senate e-mail was effectively cut off, and most employees could not access internal senate systems and information from home. At the staff meeting, Bill realized he would need to make his personal senate website (Frist.senate.gov) something of a Grand Central Station for news, posting all information as soon as it became available. That solved the e-mail problem.

Bill's staff got to work, updating the site and adding: links with information about anthrax, strategies to deal with the recent or future attacks, now-standard protocol for opening mail, references, FAQs, updated current test results, and locations where individuals could be tested. Overnight, Bill's senate site did in fact become the central source for senators and their staff members.

Given confusing televised reports about the differences between inhalation and cutaneous anthrax, everyone on Capitol Hill wanted more and better information. Textbooks provided little, if any, information, because anthrax was just too rare. "What does the skin rash look like?" "What would symptoms of inhalation anthrax look and sound like?" Even Bill, with his twenty years in medicine, had never seen a manifestation of anthrax poisoning. He called his medical colleagues around the country, asking for help. Soon it came pouring in. He posted pictures of cutaneous anthrax on his website listing the day-by-day development of the rash, blisters and potential early-warning signs. "What about pregnant women?" "What are the side effects of Cipro?" In response to Bill's previous work on bio-terrorism, and his work on the Public Health Threats and Emergencies Act of 2000, his staff had long ago created a bio-terrorism section on his site. With the framework in place, they needed only to update and expand it. They linked the site with other reputable sites (including that of the CDC) providing useful information on bioterrorism, biological agents, and public health safety. They were quickly filling the information void, which Bill knew would allay people's fears.

The Capitol physicians confirmed that more than six thousand nasal swabs had been taken in two days and with all but twenty-eight returning negative. Only those twenty-eight, who'd been exposed via their proximity to the fifth and sixth floors of the Hart Building, received the sixty-day prescription of Cipro. Over the next several days, analysts collected thousands of environmental cultures. This glut of samples stretched local laboratories—already working around the clock—to their maximum. Bill noted that the added workload surpassed the "surge capacity." In Atlanta, the CDC was so overloaded that its sputtering power system failed, causing a blackout and a delay in testing.

The news worsened. Environmental samples from the Dirksen Office Building mailroom, the Hart Building, as well as one of the House buildings, confirmed anthrax contamination. On Thursday, House leaders decided to immediately close all congressional buildings until further tests were completed. A single letter had, indeed, effectively shut down the government. Now lawmakers wondered if it would shut down the city. (The Hart Building would remain closed for three months.)

During this time, the new mail sorting protocols led to the discovery a second anthrax-laced letter addressed to Senator Leahy. Opened within the safe confines of the laboratory, the handwritten letter matched identically to the first letter sent to Senator Daschle.

Operating out of the third floor command center, Bill and his colleagues held two press conferences, six hours apart, on Thursday. Meanwhile the CDC continued to mobilize and sent new people up from

AP/World Wide Photos

Senator Bill Frist talks with his father, Dr. Thomas Frist, Sr., at a campaign rally for Sen. Frist in October 1994 in Nashville, Tenn.

AP/World Wide Photos

Vice President Dick Cheney chats with Frist on January 7, 2003, as they conduct reenactments for newly elected senators at the U.S. Capitol.

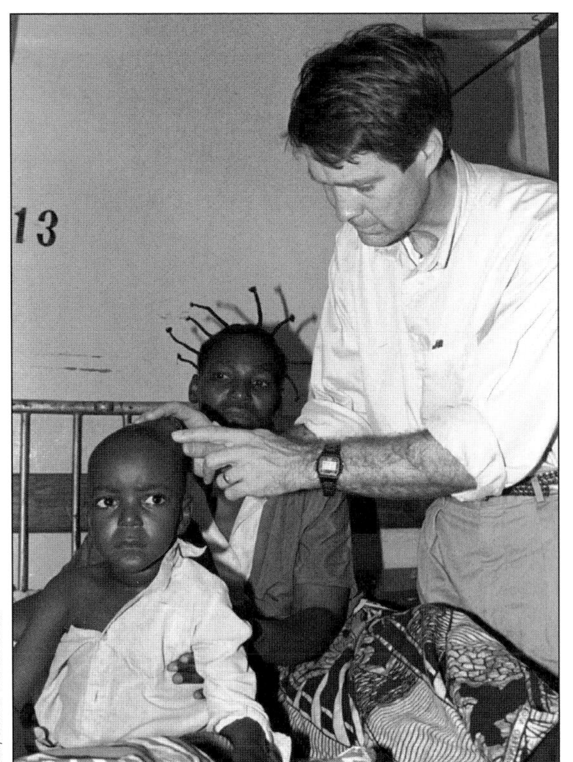


AP/World Wide Photos

Senator Bill Frist examines a child with an enlarged head at a mission hospital in Nyakunde, Congo, on January 25, 1998.

AP/World Wide Photos

Senate Majority Leader Bill Frist walks off the Senate Subway on his way to see his new office in the U.S. Capitol before the opening session of the 108th Congress, on January 7, 2003.

Reuters

Bill Frist and wife, Karyn, arrive at the U.S. Capitol to swear in newly elected senators.

AP/World Wide Photos

Frist watches as U.S. Public Health Service Commissioned Corps Readiness Force nurse Lucienne Nelson, properly disposes of the needle used to give Frist his smallpox vaccine in Washington, Friday, March 14, 2003.

AP/World Wide Photos

Bill Frist plays with an unidentified child during his visit to a Salvation Army orphanage home in Soweto, South Africa, on August 21, 2003.

AP/World Wide Photos

Frist talks with Ronny Lancaster, senior vice president of Morehouse School of Medicine in Atlanta, during commencement ceremonies on May 17, 2003. Frist was the keynote speaker.

Samaritan's Purse

Rev. David Kilel, chaplain at the Tenwek Hospital in Kenya, shakes hands with Samaritan's Purse President Franklin Graham, who presented a new vehicle to enable Rev. Kilel to expand his ministry.

AP/World Wide Photos

President George W. Bush talks after signing a bill to expand unemployment benefits in the Cabinet Room of the White House.

AP/World Wide Photos

Members of Congress bow their heads in prayer on Capitol Hill on September 11, 2003, during a ceremony making the second anniversary of the Sept. 11 attacks. In the front row, left to right, are House Minority Leader Nancy Pelosi, House Majority Leader Tom DeLay, Senate Majority Leader Bill Frist, and Senate Minority Leader Tom Daschle.

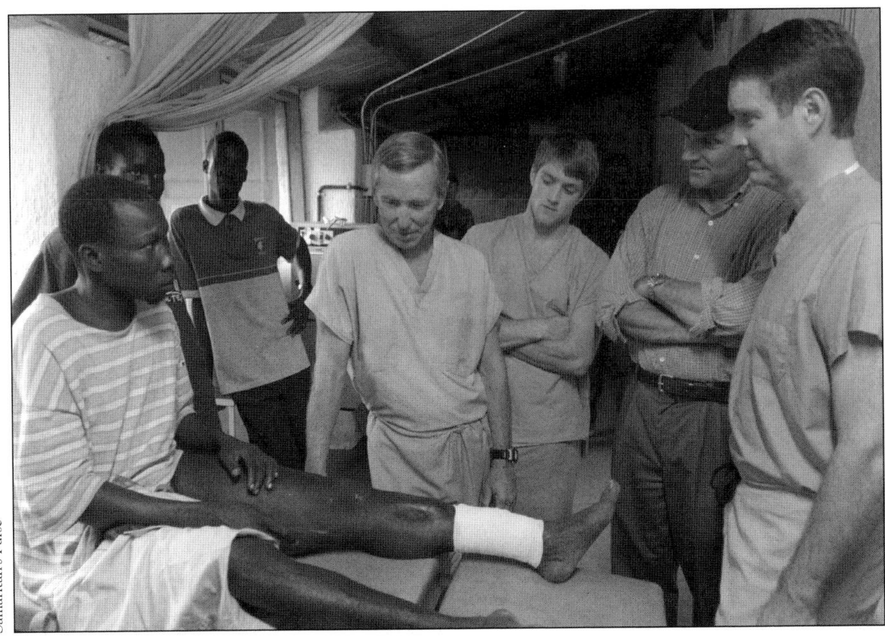

Samaritan's Purse

Bill Frist consults with a patient at the Lui Hospital operated by Samaritan's Purse in southern Sudan. With the senator (from right to left) are Franklin Graham, Frist's son Jonathan, and Dr. Richard Furman. Senator Frist has made five trips to Africa with World Medical Mission.

Reuters

Frist listens at a press conference (with Sen. Don Nickles) regarding Miguel Estrada dropping his bid for a federal judgeship.

Samaritan's Purse

Sudanese women fetch water as Bill Frist and Franklin Graham visit caves that serve as bomb shelters in the Sudanese village of Lui.

AP/World Wide Photos

Bill Frist talks to reporters in the Capitol about one of the biggest overhauls of the Medicare health insurance program for the elderly in history.

Atlanta. With these press conferences, held so closely together, officials finally felt they'd turned the corner on informing the public. The media now had a more comprehensive collection of facts regarding the basics about anthrax: risk of exposure, the available testing procedures, and, of course, treatment options (including the nature of Cipro and its side effects).

Closing Capitol Hill meant moving the central testing site. Early Thursday morning, Bill stopped in to see if the day-care center they'd chosen, could accommodate the impending influx of people. Though Bill left feeling that the facility could withstand the onslaught, he asked the director of his health subcommittee to visit the site every two hours to maintain some semblance of quality control. By late morning, the line of people stretched around two sides of a city block, requiring most to wait over an hour.

Friday brought with it a lull and a growing, (albeit false), consensus that the anthrax outbreak had been contained. People believed that officials had not only identified and were treating all who had been exposed, but that the antigen and spread of infection had been contained. Surely the crisis neared its end.

Communication had steadily improved over the five days. Consistent and up-to-date information now rolled out of the command center, and people became accustomed to the faces that had begun regularly appearing at the microphone; particularly Bill's. The public identified with and appreciated his gentle doctor's bedside manner coupled with his knowledgeable disposition. He assured. He assuaged. He soothed. And, in turn, they trusted him. Who better to have at the helm than a man who'd spent his twenty-year medical career trying to tame a sea of infectious diseases? The team candidly addressed the lingering unknowns: "How will people respond to long term (sixty-day) use of a powerful antibiotic like Cipro?" "What if they'd missed someone or, worse yet, had failed to diagnose someone?" "What if the test results were wrong?" "Was it possible for someone to visiting the Hart Building on Monday, to have returned home—somewhere in the U.S.—and taken the infection with them?"

"Could the ventilation system have spread the spores farther than once thought?" "Could the Dirksen mailroom have been infected?" "Should they have paid more attention to possible mail room contamination?"

The following day, the answer would be yes.

If the weekend brought with it a sense of calm, it was only the calm that arrives just before the storm. On Saturday morning, Bill drove to the Capitol for what he thought would be a brief meeting with the response team. They had planned to formulate additional precautionary steps for the following week.

Instead, the meeting began more like hospital rounds—with a patient history. A local community physician had contacted the CDC Friday night regarding one Thomas Morris, Jr., an employee at the Brentwood Post Office in Washington, D.C. (just a few miles from Capitol Hill), the fifty-five-year old had presented symptoms that, while usually associated with the flu, were also consistent with inhalation anthrax: shortness of breath, abnormal chest X-ray with enlarged lymph nodes but clear lung fields. Related tests had been performed but results would not be available for twenty-four hours.

The situation reminded Bill of the eight-year-old little girl he lost to burn infections during his residency. Tests told one story. Instinct told another. Bill became truly alarmed.

The ten thousand spores needed to produce inhalation anthrax would never have traveled the several miles to Brentwood—it was impossible for someone so far from the Hart Office Building to become infected. So, if this wasn't the flu and someone had become contaminated, then how and where had he been exposed? The only logical answer: *outside* the Senate Building.

Unfortunately, as Bill and the team quickly discovered, the best information that modern science currently had to offer was wrong. Dead wrong. If the test results came back positive for inhalation anthrax, then was the United States headed directly into a national catastrophe? How much of this stuff was out there and how many more anthrax-laced envelopes had been opened or handled? Would cases across the country start popping up out of the woodwork? Would the postal system have to shut down completely? Just how big of a conspiracy was this?

Bill sat in the meeting and realized nothing was certain. Right before their eyes, an unimaginable crisis continued to develop. Had it only been five weeks since the unthinkable collision of two planes into the Twin Towers?

The doctor-now-senator rose from his chair and placed a call to the White House. He asked to speak with Tom Ridge, former governor of Pennsylvania and the newly appointed director of Homeland Security. Bill reported that because the disease was now appearing and behaving uncharacteristically, the public health situation could potentially ". . . explode as a national security issue and a national public health emergency."[7] If people could become exposed simply by handling the mail without opening it, then untold numbers of workers across the country could soon present the same symptoms.

An hour later, the team reconvened for a conference call with Governor Ridge and the nation's highest officials in charge of emergency preparedness and response: Tommy Thompson, Secretary of Health and Human Services; Bill Knous, director of Health and Human Services Office of Emergency Preparedness; Dr. David Fleming, from the CDC in Atlanta; Joe Allbaugh, from the Federal Emergency Management Administration.

After Bill's opening remarks, each member of the Ridge team took approximately five minutes to deliver his brief. Despite the steepness of the learning curve, the pool of collective information had grown but there was still much they did not know. As the phone line grew quiet and tense, Bill reiterated the gravity of the new knowledge that someone outside the system had become infected. Before they hung up, Secretary Thompson told each member, "Make a list of whatever you need. It will be provided."[8]

Now recognized as the face behind the microphone, Bill found the networks fighting over his available time. Within days, he appeared on *Today*, *Larry King Live*, *Hardball* and *Fox Morning News*. Bill woke Sunday morning and as he prepared for a 10 a.m. talk show regarding the week's developments on the Hill, he learned of Thomas Morris's test results. Morris had indeed tested positive for inhalation anthrax. Within the hour, the public health command team converged at the Brentwood post office, acquiring both nasal swabs and environmental cultures. The emergence of infection outside of the Capitol convinced Bill and his team that their understanding of how the disease spread, was almost pre-industrial—that the data they'd been using had been compiled before buildings were air conditioned and before forced air was used to sort mail—and therefore outdated. They concentrated on how anthrax occurred and spread naturally, not on how it could be used by terrorists.

Two days later, Thomas Morris succumbed to the antigen. Two days after that, a second postal worker, Joseph Curseen Jr., died from the same infection, both deaths tragically unforeseeable.

The team reevaluated every assumption they had made—especially the likelihood of contracting inhalation anthrax versus cutaneous anthrax. As news of more infection spread, Bill's senate website was receiving an average of forty thousand hits a day. People devoured the information as quickly as it became available. Postal facilities began irradiating mail (gamma rays kill anthrax) and as many as ten thousand people in and around the beltway were taking Cipro. Thankfully, the federal government had negotiated with Bayer, the German company which produces Cipro, to purchase the pills for ninety-five cents each, far better than the usual retail value of four to five dollars per pill.

As Bill continued his circuit of talk shows and interviews he emphasized two themes: anthrax isn't contagious, but fear is (he admittedly borrowed this phraseology from *Newsweek* writer Jonathan Alter); and in the war against bioterrorism, information is power.

He suggested faith as a relief to the building anxiety, urging viewers: "Keep the faith. For many of us, faith was a source of comfort and strength in the wake of the unspeakable horror we witnessed [9/11]. As a medical doctor, I know the healing power of prayer. In these difficult times, prayer can help ease anxiety and bring us together. This is a time to draw strength from the traditions of your church, synagogue, mosque, or temple. Knowing that God is just and that He is in control offers great comfort when we feel so powerless."[9]

In light of the week's events, Senators Frist and Kennedy, borrowing from Bill's letter to the President dated more than a month ago, sponsored the Bioterrorism Preparedness Act of 2001. The act built on the 2000 bill and filled in even more gaps in the nation's defense against bioweapons, moving the country, "from under-prepared to appropriately prepared."[10] Highlights included the myriad city and health departments lacking up-to-date diagnostic equipment and high-speed internet access as well as the dismal condition of laboratories at the CDC in Atlanta. The nation's Center for Disease Control sported cracked and leaking pipes repaired with duct tape; a sputtering, blackout-causing power system; and the CDC's Intelligence Service—a sort of SWAT team—lacked such basic field equipment as two-way pagers.

In 2002, Bill would be instrumental in ensuring over three billion dollars in appropriations to fund antibioterrorism activities. True to his belief in satisfying a need at the point at which it exists, Bill secured more than one billion dollars to upgrade state and local public health and hospital infrastructures. A 600 percent increase over the previous year's funding levels.

In the wake of the 2001 anthrax attacks, the FBI spent more than 251,000 man hours, conducted fifteen searches, interviewed five thousand people and served four thousand subpoenas—all without an arrest.[11] Whoever was responsible knew how to remain anonymous. Some experts hesitated to attribute the anthrax attacks to Al Qaeda due to the ineffectiveness of the method, a method akin to hijacking a motorcycle and driving it into a telephone booth. Had Al Qaeda planted the anthrax, they'd more likely have blown it into an air vent and infected hundreds or even thousands of Americans.

With the initial attacks still unsolved in February 2004, terror struck again—this time in Bill's own office. Employees working in his Senate mail room discovered a suspicious grayish-white powder beneath an automatic mail-opening machine. Tests soon confirmed that the powder (mostly paper dust) contained the deadly poison ricin.

Two hundred more times potent than cyanide, ricin, a derivative of the castor bean, is a deadly poison with no known antidote. One milligram can kill an adult. Ricin reached international fame in 1978 via one of the more famous Cold War assassinations, which read more like something out of an Ian Fleming James Bond novel than a news report. Bulgarian dissident Georgi Markov died when a ricin-filled dart placed in the tip of an umbrella was stabbed into his leg as he strolled down the sidewalk. In January 2004, ricin was found in a London apartment and traced to seven men of North African origin who were later linked to Al Qaeda terrorists and Iraq. The following October officials found a package containing ricin at a postal facility serving Greenville-Spartanburg International Airport in South Carolina.

Fear and shock rippled through the Frist office and the Capitol, but past experience provided a more ready response. A specialized marine unit—the Chemical Biological Incident Response Force, or CBIRF—was deployed to Capitol Hill and sixteen employees who had been in the vicinity of the machine underwent decontamination procedures before being sent home. The Dirksen, Hart and Russell buildings were closed; their ventilation systems, though now fitted with filters sensitive enough to determine the existence and spread of biological agents, shut down as well. Because the powder had spilled around the base of the machine, no one could trace the toxin to any one letter or envelope.

At a late-night press conference, Bill assured the public that if symptoms of poisoning failed to surfaced within eight hours, contamination seemed unlikely. "Nobody is sick. We don't expect anybody to get sick."

Good news followed. The perpetrator(s) either lacked the knowledge or the quantity to have caused any serious damage. The powder found in the Frist office contained traces of ricin so minute it was difficult to evaluate for purity or particle size. It seemed more of a pesky warning by a disgruntled citizen than an all out attack by Bin Laden's Lieutenants. While this news was encouraging, by March officials would be investigating the driver of an eighteen-wheeler in Florida for the attack. Though not seemingly funded by an extremist group, in Bill's mind, the intention remained the same. Someone had tried to assassinate him and the members of his staff—a sobering thought.

# 6

UPON BECOMING MAJORITY LEADER, Bill had a mere two weeks to assemble his staff before the Senate returned to session—a tight time-frame indeed. However, as always, he hit the ground running. "Bill Frist was making brick with one hand and laying it with the other."[1]

Despite its high visibility, many consider the job of Majority Leader an unenviable position. Howard Baker once likened it to taming tigers. Tennessean Alan Murray, the former Washington Bureau Chief of *The Wall Street Journal*, opined "being Senate Majority Leader is akin to being groundskeeper at a cemetery. You have a lot of people under you but they aren't paying much attention."[2] And Tom Daschle bluntly offered that being Majority Leader is like "loading frogs on a wheelbarrow."[3]

Unlike the Speaker of the House's role in the House of Representatives, the Majority Leader has no magic arrow in his quiver—no real power—to force any of his colleagues to do his bidding. In the most exclusive fraternity in the world, each senator is often an island unto himself, accountable to no one but the electorate who speaks once every six years. It's much like a law firm where each member is an equal partner. They can ask politely for favors, give-and-take a bit, but at the end of the day, each owner maintains the power to disagree and disrupt. Of course, this is exactly what the framers had in mind when they wrote the Constitution and created the counter-balance body to the House. Naturally, it takes a gifted leader to generate consensus and influence the Senate.

Bill Frist keeps a stethoscope and several models of now antique pacemakers about the size of a common beeper, along with a reflex hammer, as paperweights on his Senate desk, as reminders of who he is and from where he's come. Framed and hanging on his wall, is an American flag painted by his son, Harrison, at age twelve; an original portrait of Andrew Jackson; gifts from transplant patients; and photographs of his family and patients.

Once selected as Majority Leader, he requested that all of his Republican colleagues obtain and learn to use a Blackberry wireless handheld device. Technologically savvy, he is seldom far from his, allowing him to maintain contact with forty-nine other senators as well as friends across the country. Ramona still merges the family schedule with the Senate schedule assuring time for his sons' interests and activities. When his sons Jonathan and Bryan began showing signs of talent as rock climbers, Bill installed a rock-climbing wall next to their house in Washington.

Taking his father's advice to heart, Bill has hired good people with strong morals. As Majority Leader, he has built a strong team that he trusts—key for a man in his position. Aside from leading the Senate, he must also track some 2,800-odd pieces of legislation, yearly. Despite the misperception that he now must be a consummate Washington insider, he still remains wary of a myopic Washington view of the world. He respects government and understands it works best when it creates an environment in which people can flourish.

Like transplantation, the Senate schedule suits Bill. Though hectic, he functions best when life is at its busiest. With every minute of every day planned for him, he eats when he can, not when he wants to for it is seldom convenient, and friends say he hasn't slowed a bit—still existing on little to no sleep. "He's the energizer bunny,"[4] they say. "He's a night owl and early bird all wrapped into one."[5]

The majority of Tennesseans agree that he has more than delivered on his campaign promises—to listen, diagnose, and fix—as evidenced by the 2000 election, in which he was re-elected by more votes and a greater majority than any elected official in the history of Tennessee politics. Even across the aisle, members agree he is a good-hearted man of integrity, who sees the best in people; a man who is trusting, filled with compassion and who has maximized the opportunities that life has offered him. He has even become an unofficial doctor to several senators—Democrats included. The bottom line? They trust him.

Despite being pulled in so many directions, Bill Frist remains focused on several key issues: Iraq, terrorism, AIDS, race relations, judicial appointments, overcoming the Democratic filibuster, passing the marriage amendment, making tax cuts permanent, Medicare, and foreign relations.

Mark Tipps explains,

> He's not one to let his guard down so Iraq and terrorism are the top two. Then, the completion of Medicare reform. That is a future catastrophe coming just based on the demographics. He knows that as well as anybody. Global AIDS is and will continue to be a major issue not only because it's the right thing to do and because millions of our fellow human beings are dying, but finding a cure and affordable treatment for HIV/AIDS is critical to the war on terrorism. People don't normally equate AIDS with world terrorism, but when you've got one out of three or four adult males dying, you, by definition, have unstable governments. When you have unstable governments you have the perfect breeding ground for terrorism, One way to begin to address it is to address the stabilization problem and one of the major threats to stabilization is AIDS. Again, it goes back to the senator's comment that "D.C. is a two-year town when it ought to be a twenty-year town." He knows that we will either face this problem now, or later. This

> isn't going to go away over night, but if we don't start thinking about it we are going to have to deal with the destabilization of an entire continent. Another issue on his radar screen is our relations with China. World security, trade, economics, each of these will be affected by China in the next two or three decades. China will be a major area of focus.[6]

Bill has an astounding ability to process information—particularly large amounts. Those who know him see him as "a forward thinker," "not lost in the forest for the trees," and "intensely focused and results-oriented." But there must be more. Plenty of doctors and senators fit the same description, so what makes Bill Frist different? Mark Tipps suggests, "Bill Frist thinks in much the same way that Wayne Gretzsky played hockey. He's not skating where the puck is, he's skating where it's going to be. Bill is focused down the road. He did that with bioterrorism, with AIDS, with the Republican Caucus and re-election and he's doing it now."[7] Barry Banker admits, "I'm not sure that brain of his has an upper limit."[8] Vanderbilt colleague John Morris remembers, "He can juggle so much. Whereas you or I can handle six or eight things at once, he's unreal. He can multi-task on an exponential scale. To say he thinks outside the box is an understatement. Whereas we normal people are limited by our own constraints, he doesn't seem limited by any of them."[9] Childhood friend John Gibson reflects, "He's like a good chess player, thinking ten to twelve moves down the board."[10] Princeton classmate and longtime friend, Ed O'Lear agrees, "Bill is a great equalizer. He's can understand and make sense of mass amounts of information and detail. Yes, he thinks outside the box, but he also looks under the hood. He'll be the first to roll up his sleeves and I've never seen him ask a staffer to do something that he either wouldn't do or hasn't done . . . He's not afraid to get his hands dirty."[11]

Another Princeton classmate, Gick Berg, emphasizes, "This guy has been so accomplished in every thing he's ever done. From Princeton, Harvard, and Mass General, to working with Shumway, he's accomplished as a visionary in science, and now he's become a visionary as

Majority leader in the U.S. Senate. I often tell people that if we are not going to support this guy, who then? This is an extraordinary man, and any of us would be pleased to see him as President of the United States. Would it surprise me to find out that, as a kid he wanted to be president but, oh by the way, he was going to be a doctor first? Absolutely not. However smart you think Bill Frist is, he's smarter. He's is able to quickly assess risk and reward, and *if* he has the ambition to become president, having that ambition does not invalidate the substance that he can bring to the office. It's like being a transplant surgeon. He knew he belonged there. If you were being cut on, would you want someone performing your transplant who didn't think he belonged there? Sure he's confident, sure he's competitive, he's one of the most competitive people I know in a nice sort of way, so I've never worried about him being the friendly humanitarian doctor getting thrown into a world of sharks. Anybody who knew him well, knew he could handle whatever they threw at him. Billy's got sharp elbows and he can take care of himself."[12]

While Bill's friends and colleagues admire the course of Bill's life, his leadership and his long list of accomplishments, they are even more impressed with Karyn. Ed O'Lear, known to Bill and Karyn's kids as "Uncle Ed," insists that "Bill without Karyn would be a very different person. She is his absolute best friend. When you get one, you get the other. She's phenomenal. They make a great team and without her, there's no Bill."[13]

Bill has limited himself to two terms, but few think that 2006 will mark the end of Bill's political career. "I've always felt that Bill had some sort of Manifest Destiny about his life. We all did,"[14] offers childhood friend, John Gibson.

Bill carries an infectious enthusiasm in everything he does that spreads to those around him. Whether at Vanderbilt or on the Hill, the teams he has built see him not so much as a Senator but as a doctor making rounds, training young residents and interns. Rather than coming away from a meeting feeling brow-beaten or stifled, they feel empowered, equipped and welcomed at the table. Vanderbilt assistant Tracy Frazier remembers, "I interviewed with Bill on a Friday and he asked me to start on Monday. I was just his assistant but he would literally stop what he was doing and ask me my opinion on something. Not only that, but he'd listen. He does it still, even today. Then and now, I felt valued, and I'm a better person for knowing Bill Frist."[15] Dr. Dick Furman, who has operated with Bill in Sudan every year since 1998, says, "All men really are equal to Bill; that's just the way he is."[16]

In recent years, Bill has become more verbal about his characteristically quiet faith. Maybe it's because he has been given far more opportunities to speak publicly. Despite the spotlight, though, he is neither talkative nor didactic. One might say he embodies St. Augustine's tenet: "We should preach the gospel at all times and if all else fails, use words." His work in the Sudan is a prime example. Bill's faith can be described as long on action and short on talk.

Transplant partner and good friend, Walter Merrill, maintains, "If he wasn't working, he was as regular as he could be in going to church on Sunday and I have no doubt that he prayed for his patients. He's a man of faith, with outstanding moral values and certainly a product of his upbringing. He's honest, forthright, well-intentioned and got enormous energy. He never seems to get tired. I can get by on little sleep compared to most people but he puts me to shame to do that consistently. He's on the high end of high-energy spectrum. He is one of the most talented, hard-driving and courageous people I've ever known. He has internal drive to try to do good works and make the world a better place. And, he didn't have to do it. He's chosen to do it."[17]

Franklin Graham says of Bill, "He's got the opportunity to do anything he wants to do and yet he's in politics because for him right now this is a calling. He really doesn't have an axe to grind. He really wants to do the right thing. He is a great encourager of people. He lifts people up, and takes time to look at what they do. He comes from a Presbyterian background, doesn't shy away from that, or hide from it. Now, he's not a preacher, he's not an evangelical minister, but as a transplant surgeon he was very clear in telling people who made that heart and who made it work. He believes. He's not ashamed of the gospel."[18]

Dr. Ogilvie comments, "Bill Frist understands that he is a riverbed for the flow of God's power, and not the river. I see many parallels between the life of William Wilberforce and Bill Frist. Both possess a great level of intelligence, then human talents, and then an openness for the supernatural gifts of God, which is a rare combination. Bill represents one of those who has this high calling. He really is concerned about the country and the issues that affect everyone. He has a tremendous ability to analyze problems and envision solutions. He recognizes there is supernatural power available to a leader who is open to receive it and he recognizes that talent is not enough and grasps with clarity that he must turn to God for help. Often, I have seen him go as far as he could go on the level of talent and intellect, but then I saw him again and again turn to God and ask for wisdom to understand and know what to do. We've never talked about any issue that took longer than five minutes that he didn't ask for prayer at the end of it. He'd pray and then I'd pray. There was a kind of reciprocity in that he was as concerned about knowing my challenges as he was in my knowing his. He knows that to lead with power and decisiveness requires a constant flow of God's spirit in and through a leader. This man cares profoundly about America and our role in the world. He is a global thinker, deeply committed to his own daily time of prayer and study of the scriptures, but also his fellowship with other leaders. He reaches out to leaders on both sides of the aisle. He is as loyal and faithful a person as I know."[19]

# 7

SITTING AT LUNCH with Karl VanDevender the afternoon before his election to Majority Leader, Bill reflected on the painful wounds that Trent Lott's comments had reopened and considered how best to heal them. Bill trusted Karl not only because his father chose Karl to lead the First Clinic in his stead, but also because his father chose Karl as his private physician. Karl VanDevender had become confidant to the Frist family. Knowing that Karl had a more liberal voting history, and had lived through the turbulent '60s, Bill asked for his opinion: "What are your thoughts? Where would you begin?"

Karl VanDevender, in turn phoned Bernard LaFayette—one of Dr. Martin Luther King Jr.'s deputies, who had been with him the day he was assassinated and the man who later recruited Jesse Jackson. Within the hour, Bernard called back, having conferenced-in Coretta Scott King, Julian Bond, and Andrew Young.

Karl informed the group, "I'm here with Bill Frist and chances are good that he'll be confirmed tomorrow as Majority Leader. He would like to talk with you, to ask your advice on how to counterbalance Trent Lott's comments."[1]

Bernard responded, "Bill, we are all Democrats and we understand that you are coming to us in good faith, but we're willing to get behind you because you reached out to us and asked us."

Seeing an open door, Bill gently prompted, "What specifically, can I do?"

Again, Bernard spoke, "Senator, you can listen when we call. We don't necessarily expect you to do what we ask, but you can listen when we call."

Bill was given a chance to listen on February 13, 2004, when the Faith and Politics Institute sponsored their yearly Civil Rights Pilgrimage, led by Georgia Congressman John Lewis, to cities in Alabama and Tennessee where they retraced the steps and history of the civil rights movement. The Institute asked Bill to co-lead the pilgrimage comprising some ten other senators, nineteen congressmen and -women, as well as some of the public figures of the original movement: Bernard LaFayette, Fred Shuttlesworth, Dorothy Cotton, Diane Nash, Bettie Mae Fikes, Fred Gray, Ruby Sale, Johnnie Carr and Bob Mants.

Whether traveling on the bus or visiting one of the historic locations, Pilgrimage participants hoped to honor their predecessors and fallen colleagues by retelling the story of their struggle. One such story was that of the events of March 7, 1965, when six hundred protesters marched fifty-four miles from Selma, Alabama to Montgomery, Alabama. Mounted on horses, Alabama State Troopers met the protesters at the Edmund Pettis Bridge with tear gas and clubs in what would later be called "Bloody Sunday." Congressman John Lewis was first in line and the first to take a blow from the billy club.

On Saturday, Congressman John Lewis again led a group across the Edmund Pettis Bridge in Selma, Alabama. When he reached the other side, John Lewis knelt at the spot where State Troopers had first struck him, spilling his blood across the pavement. Bill and the other senators knelt too and the entire delegation showered the street with their prayers.

Bill would later comment, "It is difficult for me to find the words to express the power of standing shoulder-to-shoulder with Congressman John Lewis as we crossed that bridge—that bridge where over forty years ago John Lewis suffered a savage beating. . . . We walked in the footsteps of giants."[2]

One day later, at an evening symposium held at the Nashville Public Library, Dorothy Cotton retold her story. Karl VanDevender remembers, "She was tough. She told it like it was and really stuck it to the Republicans and the White House, but Billy listened, taking it all in stride. When given a chance to respond, he said that we'd not done enough. You could tell that he had heard her. He also acknowledged that it's not a one man job and that there's more to be done."[3]

Following the symposium, several speakers and attendees milled about the stage. Bernard LaFayette tugged on Bill's sleeve, pulling him aside to a quiet corner. He tapped Bill in the chest and said, "Senator, I knew your father. He was not the greatest doctor because he knew more about pills than anyone else, he was a great doctor because he listened, and you," Bernard tapped him again, "are his equal. From this moment on, we in the black community are going to start calling you, "The Great Listener."[4]

Reflecting on that day, Bernard LaFayette says, "He was able to listen to a lot of things that he might have disagreed with. In fact, I'm sure he did. They were very critical of certain policies, of the administration. The Senator was open and listened without reacting or being offended. That's a very important quality when it comes to differences. Senator Frist is able to see the problem through the eyes of the other person. That makes me encouraged and hopeful. He had a real sensitivity to the issues and even started reading some of the books, like *The Children* [by David Halberstam, chronicling the Nashville civil rights movement] that talked about the plight that we endured during the non-violent movement. There is a growing interest among people to understand the civil rights movement and I think the Senator is on the cutting edge . . . I like his demeanor and personality, the way he treats other folks . . . We need more leaders like Senator Frist in the public arena. He's genuine, no hidden motives, and he has won my trust. When they made him Majority Leader, they found the best."[5]

---

HAVING TREATED TENS OF THOUSAND of patients and understanding well the needs of the sick and dying, Bill knew that the first step in facilitating healing was to listen to the patient. To his credit and others' surprise, Bill is listening, both to those who need to be heard and to the Proverb he knows by heart, "In his heart a man plans his course, but the Lord determines his steps."

As long as there are leaders with the temerity to lead, critics will question their actions, considering their ambitions as career advancements. Thus is the nature of politics, but whether it's moving back to the house on Bowling Avenue, or a big white house in Washington D.C., Bill—and Karyn—will be responding to another's need and His call to lead.

Bill Frist has been "on call" most of his life, but even now, as a citizen-legislator and Majority Leader, he still sees life through the lens of a physician. When Bill left Vanderbilt and turned in his beeper, he simply traded it in for another. Today, rather than jetting through the night to retrieve a heart for a dying man or woman in Nashville, he takes calls from President George W. Bush, senators, a host of congressmen and congresswomen, and thousands of constituents. Their needs are various and the pressure on Bill to be all things to all people grows every minute. Regardless, Bill is focused on the one thing he knows beyond a shadow of a doubt that God made him to do: bring healing to the sick. In today's partisan and divided environment, America needs leaders who can heal.

Of Bill's future plans, actor and former Senator Fred Thompson states, "The nation has gone through hard times. There's a lot of negative thinking around the world that has bred cynicism about our nation and leaders. What this nation needs more than anything else is to be inspired, to be reminded that we are a great nation, that we remain a great nation, and that leaders worthy of that nation can rise to the top. Bill is the kind of guy who proves that, out of the midst of America, from other walks of life, people like that can come and be great leaders and not have the baggage of people who have made their entire lives trying to figure out which way the wind is blowing. Ambition in and of itself is a neutral term and can be channeled either in good or bad ways. I'd say that a guy who spent his life saving other people's lives would compare pretty well in the ambition game when competing against guys who've spent their whole life trying to get re-elected."[6]

It seems fitting for Bill Frist's own words to close this book. At the conclusion of that afternoon conference call with Bernard LaFayette, Coretta Scott King, Julian Bond and Andrew Young, Bill was invited to speak to the distinguished attendees at a Congress of Racial Equality (CORE) dinner in New York City on January 20. It would be one of Bill's first speeches as Senate Majority Leader. The following is a transcript of that speech:

> In his Letter from a Birmingham Jail, Martin Luther King wrote, "Like a boil that can never be cured so long as it is covered up, but must be opened with all its ugliness to the natural medicines of air and light, injustice must be exposed, with all the tension its exposure creates, to the light of human conscience and the air of national opinion . . ."
>
> I'm a doctor. And when I graduated from medical school, I—like all my classmates—took a solemn oath of professional ethics—the Hippocratic Oath. It has been the foundation deeply embedded in my profession since ancient Greece of equal respect and treatment.
>
> That foundation—combined with my own faith and deep personal belief in global service—leads me at least once a year to the heart of Africa. Not as a United States Senator. But as a doctor, from America. I was there last January. And I'd like to share with you a story about one Sudanese man for whom I cared.
>
> Sudan is in the midst of a civil war lasting eighteen years, killing two million people, and displacing from their homes another five million families. Our medical mission team landed our single-engine plane in a field three hundred miles from the nearest health clinic. The children and

tribal leaders who approached the plane were wasted and malnourished.

Several villagers were carrying a man who was deathly sick—pained, feverish, and stick thin. Except his leg. It was huge—inflamed and swollen enormously with what to my eye was a deep-seated abscess. A boil buried deep and "covered up" by muscle and skin. The infection would bring certain death if not opened and drained. The tribal medicine man did not have the experience to cure such an "ugly" wound.

So I took a scalpel and folded it in the man's hand. I then held his hand and together we incised the skin, pushed deep into the wound—through the swollen underlying tissue, then through the muscle. Sensing his hesitancy, I assured him it was okay. We were doing it together—hand grasped over hand.

Carefully, respectfully, steadily, we pushed deeper. The patient's pain was intense. But suddenly we struck the pocket of infection. All its ugliness gushed forth and was exposed to the air and light. At that instant the hurt flowed out. The healing began. And I saw, in the eyes of a patient facing death, the hope that shines with new life.

Like the boil deep in that man's leg, America's wounds of division run deep. They have festered long. Too long. And we as a people have paid a terrible price throughout our history. Nearly thirty-five years ago Martin Luther King paid with his life. Tonight we honor his sacrifice. And celebrate his bold commitment to lifting up the less fortunate among us. But we also have a duty—a duty to act.

My title is Majority Leader of the United States Senate. It is not a position I sought. It is not a position for which I ran. And of course no one wished for the event that led to my ascension. But I do feel deep inside—just like in Africa—that my hand can now be grasped by others to seize an unprecedented opportunity. To dig deep into America's soul and lift up our dialogue to a higher and more robust level. This may cause tension. But by letting air and light into our dialogue, I believe we will find a new optimism to help heal our wounds of division.

Martin Luther King elevated the dialogue about civil rights and uplifting all people. And he propelled it with soaring words. But his words had purpose. Though his dialogue was cut short, he changed how people think. And, above all, he moved people and government to action.

Those of us in public service must answer Dr. King's call to action. We must build the trust, find the energy, and summon the will not to succumb to the rhetoric of division that paralyzes discourse and separates us as a people, but to push for real and sustained and bold action. So all Americans can lift themselves up to reach their dreams.

What type of action?

Equality. No child should be left behind in our public schools. The President has spoken loudly. The next generation must learn to read and write and do math. It empowers them more than anything else. So they can get good and rewarding jobs when they come of age.

Disparity. As a doctor, when I see a forty-year-old African-American with prostate cancer, why do I have to tell him he has twice the chance of dying than a white male the same age? Or the thirty-five-year-old Hispanic mother with diabetes, who is twice as likely to die as her Caucasian counterpart? We cannot tolerate such health disparity. We can change that. And we will.

Injustice. And those in our communities suffering from poverty and despair. President Bush and the United States Senate will aggressively support faith-based initiatives and organizations so they can reach out, give back and lift up. Indeed, Martin Luther King's journey and all the good it did was grounded in faith.

Tonight I ask you, I ask my colleagues in the United States Senate, indeed I ask every American to join together. To shatter past assumptions. To dig deep within our souls. And to open our hearts and minds to a new optimism.

As Martin Luther King wrote while sitting in a Birmingham jail, such an exposure will cause tension. But with light and air, healing will come. And when it does, and I know it will, we will have learned together and grown together and rededicated ourselves to coming together. As one people. Inseparable. Free. Equal. And just.[7]

# In His Own Words

Today, bill frist finds himself in the powerful yet often unenviable position of Senate Majority leader—a job which by its very definition means that by pleasing one group he often alienates another. An impossible place. This place is even more complicated when one understands that America is a country where half the electorate don't vote, ninety-six percent don't contribute money to the political system, and forty percent don't know the name of the Vice President. This fact has given rise to the description that the electorate is complacent, aloof and ignorant—a fitting description for many of the patients Bill Frist has seen walk into and out of his office. As any Majority Leader inevitably does, Bill Frist has both built consensus and drawn lines in the sand.

As Bill Frist has climbed the political ladder, his positions on various issues have garnered more and more attention. And as with any man or woman in public service, his own words have been used to both praise and criticize him. Rather than summarize those words into sound bites, the following chapters come from his own speeches, press releases, weekly columns, op-ed columns, and other forms of public communication in which Bill Frist states his own position. Through his own voice, word choice, and the stories he tells, the reader gains a better sense of what he values and where he stands in today's boiling pot of partisan politics and why he has chosen that stance.

# Speech to the National Prayer Breakfast

*February 1, 2001*

Before coming to the U.S. Senate, my job was transplanting hearts. A typical night: I'm in bed and the telephone rings. A faceless voice on the other end of the line said, "Dr. Frist, we've got a heart for you. Blood type A. Donor 140 pounds. Sounds like a match for Mr. John Majors." I'd receive a call like this, usually late at night, one or two times a week from the national organ donation registry.

John was a fifty-five-year-old patient, and also a friend, with a fatal heart disease. In bed and wasting away, he'd waited months for a transplant. He'd begin each day with a prayer that he would not die before someone, somewhere, would make the gift of a heart for him. With that call, John's prayers had been answered. God blessed him with a second chance at a full life—if my transplant team did a good job.

Excited, I got out of bed, kissed my wife, Karyn, goodnight, checked on my three boys who were sound asleep, and rushed to the hospital to give John the good news myself, news I knew he and his wife feared they'd never hear. An hour later, I was on a chartered plane, flying through the black night to Chattanooga to remove a healthy heart from a twenty-three-year-old woman who'd died just several hours earlier in a tragic car accident. From the plane, I jumped into a waiting ambulance and rushed through the still night to a hospital I'd never seen, to operate alongside surgeons I'd never met. I scrubbed, opened the chest and exposed the heart. Every eye in the room focused on that heart—powerful and inspiring as it beat in perfect rhythm, expanding and contracting, pumping blood through thousands of miles of capillaries in the human body—a living, vigorous miracle of God that exists in every one of us in this room. I cross–clamped the aorta, infused cold cardioplegia, and instantly, the powerfully pulsating heart stopped! Suddenly, it was completely motionless—still, and quiet. That heart, the energy source of our physical life, was now asleep. That's when my own adrenaline started to pump. I began to operate as fast as I could, because I knew I had only four hours to take out the heart, fly back to Nashville, and get it beating again. A mistake, a delay—anything that took more than four hours—meant that heart would never restart, and John would never see his family in this world again.

Within ten minutes, I'd taken the heart out, placed it into an Igloo ice chest, and dashed to a waiting ambulance. We raced again, under swirling lights and loud sirens, to the plane whose engines were already roaring. Back to Nashville, and another bumpy ambulance ride to the hospital where John was asleep in the OR. Carefully, I excised John's old, worn-out heart, and respectfully placed the new healthy heart in the empty chest cavity. I sewed the blood vessels together, and filled the heart with blood. And then the precious moment had come, the wait for the heart to come alive again. The room became hushed.

This is a precious moment, but one that always—in every case—strikes fear deep in my soul. Will the heart come back to life? What if I'd taken too long? What if someone had made a mistake in the blood type?

Every time I reach this moment, I say a silent prayer. The wait lasts only about two minutes, but it seems like an eternity. We wait anxiously, with a profound sense of humility, peering down at the flaccid heart, boldly spotlighted by the bright OR lights, waiting—waiting for that first sign of life. Waiting to be reborn.

Now what's the message of this story? I'll mention two: Giving. The first is about giving, one person to another. A gift is the ultimate expression love, and organ donation is the ultimate gift. Who was that twenty-three-year-old woman, killed in the car accident, who acted so selflessly, literally giving of herself to others, whom she had never met and would never know, might live?

Now all of us try to find ways to give that are within our power. But sometimes we just think about it and don't do it. Organ donation is a way to give something that costs us nothing, not money, or time, a gift greater than any other . . . the gift of life. Jesus tells us in John 15 that there is no gift greater than this. He said, "Greater love that this no man hath, than a man lay down his life for his friends." [John 15:13].

And he also told us to give freely, purely, out of love, without thought of reward: "Do not do your 'acts of righteousness' before men, to be seen by them . . . When you give, do not announce it with trumpets . . . Do not [even] let your left hand know what your right hand is doing, so that your giving may be in secret. Then your Father, who sees in secret, will reward you." [Matthew 6:1–4].

There is no gift purer or more selfless than the gift of a heart, or a kidney, or a lung. Neither the donor nor her family receives or expects anything in return. And yet the donor who gives such an intimate and priceless gift is rewarded with something just as priceless-a gift that transforms a moment of death into new life that continues long after the physical presence of that donor, and even the recipient, is gone.

It's a little like the light of the Lord that, once shared with another, radiates out from person to person until all within its reach is lit by the life of love. How many of you have signed an organ donor card? Raise your hand. Only about 1 in 50.

The message: each one of us has the capacity to give the most powerful of all gifts—in this case the gift of life—but we haven't acted. And let's think of the other gifts we haven't given, the compliment to your spouse, the meal to the hungry, encouragement to the troubled.

**Miracles.** Second, this story says something about miracles. Now, in our everyday lives, getting up, getting the kids off to school, going to work, buying groceries, working at the office, miracles often seem like legends left over from childhood. But miracles are not only the stuff of the great stories of the Bible—making the blind see, the lame walk, the dead rise.

Miracles are the manifestation of God in our everyday lives. As a transplant surgeon, I was blessed to see it, day after day. How can an inert piece of muscle, stored in an ice chest for three hours, separated entirely from its blood supply and transported across the country, explode back into life when placed in some other person's body?

Physicians can describe it, but they can't explain it. Scientists can define it, but they can't understand it. But God knows. And, with God's help, we can give life and encourage miracles in other ways as well. And I say "with God's help" because God really does guide our steps—often without us even realizing it.

And again, it happens most often, not through public service, like my work in the Senate or my practice as a physician, but through our "secret" acts of love through each other and to the Father.

**Sudan.** Now, shift gears, and imagine yourself flying in deepest Africa in a small plane, loaded to gross weight with medical supplies, at four hundred feet above the tree tops with the destination being a small makeshift hospital in war-torn Sudan.

We're flying low to avoid being sighted by aircraft who indiscriminately and regularly bomb the villages below. We're on a medical mission trip with Dr. Dick Furman, founder of World Medical Mission and my friends from Samaritan's Purse, an international Christian relief organization, run by my good friend Franklin Graham.

I landed the plane on a dirt strip, drove five bumpy miles past the boarded-up, old hospital (deserted and empty for twelve years because of active land mines placed during the war). We finally arrived at the old dilapidated two-room school house converted into a clinic.

Proverbs 16:9 tells us, "In his heart a man plans his course, but the Lord determines his steps."

Indeed, I came to Washington in my heart to serve in the U.S. Senate, but after arriving my steps have taken me far from the floor of the Senate, on medical mission trips to Africa—to the Congo, Uganda, Kenya and the Sudan. Six weeks prior to our arrival, Samaritan's Purse had courageously opened a small medical clinic in Sudan, where over two million people have died and more than four million have been displaced by the war.

We performed surgery where no care had been delivered in over a decade. The conditions were primitive. A minimum of surgical instruments. No electricity. No running water, ether for anesthesia. Patients would walk or be carried for days when they heard that we were there.

But the real image I want to share occurred in the small one-room building next door, used as a recovery room for the sick and injured. It was there that the real evidence of God's power at work in our lives came.

It was late and we were just finishing our last operation of the day—so late that we were operating under hand-held flashlights. We were to leave the next day and I was weary, looking forward to going home. A message came that a patient, a man from the Dinka tribe I had never met, wanted to see me, "the American doctor." I was exhausted and honestly just wanted to go to bed. But I went anyway.

Dusk had settled in. I brushed aside the curtain which served as a door, and it was almost pitch black dark inside. As I approached the voice in the corner, I could see only the vague silhouette of a man in bed. I could see little except the bulky white dressings covering the obvious stump of a left leg and injured right hand. And then the *smile*. It was a smile that pierced the darkness of the room.

Pulling my eyes from that luminous smile, I noticed the Bible beside his bed, and then the interpreter, who began to relay his story. I asked him why he wanted to see "the *American* doctor." He told me that two years ago, his wife and two children had been murdered in the war. Yes, I nodded. And that captivating smile seemed to grow even bigger. A smile of caring—a smile of love.

Eight days ago, he said, "I lost my leg and fingers to a land mine."

Yes, I nodded, wondering to myself how could anyone who had lost his family to a war—and now his leg and most of his hand—still smiled. And yet the smile seemed to grow even broader—a beautiful shining light in the night.

Finally, I had to ask, "Why are you smiling—how can you be smiling?"

For two reasons, he said. First because you come to us in the spirit of Jesus of Nazareth, and second, because you are an American doctor. (Now, in the transplant world, I'm accustomed to people thanking me for replacing a heart, but not because I'm an American).

I asked, "What do you mean?"

Lifting his mutilated limbs for me to see—limbs lost fighting for his religious freedom—he replied, "Everything I've lost—my family, my leg, my hand—will be worth the sacrifice if my people can someday have what you have in America: freedom. The freedom to be and to worship as we please.

It struck me that the freedoms and liberties which this nation has come to enjoy were obviously not bestowed by men, but have been endowed by our Creator. Our freedom is not based on anything given to us by government, but on the inalienable rights bestowed on us by God.

I've been back to the Sudan since then on another mission trip, operated at the same hospital, which has grown in size, though sadly, it has been bombed every few months. I never saw that Dinka man again. But I'll always carry with me that smile.

In fact, that smile and his words echoed through my consciousness as I sat on the West Front of the Capital a week and a half ago, looking out over that magnificent Mall, observing the swearing-in of President George W. Bush, listening to his words as he reminded us what a gift we have in freedom, and why it is a gift we mush share. "Once a rock in a raging sea, it is now a seed upon the wind, taking root in many nations . . . an ideal we carry but do not own, a trust we bear and pass along."

How true. Man's freedom does not begin with America, but we have an obligation to pass it on. And, as President Bush also reminded us that same day, "His purpose is achieved in our duty, and our duty is fulfilled in service to one another."

Mr. President, Mrs. Bush. Mr. Vice-President, Mrs. Cheney. May God continue to bless and guide you now and all the days of your life.

Oh, I almost forgot. What about John? We were in the operating room. I'd just given a prayer that the new heart would be infused with life. The room was silent—no one was moving, and all eyes were expectantly focused on the motionless, lifeless heart in John's chest.

Suddenly, the still heart began to quiver—ever so little. Then, the quivering began to coarsen into a stronger ripple. The ripple began to synchronize into a gentle beat. Then . . . BANG! The heart jumped, and took a strong and powerful heave—and the bold rhythm of life once again was reborn. Another miracle. And it all started with a gift.

# ON HIV/AIDS

*July 2002*

I SPENT THE FIRST TWENTY YEARS OF MY CAREER studying and working in medicine. I graduated from medical school in 1978. After that, I trained as a surgical resident for eight years. I then worked as a heart and lung transplant surgeon until I was elected to the United States Senate in 1994. During that time, HIV/AIDS went from a disease without a name to a global pandemic claiming nearly twenty million people infected.

It's hard to imagine an organism that cannot survive outside the human body can take such an immense toll on human life. But HIV/AIDS has done just that—already killing thirteen million people. Today more than forty million people, including three million children, are infected with HIV/AIDS. HIV/AIDS is a plague of biblical proportions.

And it has only begun to wreak its destruction upon humanity. Though one person dies from AIDS every ten seconds, two people are infected with HIV in that same period of time. If we continue to fight

HIV/AIDS in the future as we have in the past, it will kill sixty-eight million people in the forty-five most affected countries between 2000 and 2020. We are losing the battle against this disease.

There is neither a cure nor a vaccine for HIV/AIDS. But we do have reliable and inexpensive means to test for it. Also, because we know how the disease is spread, we know how to prevent it from being spread. We even have treatments that can suppress the virus to almost undetectable levels and significantly reduce the risk of mothers infected with HIV/AIDS from passing the disease to their children.

We have many tools at our disposal to fight the spread of HIV/AIDS. But are we using those tools as effectively as possible? The gloomy statistics prove overwhelmingly that we are not. What we must do is focus on what is truly needed and what is proven to work and marshal resources towards those solutions. We have beaten deadly diseases on a global scale before; we can win the battle against HIV/AIDS too.

## A Global Problem Requires Global Leadership

More than 70 percent of people infected with HIV/AIDS worldwide live in sub-Saharan Africa. But the devastation of the disease—and its potential to devastate in the future—is by no means limited to Africa. HIV/AIDS is global and lapping against the shores of even the most advanced and developed nations in the world.

Asia and the Pacific are home to 6.6 million people infected with HIV/AIDS—including one million of the five million people infected last year. Infections are rising sharply, especially among the young and injecting drug users, in Russia and other Eastern European countries. And the Americas are not immune. Six percent of adults in Haiti and four percent of adults in the Bahamas are infected with HIV/AIDS.

I believe the United States must lead the global community in the battle against HIV/AIDS. As Sir Elton John said in testimony before a committee on which I serve in the United States Senate, "What America has done for its people has made America strong. What America has done for others has made America great." Perhaps in no better way can the United States show its greatness in the twenty-first century—and show its true selflessness to other nations—than leading a victorious effort to halt the spread of HIV/AIDS.

But solving a global problem requires global leadership. International organizations, national governments, faith-based organizations and the private sector must coordinate with each other and work together toward common goals. And, most importantly, we must make communities the focus of our efforts. Though global leadership must come from places like Washington, New York and Brussels, resources must be directed to where they are needed the most—to the men and women in the villages and clinics and schools fighting HIV/AIDS on the front lines.

## Significant and Sustainable Progress

Adequate funding is and will remain crucial to winning the battle against HIV/AIDS. But just as crucial as the amount of funding is how it is spent. Should we spend on programs that prevent or lower the rate of infection? Should we spend on treatments that may prolong the life of those who are already infected? Should we spend on the research and development of a vaccine? The answer is yes . . . to all three questions.

We can only win the battle against HIV/AIDS with a balanced approach of prevention, care and treatment, and the research and development of an effective vaccine. HIV/AIDS has already infected tens of millions of people and will infect tens of millions more. We need to support proven strategies that will slow the spread of the virus and offer those already infected with the opportunity to live as normal lives as possible. And if our goal is to eradicate HIV/AIDS—and I believe that is an eminently achievable goal—then we must develop a highly effective vaccine.

But even with proven education programs or free access to anti-retroviral drugs or a vaccine that is 80 to 90 percent effective, our ability to slow the spread of HIV/AIDS and treat those already infected would be hampered. The infrastructure to battle HIV/AIDS in the most affected areas is limited at best. We need to train healthcare workers, help build adequate health facilities, and distribute basic lab and computer equipment to make significant and sustainable progress over the long-term.

## Not Only the Disease Itself

To win the battle against HIV/AIDS, we must not only fight the disease itself, but also underlying conditions that contribute to its spread—poverty, starvation, civil unrest, limited access to healthcare, meager education systems and reemerging infectious diseases. Stronger societies, stronger economies and stronger democracies will facilitate a stronger response to HIV/AIDS and ensure a higher quality of life in the nations most affected by and most vulnerable to the disease and its continued spread.

And we can make significant progress without vast sums of money and burgeoning new programs. Take, for example, providing something as basic and essential as access to clean water. Three hundred million, or 45 percent of, people in sub-Saharan Africa don't have access to clean water. And those who are fortunate enough to have access sometimes spend hours walking to and from a well or spring.

It costs only one thousand dollars to build a "spring box" that provides access to natural springs and protects against animal waste run-off and other elements that may cause or spread disease. Eighty-five percent of the ten million people who live in Uganda don't have access to a nearby supply of clean water. It would cost only twenty-five million dollars to build enough "spring boxes" to provide most of the people living in rural Uganda with nearby access to clean water.

Providing access to clean water is just one of the many ways in which the global community can empower the people most affected by and most vulnerable to HIV/AIDS. In some cases, such efforts—like supporting democracy and encouraging free markets—may cost little or take a long time, but they will make a significant difference in the battle against

HIV/AIDS and the quality of life of billions of people throughout the world.

## Our Stand Against HIV/AIDS

We have defeated infectious diseases before—sometimes on an even larger scale. Smallpox, for example, killed three hundred million people in the twentieth century. And as late as the 1950s, it afflicted up to fifty million people per year. But by 1979 smallpox was officially eradicated thanks to an aggressive and concerted global effort.

What if we had not launched that effort in 1967? What if we had waited another thirty-five years? Smallpox likely would have infected 350 million and killed forty million more people. That is a hefty price for inaction—a price that we should be grateful we did not pay then, and we should not want to pay now.

Right now we are losing the battle against HIV/AIDS. But that doesn't mean we can't win it in the end. Indeed, I believe we will ultimately eradicate HIV/AIDS. We have the tools to slow the spread of the disease and provide treatment to those already infected. And we have the scientific knowledge to develop an effective vaccine. But we need to focus our resources on what is truly needed and what is proven to work. And we need global leadership to meet a global challenge.

In 2020, when it is estimated that more than eighty-five million people will have died from HIV/AIDS, how will we look back upon this day? Will we have proven the experts right with inaction? Or will we have proven them wrong with initiative? I hope that we will be able to say that in the year 2002 we took our stand against HIV/AIDS and began to turn back what could have been, but never became the most deadly disease in the history of the world.

# On Stem Cell Research

*July 15, 2001*

In my work as a heart and lung transplant surgeon, I have for years wrestled with decisions involving life, death, health and healing. Having taken part in hundreds of organ and tissue transplants, I've experienced the ethical challenges involved in end-of-life care on numerous occasions. I've seen families faced with the most difficult decision of saying farewell to a loved one. Yet I have also seen their selfless acts in the midst of this sadness to consent to donate living organs and tissues of their loved ones to the benefit of others. Like organ donation, stem cell research forces us to make difficult decisions. While holding great potential to save lives, it also raises difficult moral and ethical considerations.

I am pro-life. My voting record in the Senate has consistently reflected my pro-life philosophy. As a physician my sole purpose has been to preserve and improve the quality of life. The issue of whether or not to use stem cells for medical research involves deeply held moral, religious and ethical beliefs as well as scientific and medical considerations. After grappling with the issue scientifically, ethically and morally, I conclude that both embryonic and adult stem cell research should be federally funded within a carefully regulated, fully transparent framework. This framework must ensure the highest level of respect for the moral significance of the human embryo. Because of the unique interaction between this potentially powerful new research and the moral considerations of life, we must ensure a strong, comprehensive, publicly accountable oversight structure that is responsive on an ongoing basis to moral, ethical and scientific considerations.

Embryonic stem cell research is a promising and important line of inquiry. I'm fully aware and supportive of the advances being made each day using adult stem cells. It is clear, however, that research using the more versatile embryonic stem cells has greater potential than research limited to adult stem cells and can, under the proper conditions, be conducted ethically. The prudent course for us as policymakers is to provide for the pursuit of both lines of research—allowing researchers in each field to build on the progress of the other.

To achieve this, we must significantly strengthen the National Institute of Health's guidelines so that they include appropriate safeguards. Federal funding for stem cell research should be contingent on the implementation of a comprehensive, strict new set of safeguards and public accountability governing this new, evolving research. This process will ensure the progress of this science in a manner respectful of the moral significance of human embryos and the potential of stem cell research to improve health.

# On Heroes

*July 2000*

I've heard it said, over the course of the last decade or so, that America has lost all her heroes, that our children today look to sports figures and rock stars and movie actors, where before there stood great generals, presidents, and other leaders for them to imitate and admire. All the heroes, they say, have disappeared.

Well, I don't believe that's true.

And the reason I don't believe it's true is because, over the course of the last six years, as I've traveled the length and breadth of Tennessee, I've met hundreds and thousands of ordinary people, and all of them are heroes.

No, they're not people with well-known names or high profiles, but they are people who give generously of themselves, who exemplify the essence of what it means to be an American: a helping hand, a caring heart, a willingness to give of one's time and energy and spirit to help another.

That's the real definition of a hero and, from the frontier days until today, they have always existed in Tennessee. In my family, there were at least two such heroes. The first was my grandfather, Jacob Frist Jr.

"Jake," as he was known, worked the railroad during the great "Steam Age," when railroading was one of the most labor-intensive industries in America. As you might expect, he traveled around a bit, moving from his home in Chattanooga, where his father, my great-grandfather, was one of the city's fifty-three original settlers, to New Orleans and later to Meridian, Mississippi, where my father was born. Along the way, he propelled himself professionally as well, rising to conductor, and eventually, station master which, at that time, was a job with considerable responsibility.

One day, February 14, 1914, to be exact, an older woman from New Orleans arrived at the Meridian station with her youngest child, who was just three years old at the time. Fascinated by the trains, the boy drifted out onto the tracks. As his terrified mother ran after him, an incoming train came speeding towards them, paralyzing them both with fear. Without a thought for his own safety Jake barreled out onto the tracks, pushed the child to safety, and took the blow himself.

The head and spinal injuries he sustained totally immobilized him for nine months. But his bravery didn't go unnoticed. He was awarded two medals: the first, the Carnegie Hero Award, from the railroad; the second, the Congressional Medal of Honor, from Woodrow Wilson, the President of the United States. Jacob Frist died five years later from complications related to the accident. He left behind his wife, Jennie, and two sons, John Chester and Thomas, my second hero and father.

After her husband's death, Jennie Frist turned their large home into a boarding house to support her family. One of the boarders was a physician, whose evening stories about the importance of kind and compassionate care, the gentleness of the person drawing blood, the smile that accompanied the breakfast tray each morning, and the orderly who tidied the wards every night, kindled Dad's interest in medicine.

Taking the good doctor's advice, Dad eventually went to work in the local hospital as an orderly, where he was able to observe these everyday heroes in action. Still supporting his mother and my future aunts and uncles, he worked his way through college and medical school. After graduation, he became a family physician and traveled the state, treating patients for just three dollars a visit.

Dad practiced medicine for nearly sixty years, and if there was one thing that characterized him, it was the compassion he felt for his patients, sometimes driving one hundred miles in the middle of the night to sit by the bed of a dying patient. Most people know my Dad as the man who founded HCA. But it was these things that made HCA possible.

I'll never forget the day I took my oath of office as a United States Senator. Dad came up to watch my swearing-in, and afterwards, we took a tour of my office. Not enamored with politicians generally, and certainly not all that excited that I had put my life in medicine on hold to go to Washington, I could tell nevertheless, as he walked those marbled halls for the first time, that he was proud of his son.

Until, that is, he glanced up at the prominent nameplate under the large ornate Tennessee Seal on the door. It read, Bill Frist, United States Senator. He took me by the arm, looked me in the eye, pointed to the nameplate, and said: "Something missing?" He meant, of course, the initials, "M.D."

As we all know, dads don't have to say much to communicate their point. And Dad's point was unmistakable: He wanted me to remember not only where I came from, but the values, the ethics, the compassion, that are the essence of our profession.

In his subtle but crystal-clear way, he was telling me never to forget that the well-being of people must be the ultimate goal of all public policy. I never have.

Two men. Two kinds of heroes: the ordinary man who commits an extraordinary act of courage placing himself in the path of an oncoming train to save the life of another; and the ordinary man whose everyday acts are themselves extraordinary, because they are done solely for the good of others.

Has America lost all her heroes? No, she has not, at least not in Tennessee.

A couple of months ago, I had the opportunity to speak to a "Health Care Heroes" conference in northeast Tennessee. Like the pioneer heroes of our past, they also have a vision of the future, and they're working to make it come true.

One part of that vision is a twenty-first century medical corridor that will one day link health care delivery systems and related research with high tech business. Another part is a communications network that will overcome the digital divide and establish new opportunities for jobs and businesses. Some, like those at King Pharmaceuticals, are turning out some of the best medicines in the world. Others, like those at ETSU, are training some of America's finest physicians.

But what makes it all work is the people, whether descended from those who first carved out a life on the frontier, or those who arrived more recently, all of them, all of you, find a special quality of life here that enables you to be modern-day frontiersmen: independent, creative, visionary, but even more importantly, kind, loving, and compassionate.

You know, when someone mentions the word "hero," specific images usually come to mind: We picture a young soldier in uniform, laying down his life for his country, or standing sentry on the frontiers of freedom. We imagine a policeman, or a fireman, risking his own safety to secure the lives and property of others. But the real heroes are those whose deeds never make the morning papers, whose acts of heroism go unnoticed. They are the ordinary people who do extraordinary things, not because they are soldiers, or policeman, or firefighters, but because they are people who hear a cry, see a need, and feel the pain of another, and so they reach out and touch that neighbor, hand-to-hand and heart-to-heart. They not only stand for American values, they are the lifeblood of the American spirit.

William Makepeace Thackeray once wrote that "to endure is greater than to dare; to tire out hostile fortune; to be daunted by no difficulty; to keep heart when all have lost it. Who can say," he said, "that this is not greatness?"

Who, indeed? Or as someone else once put it, "The courage of very ordinary people is all that stands between us and the dark."

Aren't we lucky there is so much light in Tennessee?

# On Infectious Disease

*April 2002*
*Keynote Address at the Third Annual American Transplant Congress*

It's good to be among so many friends. I know that each of you share a passion for the health and well-being of the American people. That is reflected in your daily work, as captured by the proceedings of this meeting, and reflected in the work of the American Society of Transplantation and the American Society of Transplant Surgeons. Your two societies have been stalwarts in the effort to increase the number of organs for transplantation and to improve the allocation process for patients. I thank you for your leadership.

And I thank you for your support. In February, I introduced the Organ Donation and Recovery Improvement Act. This bill offers a comprehensive approach to increase organ donation while improving the overall process of organ donation and recovery. It will: improve coordination among existing federal organ donation and transplantation research activities; establish pilot projects to discover new opportunities to increase organ donation; and, enhance the coordination of public awareness and the education of health professionals.

We will begin looking at the bill in committee within the next month, and—thanks to your support and the broad support of the transplant community—I am hopeful that it will soon become law.

As you know, there is more work to do in the field of transplantation, and you are not waiting on government to do it. In fact what you need most is for government to simply stay out of the way and let you do your work.

I commend you for your work to remove disincentives for living donors, especially your efforts to encourage employers to support these heroes with medical leave from their jobs. And how pleased you must have been to hear the news that the number of living donors has outpaced those of cadaveric donors for the first time in history. Congratulations on a job well done.

Indeed, we are all stewards of what I believe is a great public trust—the knowledge and experience and investment of countless generations coming together to enable the miracle that is transplant medicine. And I believe we have the capacity not only to improve one life at a time, but as many lives as we can—hundreds, thousands, even millions of lives over the course of our lifetimes.

You do that by your teaching, by your research, by your probing of the unknown, by being at this meeting today and sharing ideas.

That same commitment is what led me from the practice of transplant surgery at Vanderbilt to the arena of public service right here in Washington. We in transplantation are uniquely equipped to participate in this mission beyond the practice of the individual transplant. You have the tools to do so. You have the will and the compassion.

Let me begin by stating something you already know. Almost all of you in the room are experts in infectious disease. You have to be. You are the experts in immunosuppression.

Today, infectious disease—viruses, bacteria, and other microorganisms—are emerging as a threat not only to the health of millions of people, but to the security, stability and prosperity of all humanity. Ancient killers like malaria and tuberculosis are evolving and re-emerging in drug-resistant forms. New killers like HIV/AIDS are spreading so rapidly that they have taken hold of entire continents. And the worst of disease and the worst of war are coming together to make bioterrorism a very real and increasing threat to the very communities in which your families live—indeed making our nation vulnerable.

If we do nothing more than what we are already doing, within the next ten years infectious diseases will cause some economies in Africa to lose 20 percent of their GDP, nearly forty-two million children in twenty-seven countries to lose one or both of their parents, and the average lifespan to drop by as much as ten, fifteen, twenty, or even thirty years in countries in Asia and Africa, and even the Americas.

My friends, this is the spread of disease on a biblical scale and it must be stopped. History will judge us on how this generation responds to this moral crisis. With the eradication of smallpox in 1978, the global health community scored a major victory against one of the most ruthless killers in history. In the twentieth century alone, smallpox claimed a half billion lives—more than all wars and all other diseases combined.

The United Nations was so impressed with the success of this effort and a host of other factors that it predicted a health revolution by the new millennium in which infectious diseases would no longer pose a major threat to human health.

But this optimism led to complacency—and to carelessness in the battle against infectious diseases. The overuse of antibiotics in humans and animals led to the rapid evolution of more deadly and drug-resistant bacteria. Global trade and travel enabled diseases like West Nile virus to journey from the swamps of Uganda to the streets of New York City. Poor land management brought humans closer than ever to insects and animals that carry and spread diseases, such as malaria, yellow fever and Rift Valley fever.

Indeed, we are living through a health revolution; but just the opposite of what we expected. Over the past thirty years, twenty diseases have reemerged in more deadly and drug-resistant forms. And scientists have discovered thirty new diseases that never before existed in humans. This has ensured infectious diseases their place as a leading cause of death globally. Between a fourth and a third of all deaths worldwide are caused by infectious diseases.

And the United States is not immune to this growing threat. After dropping to an all-time low in 1980, deaths from infectious diseases has doubled—to 170,000 per year in 2000. Infectious diseases are a deadly problem that is not getting better, but much worse, everywhere. And remember—you in this room are the experts.

We are losing the global battle against another new virus—HIV/AIDS. Right now about forty million people worldwide have HIV/AIDS. And as one person dies from AIDS every ten seconds, two new people are infected with HIV. And 9 out of 10 don't know they are HIV positive. We are losing the battle. HIV/AIDS is a plague of biblical proportions: it is not just killing millions; in Africa, it is killing a continent.

Once or twice a year, I travel to Africa to do medical mission work. Last January I operated in the Sudan and in Uganda and traveled to Tanzania and Kenya. In the clinics and in the villages, I saw first-hand the level of destruction and havoc caused by HIV/AIDS and other infectious diseases.

As I walked through the villages, I saw children—many of whom contracted HIV from their mothers and won't live to be teenagers—and very old grandparents. What I did not see were vibrant young men and women and adults who are middle–aged. That's because their generation is being literally decimated by AIDS or AIDS-related illnesses. HIV/AIDS is wiping out an entire generation of teachers, military personnel, civil servants—and it will wipe out another and another and another as long as we let it fester among the impoverished peoples of the world.

But the massive loss of life is only the immediate threat of the HIV/AIDS pandemic; the breakdown of civil society is a long-term issue about which we all should be concerned. Grandparents cannot defend borders and police cities. Newborns cannot plant crops and work in factories. And nations cannot build schools and roads and clean their water if they must spend all their money just keeping their people alive. The rise of HIV/AIDS is bringing a demographic disaster that will result in all-too-fragile democracies being tested to their limits.

And what more fertile ground to grow terrorists than a country with no civil order, no parents, no mentors, no civil society? Three years ago, people laughed when we said that infectious diseases could spark political instability and threaten international security. Today it is accepted as a reality. And remember: it is you in this room who know more about infectious diseases than 99.99 percent of people in this country.

And the events since September 11 have brought the reality into even sharper focus. Just a year ago (except for a few of us who in a bipartisan way were trying to call attention to it), the risk of bioterrorism on our soil—and the use of viruses and bacteria as weapons of mass destruction—was felt to be negligible.

Today, bioterrorism on our soil has become a reality. And the risk of more attacks against us real; it is increasing and our vulnerabilities as a nation remain high. Although the United States is not unprepared for a biological attack, we are clearly under prepared.

Last October, our vulnerability to bioterrorism was exposed for the entire world to see. A terrorist—or group of terrorists—mailed letters laden with anthrax to media outlets in Florida and New York and to the offices of Senators Daschle and Leahy here in Washington. The attack shut down the US Postal Service, pushed our public health system to the limit, and paralyzed the federal government. Sadly, it was also a deadly attack, infecting twenty-two people and killing five, including two innocent postal workers responsible for mail delivered to this building.

What was once a remote possibility is now a brutal reality: bioterrorism is alive in America. The terrorist or terrorists who launched the anthrax attacks are still out there. They could be in your community or my community or anywhere in America. They have tasted success. They are cold-blooded killers. They likely have more anthrax in their arsenal. And there is no reason to believe that they will not strike again. And there is no reason to believe that other terrorists—domestic or international—won't chose biological weapons for their next attack.

I believe the threat of bioterrorism is increasing and so does our intelligence community. The National Intelligence Council recently wrote in an unclassified report: The biological warfare capabilities of state and non-state actors are growing worldwide. This trend leads us to believe that the risk of an attack against the United States, its interests and allies will increase in the coming years.

Why?

First, at least eleven and as many as seventeen countries have active biological weapons programs. Many of these countries are not, to say the least, among our most trusted allies: Iraq, Iran, Libya, Syria, Cuba, China, North Korea and Sudan. Some of these countries have developed, produced and weaponized deadly agents such botulinum toxin, the plague and smallpox. Russia has even experimented with Ebola—a virus that kills 90 percent of its victims, and one which we know almost nothing about.

There are of course non-state actors—including terrorists, religious cults and other extremist groups—who may already have or are trying to develop biological weapons. Just last month, it was reported that American forces uncovered a lab near Kandahar that Al Qaeda was building to develop biological agents. But this should come as no surprise: Osama Bin Laden has repeatedly said that it is his religious duty to acquire weapons of mass destruction.

Second, the proliferation of technology and expertise has made biological agents easier not only to develop, but to make more lethal and deliver as weapons. Imagine being able to buy the expertise of one of seven thousand former Soviet "bioweaponeers" for one hundred dollars per month. Imagine being able to genetically alter a strain of anthrax so that it is resistant to ciproflaxin, doxycycline and every other antibiotic. Well, you don't have to imagine either of these scenarios, because they have in all likelihood already happened.

Third, biological agents can make far better weapons than chemical, nuclear or conventional weapons. You know better than anyone the deadly nature of these agents. You can't smell anthrax. You can't see botulinum toxin. You can't hear tularemia. If a terrorist strikes with smallpox, victims will not show symptoms for a week, which provides ample time for a perpetrator to escape.

And if distributed at the right time, in the right place and under the right conditions, a biological weapon can be even more deadly than the hydrogen bomb. For terrorists, biological agents are the ideal weapons.

Fourth, terrorists know that the United States is highly vulnerable to biological attack. The anthrax attacks proved that bioterrorism could cause widespread panic and paralysis and strike fear in the heart of every American. Why then should Al Qaeda test the heightened security at our airports by hijacking another commercial jetliner, or attempt to import a "dirty nuke" under the watchful eye of the US Coast Guard, when they have a much better chance of success by sending an anthrax-laden letter through the mail or spraying botulinum toxin in the air above our cities?

Indeed, the United States is highly vulnerable to bioterror attack. Let me share with you just a few facts about our public health system: nine of ten public health departments don't have staff fully trained in bioterrorism; one-third of public health departments serving 25,000 or fewer people have no Internet access and one-quarter of public health staff have no e-mail; and less than one percent of our food imports—a prime vehicle for bioterrorism that can harbor two hundred different diseases—are properly inspected. Although we are not unprepared for a bioterror attack, we are under-prepared.

There is a special role for each of you as we face the growing threat of bioterrorism, the HIV/AIDS pandemic and emerging infectious diseases. Everyday you face the realities of what infectious diseases can do to the human body—especially a body that is weak and without its natural defenses. I believe you—the stewards of the modern miracle that is transplant medicine—have the power to save hundreds, thousands and millions of lives as we battle infectious diseases over the next decade and beyond.

My friends, I urge you to renew your dedication to saving lives, but on a scale that reaches beyond your clinical practice and into Siberian prisons where multi-drug-resistant tuberculosis runs rampant, into the villages of sub-Saharan Africa where AIDS has stricken a generation, and—although less exotic—into your local public health offices where the first signs of a bioterrorist attack will likely appear.

And I urge you to take part in the public debate on the other prominent medical and scientific issues of the day. You are uniquely equipped, not just in infectious diseases directly, but also in issues such as the potential misuse of antibiotics in agriculture. Is it breeding anti-microbial resistance that will be harmful to humans? If so, do we need to propose new national policies on the use of antibiotics in animal feeds and agriculture?

We already see consumer-oriented commercial companies modifying their purchasing and marketing practices. While the science may or may not yet be conclusive, trends are emerging. Those of us in Washington need your experience and expertise to craft an appropriate policy based on sound science—one that protects against microbial resistance while protecting the prosperity our economy.

Once we have three hundred million doses of smallpox vaccine—a dose for every American—should we allow voluntary vaccination? Or should we vaccinate everyone if the threat is real? You need to be at the table to help develop that policy. You are uniquely equipped to evaluate and explain to the American people the side effects, the risks, dangers, and benefits.

We need the same help on the issue of Medicare reimbursement. More and more doctors are leaving practices because of inadequate reimbursement. You know the reality because you see it every day: Too often government is not paying doctors a fair and equitable price for the services they provide. Just like every workingman or woman, doctors must make a living. Just like every small business, a medical practice cannot continually operate at a loss.

And prescription drug coverage in Medicare. You know the absolute necessity of coverage for immunosuppressive drugs, yet you also know that the financial solvency of Medicare cannot be sustained when we have a doubling of the number of seniors over the next thirty years unless we modernize the program.

Perhaps in no other area can we use your insight and experience than the ethical issues that surround the new research techniques that allow us to manipulate the genetic restructuring of life. We simply cannot adopt a policy of science at any cost. We need an ethical framework in which to proceed in this age of rapid scientific and medical advances.

You in the transplant field have the practical experience of developing and working within comprehensive ethical frameworks. Your unique experience includes: the definition of brain death in the late 1960s, the decision-making of whom to transplant throughout the 1970s, the allocation system for organs in the 1980s, and informed consent for pediatric and infant transplantation in the 1990s.

As science progresses even more rapidly and the power to manipulate the basic building blocks of life become even more commonplace, we need you to help define the reasonable, moral and ethical bounds to allow science to progress as fast as safely possible on issues such as stem cells and human cloning.

In closing, most of what I have spoken about is the harsh reality of infectious diseases in today's world. It is scary and sobering news, but we must not lose faith in our ability to fight, defend against and ultimately defeat infectious disease.

We are America. We are the most innovative and the most resourceful nation in the world. But the response must start with each of us as individuals.

My call to action for each of you today is to stay at the table—and even increase your participation in the public policy arena. Our challenges are growing—in the use of scarce resources, the emerging infectious diseases, antibiotic resistance, HIV, bioterrorism. You are uniquely equipped. Your guidance and your genius can make the difference. And history will judge us as a profession and as a people as to how we respond.

# On Cloning

*June 4, 2002*

Can one be an advocate for embryonic stem cell research while opposing human cloning experimentation? That's the question facing about thirty United States senators who have not taken a final position on human cloning legislation to be brought before the Senate.

But we must first understand the similarities and distinctions between the two. It's important to understand that human "therapeutic" or "research" cloning is an experimental tool often confused with, but distinct from, embryonic stem cell research. Only then can we appropriately dissect a debate on the potential of the science versus the restraint defined by ethics and moral concerns.

Most agree that human reproductive cloning, or the cloning of human beings, should be banned. The contentious issue is whether this ban should extend to all human cloning, including human research cloning experimentation, a brand new field. Advocates point to its potential to develop tissues that will not be rejected by a patient's immune system. They also argue for human cloning as a source of genetically diverse stem cells for research. Moreover, they say such experimentation will further our basic understanding of biology and life's origins.

However, regardless of our religious background, most of us remain extremely uncomfortable with the idea of creating cloned human embryos to be destroyed in an experiment. As a physician and legislator who struggles with this inherent tension between scientific progress and ethical concerns, I focus on two fundamental questions:

1. Does the scientific potential of human research cloning experimentation justify the purposeful creation of human embryos, which must be destroyed in experiments? and
2. Does the promise of human embryonic stem cell research depend on experimental human research cloning?

At this point in the evolution of this new science, I cannot justify the purposeful creation and destruction of human embryos in order to experiment on them, especially when the promise and success of human embryonic stem cell research does not depend on experimental research cloning.

President Bush last August outlined a scientifically and ethically balanced policy that allows federal funding of embryonic stem cell research for nearly eighty stem cell lines. This has opened the door to a significant expansion of embryonic stem cell research. Further, there are no restrictions on private research using stem cells from the thousands of embryos left over after in vitro fertilization. This research, too, is underway. The promise and hope for new cures is being investigated. And the promise of this research does not—I repeat, does not—depend on human cloning.

Human cloning would indeed provide another source of stem cells—this time by asexual reproduction. But a human embryo still has to be created—then destroyed—to produce these stem cells. Moreover, there has been very little research cloning experimentation in animals—a prerequisite to any demands for such work in humans. Given the early state of this uncharted new science, the large number of federal cell lines and the unlimited number available for private research, I believe there is presently a sufficient number and range of cell lines.

As a heart transplant surgeon, I know intimately the challenges of transplant rejection. But I also know that there are multiple promising strategies to address this issue, such as the development of "tolerance strategies," improved pharmacologic immunosuppression, and the manipulation of cell surface structure to make cells "invisible" to the immune system, none of which carry the ethical burdens attached to human cloning.

No one can deny the potential human cloning holds for increased scientific understanding. But given the serious ethical concerns this research raises, the fact that promising embryonic stem cell research will continue even under a cloning ban, the lack of significant research in animal models, and the existence of promising alternatives, I am unable to find a compelling justification for allowing human cloning today.

The fact that we are even engaged in this debate testifies to the rapid and encouraging progress of science. As it moves forward, we will undoubtedly be forced to reexamine this issue. For now, the proper course is to stop short of allowing cloning research in humans, but to enthusiastically embrace the ongoing public and private stem cell research that holds such great hope for those who suffer from a wide range of diseases and conditions such as Alzheimer's disease, Parkinson's disease, and diabetes.

# On Smallpox Vaccinations

*August 9, 2002*
*Op-Ed Column, New York Times*

Should americans be allowed to make an informed choice to receive the smallpox vaccine? I believe they should and that individual choice should become the central component of a new national policy aimed at protecting us from the possible use of smallpox as a weapon of mass destruction by terrorists.

Smallpox as a disease does not exist today. But the highly contagious and infectious virus that causes it does. And that is the problem. We know that stores of the virus exist in the United States and Russia, and some experts believe the virus also rests in the hands of people not friendly to the United States. At a recent Senate hearing, the former head of the United Nations special commission charged with evaluating Iraq's capability to build weapons of mass destruction said Saddam Hussein could well have smallpox in his biological weapons program. Who doubts Saddam Hussein's willingness to use such a weapon?

Our vulnerabilities to smallpox, one of the deadliest diseases, today are higher than ever, and terrorists know this. Most adults are no longer protected by the vaccination they received as a child, and the mobility of our society would facilitate rapid spread of the highly contagious virus. Advances in technology have made it easier than ever to deliver smallpox as a weapon of mass destruction.

The good news is that President Bush has signed into law legislation that would enhance our response to a smallpox attack. Increased federal tax dollars will be spent to improve America's long-neglected public-health defenses at the local, state and national levels. With the cooperation of major drug companies, large quantities of vaccine are being manufactured and stockpiled, enough to vaccinate every person in America.

The major policy question is this: Who should receive this vaccine, and when? The answer affects the health of individuals, but it also carries national security implications. Allowing individuals to choose whether to get smallpox vaccinations will help reduce the threat of biological terrorism. The more people who choose to be vaccinated, the fewer people susceptible to the disease and the more effective our efforts to contain a smallpox attack.

As soon as sufficient quantities of licensed vaccine become available (most likely within eighteen months), we should allow every American to make an informed choice as to whether to be vaccinated. We should immediately vaccinate all military personnel at a high risk of exposure, and allow voluntary vaccinations for those at lower risk. Health professionals and other first responders should also be vaccinated on a voluntary basis, beginning with those at highest risk of exposure, and we should develop a national plan under which every American at risk could, within thirty-six to forty-eight hours after exposure to smallpox, be vaccinated.

We must also immediately begin a nationwide public education program to explain the substantial risks and benefits of choosing to receive vaccinations even before being exposed to smallpox.

This comprehensive smallpox vaccination policy recognizes the very real risks we face of a bioterror attack. It would ensure that those who are at the highest risk of exposure receive the vaccine first; at the same time, it can be carried out in a way that would make possible the delivery of the vaccine on a massive scale in a timely fashion.

The plan could enable medical scientists to accumulate data to study the vaccine's serious potential side effects and provide the general public with the most accurate information about the risks of vaccination. But in order to implement this approach, we will have to integrate the knowledge and the initiative of our public health community with that of our national security agencies.

Educating the public will be crucial to this effort. Smallpox vaccinations do not come without risks. Of every million people who receive the vaccine, two to four people will die from its complications. Five times that number will become seriously ill from the vaccine. And the vaccination cannot be given to the millions of people with suppressed immune systems, including those with HIV or AIDS, certain cancer patients and organ-transplant recipients.

I believe the threat of a smallpox attack outweighs the risks of providing smallpox vaccinations to a well-informed public. Along with the phased-in vaccination of military personnel and first responders, every American should be given this option. Such a policy is a sensible public health response that would enhance our national security.

# On September 11, 2001

*September 11, 2002*
*Senate Floor*

Mr. President, though we would never wish to relive the horror of September 11, 2001, we must dedicate ourselves to remembering it. That is the task we begin with this first anniversary of that darkest of days—to properly and lastingly honor the sacrifice of the more than three thousand innocent men, women and children who perished at the Pentagon, the World Trade Center and the crash site of Flight 93 in Shanksville, Pennsylvania.

September 11 will be a day of mourning for many years to come. And it should be. For the grief of those who lost loved ones on that day will pass only with their own passing. Nothing can wipe away the memory of a friend or family member taken before their time. The victims of September 11—both those who died, and the friends and family who survive them—deserve our enduring respect.

Though the attacks were carried out in New York, Washington and Pennsylvania, no American was untouched by the tragedy, including the men and women of my home state, Tennessee. John and Pat Lenoir of Knoxville lost their son, Rob, when the World Trade Center collapsed. Frances Hall of Knoxville lost her sister-in-law, and Otis and Nancy Tolbert of Brentwood lost their son when Flight 77 crashed into the Pentagon. We keep these Tennesseans in our thoughts and prayers today.

It is entirely appropriate that the President and First Lady began their September 11 by attending a church service. I hope that many Americans follow their example by spending some part of their day in a house of worship, or on bended knee in prayer. Regardless of the God we may worship, faith in a higher power can help heal, explain, console, and reassure us today . . . just as it did a year ago.

Though the September 11 attacks brought one of the darkest days in our history, a few rays of light did shine through. Americans rallied to help those in need by waiting hours to give blood, donating supplies to the rescue effort, and digging deep in their pockets for 9/11 charities. I'm especially proud of the Tennessee Baptist Convention who sent thirty volunteers to help prepare food for the rescue workers at the World Trade Center.

And I am still moved to this day by the members of Tennessee Task Force One who helped search for survivors and recover the fallen at the Pentagon. America will always remember the men and women who risked their lives to save the lives of others on September 11. The thousands of firemen, police officers, and medical personnel who rushed into harm's way forever touched our hearts with their heroism. Their example was an inspiration to us all; it must remain so for generations to come.

Britt Brewster, a twelve-year-old Tennessee girl who sang the national anthem at the Pentagon this morning, said earlier this week, "The one good thing [about September 11] was that America started coming together as one." I remember visiting Ground Zero with about forty of my fellow Senators a couple days after the attacks. Smoke was still rising from the debris and almost everything was covered with ash. The only color other than the workmen's bright yellow hats was from the American flags proudly posted on surrounding buildings. We should fly our flags on this anniversary and again show our common love for country and our fellow countrymen.

There has been much debate about what we should teach our children on this first anniversary of the September 11 attacks. I believe they deserve the truth. I took my three sons to Ground Zero two months after the attacks. I wanted them to see the destruction with their own eyes, and remember—long after I am gone—what evil once did, and can do again to our country. And I will take them back to New York. I was just there five days ago and saw the rebirth of that remarkable city. I also want my sons to see what good has done, and can always do in our country.

The Gettysburg Address is considered the most powerful piece of funeral oratory ever delivered on American soil. But as Lincoln himself admitted, even he could not dedicate the battlefield beyond what those who fell there had already done. Instead, he urged his audience to dedicate themselves: "That from these honored dead, we take increased devotion to that cause for which they here gave the last full measure of devotion."

The terrorists attacked on September 11 and continue to make deadly threats because they hate our country and all we represent. The three thousand men, women, and children who died on that horrible day did so for the same cause as those who fell on the Battle Green of Lexington, in the forests of Argonne, and on the beaches of Normandy—justice, equality, liberty, democracy.

I urge every American to offer their respects to families who lost loved ones, to put those who perished in their prayers, and to show their patriotism by unfurling an American flag. But, above all, I hope we will rededicate ourselves to the values that have been the core of our greatness for more than two and one quarter centuries. For those values may be threatened again sooner than we think. And if they are, we will find strength and hope and resolve in remembering—properly and lastingly—September 11, 2001.

# On Partial-Birth Abortion

*March 11, 2003*
*Floor Statements*

Mr. President, I rise in support of the Partial Birth Abortion Act of 2003. And I do so with a deep passion not only for the protection of life, but also for the ethical practice of medicine. Before coming to the Senate, I had the opportunity to study and practice medicine for twenty years. And though I am not an obstetrician, I have delivered babies. I've seen many times—as all parents have seen, including myself as the father of three boys—the undeniable miracle of newborn life. I've also mended the hearts and vascular systems of premature babies only days after delivery. These were human beings in their most defenseless and desperate state. Their natural place was in the womb, yet once in the world they fought to survive. As a surgeon, I have studied and performed thousands of surgical procedures. I know there are ethical bonds to the application of surgical procedures—bonds that in a moral sense should never, ever be crossed by a surgeon. Indeed, I took an oath to treat every human life with respect, with dignity, and with compassion. But abortion takes life away.

And partial-birth abortion does so in a manner that is brutal and barbaric and morally offensive to the mainstream medical community.

Today, I do not wish to debate the politics of partial-birth abortion. Instead, I will discuss the disturbing facts of partial-birth abortion as a surgical procedure—a surgical procedure, to my mind, that should and must be banned. The fact is that partial-birth abortion is a repulsive procedure. It begins by turning the living fetus around, partially pulling it out of the uterus feet first, and then thrusting the base of its skull deeply with eight-inch long scissors. Next the scissors are forcibly opened in the skull of the fetus to create a hole large enough to evacuate the brain and the contents of the head. Once the skull is collapsed, the now dead infant is pulled from the uterus through the birth canal.

This procedure is most commonly performed in the second trimester of pregnancy, from twenty to twenty-seven weeks. How developed is a fetus during this period? The survival rate for premature babies born at twenty-three weeks is 30 to 50 percent. For those born at twenty-four to twenty-five weeks the survival rate is between 60 percent and 90 percent. Experts also believe that an infant begins to feel pain at this stage and, in fact, does feel horrific pain during the forcible manipulations and the stabbing of the skull during partial-birth abortion. It is hard to imagine a more grotesque or tortuous treatment of what—if delivered fully without first being killed—would have a fighting chance to become a healthy human being. Yet partial-birth abortion exists.

The procedure is performed in America—every day. The reason I describe this procedure in detail is not to shock, but to inform. As a medical doctor, board-certified in surgery, that is my responsibility. It's critical we debate this issue within a framework of reality, no matter how disturbing that reality is. That includes dispelling the myths some opposed to this bill present as facts.

First, some say partial-birth abortion may be necessary to preserve the health of the mother. That's just not true. Never has partial-birth abortion been the only procedure or the best procedure available in case of a medical emergency. It is time consuming; it takes three days. And it is dangerous. The only advantage of partial-birth abortion—which is a disturbing advantage—is the guarantee of a dead infant. Still, in the remote chance a partial-birth abortion would be required to save the life of a mother, the ban would not apply.

Second, some say partial-birth abortion is the best option to preserve the health of the mother. That's just not true. Let me paraphrase an article in the *Journal of the American Medical Association* published on August 26, 1998: There are "no credible studies" on partial-birth abortion "that evaluate or attest to its safety" for the mother. Partial-birth abortion is more dangerous to the health of the mother than alternative procedures. There is a greater danger of over-extending the cervix and causing cervical incompetence; a greater danger of slashing or puncturing the uterus because of the blind insertion of scissors; and a greater danger of infection because of the increased use of surgical instruments in the birth canal.

Third, some say the medical community opposes this bill because it infringes on the doctor-patient relationship and specific medical procedures should not be banned by Congress. That's just not true. As a doctor, I, too, am concerned about government intruding excessively in the practice of medicine. There is nothing more precious to me—other than protecting and improving lives—than preserving the doctor-patient relationship. But, in this case, the bill would ban a rogue procedure that is never medically necessary and is condemned by the medical community. It has absolutely no place in the doctor-patient relationship. The doctor-patient relationship is built on trust and moral behavior. This procedure is not moral. And let me set the record straight about the American Medical Association: statements that the AMA does not oppose the partial-birth abortion procedure are inaccurate. The AMA has supported a ban in the past. They oppose this specific bill because of its criminal provisions.

Fourth, some say making the specific technique of partial-birth abortion a crime would make performing all late-term abortions almost impossible and discourage doctors from performing legal abortions in all circumstances. That's just not true. This bill is tightly worded to prohibit only the very specifically defined partial-birth abortion procedure. Though I also find the alternative abortion procedures morally offensive, they will still be legal. And those alternative methods are safer.

Fifth, some say that partial-birth abortion is accepted as mainstream medicine. That's just not true. Partial-birth abortion is a fringe procedure. It is not found in common medical text books. It is not taught in medical schools or surgical residency programs. Only 7 percent of obstetric and gynecologic residency programs provide routine training for even the mainstream second trimester abortion procedures. Today's doctors are not trained in the partial-birth abortion procedure because it is dangerous, because it is a rogue procedure, and because it is outside the mainstream of generally accepted medical and surgical practice. In fact, the most prominent performers of partial-birth abortions are not trained obstetricians, but general practitioners.

Partial-birth abortion is an affront to the safe and reputable practice of medicine. The question often arises: how often are partial-birth abortions performed in the United States? Surveys indicate it's not as uncommon a practice as one might think. In 1996, the research arm of Planned Parenthood asked doctors for the first time a partial-birth abortion question. The results produced an estimate that 650 such abortions were performed annually in the United States. The same survey recently found that 2,200 partial birth abortions were performed in the United States in 2000. It is also worth noting that in Kansas—the only state that requires separate reporting of partial-birth abortions—182 procedures were performed on viable fetuses in 1999. And all 182 procedures were performed for mental health reasons. None were performed for physical health reasons, such as the life of the mother.

A vast majority of Americans support a ban on partial-birth abortion. And their will was reflected in the 104th and 105th Congresses. In both Congresses, the House of Representatives and the Senate approved bans on this procedure. Sadly, both efforts were vetoed by then President Bill Clinton. Today, partial-birth abortion remains the law of the land. And we will change that. The time has come to ban this morally offensive procedure. We as a society respect human life far too much to let it be ravaged in such an inhumane way—a living infant, partially-delivered, stabbed with eight-inch scissors, emptied of the contents of its skull, and then pulled from its mother . . . dead. Never has this procedure been the only one or the best one available to protect the health of a mother. In fact, partial-birth abortion carries with it a greater danger of doing harm. That is why partial-birth abortion is morally offensive to doctors not only as individuals, but as professionals.

So I ask my colleagues, as we debate this bill, to do so with the brutal and barbaric reality of this heinous procedure in mind. And to not be sidetracked by the myths of partial-birth abortion, especially those that would imply this is an accepted, mainstream medical procedure. It simply is not. Instead, let us simply ask the question: does partial-birth abortion carry the danger of doing unnecessary harm—to a mother, to an infant, and to our conscience as a nation that values the sanctity of human life? The answer is yes. That is how I will vote. And I urge my colleagues to vote the same.

# On the War in Iraq

*March 7, 2003*
*Floor Statement*

ON THIS DAY, in the hall of the United Nations Security Council and in the distant lands of the Middle East, the United States is making a stand for the causes of freedom and democracy, for order and peace. The President and the Congress have made clear that we will no longer tolerate Saddam Hussein's production, or possession, of weapons of mass destruction. Further, it is our solemn belief that the people of Iraq deserve to live in freedom. They have suffered long enough under the oppression of a tyrant.

As is so often the case, challenging the status quo is not easy, even when the status quo is a dictator pursuing and possessing weapons of mass destruction explicitly prohibited by the United Nations Security Council. We are fast approaching the moment of reckoning with Saddam Hussein. If he were to voluntarily disarm, it would be welcome, but he will not. If he flees his country, the chances for peace are much better, but he will never flee unless he is convinced there are no other options for his survival. If individuals within Saddam's regime rise up and overthrow him, there will be an opportunity for a new beginning in Iraq. But none will take this brave step if they doubt the fortitude of the United States and the international community.

Let there be no mistake about our nation's purpose in confronting Iraq—Saddam Hussein's regime poses a clear threat to the people of United States, its friends and its allies, and it is a threat that we must address now. Recall that in 1991 we were concerned that Saddam would use weapons of mass destruction to accomplish his expansionist designs in the Middle East.

Now, a decade later, we live with the reality that terrorists may acquire and use such weapons on our soil. I have no doubts that terrorists seek such weapons to use against this nation. I am equally certain that Saddam Hussein possesses such weapons, and would provide them to terrorists if he has not already. It is this nexus of a tyrannical dictator, his weapons of mass destruction, and terrorists who seek to inflict grievous harm upon the American people that compels us to act. The Senate and the House voted overwhelmingly last fall to authorize the President to use force against Iraq if Saddam Hussein did not disarm. In those votes the Congress stated, unambiguously, that the United States will not tolerate the pursuit and possession of weapons of mass destruction by Saddam Hussein. Nothing has changed fundamentally, with the possible exception that we have even further evidence that Saddam Hussein will not voluntarily disarm.

Last fall, to reaffirm the broad international commitment to disarm Iraq, President Bush successfully pursued a United Nations resolution that offered Saddam Hussein a final chance to meet the demands of the world community, or face the consequences. Saddam his missed his final chance. Now, we are told, that the United States must pursue a second resolution before Iraq can be disarmed. The United Nations Security Council has on seventeen occasions over a twelve-year period demanded the disarmament of Iraq. For the record, this will not be a second resolution, but the eighteenth resolution. Nothing in history has ever been made more meaningful by being repeated eighteen different times. In the end, it is not a multilateral approach that our opponents seek—for the United States is already joined by a multitude of others who share our commitment to disarm Saddam. No, it is the false comfort of unanimity to which they aspire. When everyone is responsible, nobody is accountable.

My friends, the hour has arrived for democratically elected leaders to stand up and be counted. Will the free world tolerate Saddam Hussein's continued brutality, his possession of weapons of mass destruction, and his continued defiance of the international community, or will we act to stop it now? To those who would suggest we are acting in isolation to confront Saddam's evil, I remind you that we are not alone in the conviction. In the past month the leaders of eighteen European countries have publicly endorsed the U.S. call for final action, including force if necessary, to disarm Saddam Hussein. Over two dozen countries are providing basing for our troops, access to our aircraft, and material support in preparation for a possible conflict with Iraq. And if it comes to that, with allies such as the United Kingdom, Australia, Spain, Italy, Denmark, as well as many of the new democracies in Eastern Europe on our side, we will not carry this burden alone.

America is at its strongest when it is standing in common cause with its friends and allies. The inverse, of course, is that America's allies are at their strongest when they are standing with us. To those leaders who have spoken out with us against the threat posed by Saddam Hussein, I commend your courage. As America has risen to challenge the threat posed by Saddam Hussein, you chose to stand by her side. Such loyalty and leadership will not soon be forgotten. Some of our erstwhile allies would be well advised to recall that their own freedom was regained by such courage and conviction.

I would remind them that their own liberation in World War II was a less popular undertaking than a possible war in Iraq. According to polls from that time, in October 1939, when asked whether the U.S. should enter the war in Europe, only 16.8 percent of Americans responded yes;

17.2 percent said yes in December 1939; and 26.9 percent said yes in July 1940. After winning reelection in 1940, President Franklin Roosevelt tried to move public opinion toward greater U.S. involvement, while offering significant material support to the allied war effort. Yet, asked again in January of 1941 whether they would support a declaration of war, only 14 percent of the American people responded yes. As late as October 1941, President Roosevelt commented that 70 percent of Americans wanted us to stay out of the war in Europe. Sadly, many around the world recoiled at the thought of confronting Nazi Germany. After all, it was Europe's war, not ours. And Hitler was killing foreign Jews, not Americans. Many leaders of the day demanded that we look after America first. They called for our country to stay within its own borders, protected by the false security of two oceans.

But then, as now—on December 7, 1941 and September 11, 2001—we were reminded that America is most vulnerable to attack when it is in retreat. President Roosevelt demonstrated then, as President Bush does today, the essential measure of a world leader is not in his ability to chase public opinion, but his courage to make the country safer by leading public opinion in the right direction. President Bush deserves much credit for confronting the grave and growing threat posed by the mad pursuit of a ruthless tyrant for the world's most deadly weapons.

The President is right when he says that neither more time nor more inspections will stop Saddam. The consequences of a war in Iraq cannot be certain. But our goals and motives must be understood for what they are: we seek to defend our own people from horrific attack, we seek the liberation of the Iraqi people, we seek the foundation of democratic government in Baghdad, and we seek the spread of peace in the Middle East. These are goals worthy of a great nation, and they are goals worth fighting for.

# On Medicare and Prescription Drugs

*November 24, 2003*
*Floor Statements*

MR. PRESIDENT, today we stand on the threshold of a truly historic moment. Not for Republicans. Not for Democrats. Or for the House of Representatives. Or the United States Senate. But, for over forty million American seniors and individuals with disabilities, who may finally be getting prescription drug coverage under Medicare.

Saturday morning, the House of Representatives passed H.R. 1, the "Medicare Prescription Drug, Improvement, and Modernization Act of 2003."

Also Saturday, President Bush called upon the Senate, once again, to finish the job. He urged us to send him legislation that will provide badly needed prescription drugs to seniors.

For years, Congress has debated whether, and how, to provide prescription drug coverage to seniors and to strengthen and improve the Medicare program. Now, it is time for us to act.

Mr. President, this generation of seniors survived the depression, fought World War II, and helped make the United States into a prosperous and thriving nation. Time and again, they stepped forward to serve. Now, is the time to fulfill our duty to that great generation. Now is the time to answer their call.

What President Lyndon Johnson said in 1965 still stands: ". . . No longer will this nation refuse the hand of justice to those who have given a lifetime of service and wisdom and labor to the progress of this . . . country."

Let us not stay that hand of justice now. Let us not turn our back on America's seniors and individuals with disabilities.

There are nearly one quarter of a million seniors in my home State of Tennessee who have no prescription drug coverage. There are millions more across the nation for whom this legislation, literally, means the difference between life and death. They cannot afford to wait any longer. I have treated thousands of Medicare patients. And I know firsthand that, without Medicare, millions of seniors would not have received needed medical services. Millions more would have faced financial ruin. Medicare has helped save and heal lives.

But this cherished program has failed to keep pace with medical and scientific progress. Prescription drugs are an integral part of modern medicine. They are as important as the surgeon's knife. Yet, they are not part of the Medicare program.

In the nearly four decades since the Medicare program was created, the American medical system has been transformed from one focused on treating episodic illness in hospitals to one characterized by an increasing emphasis on managing and preventing chronic disease in outpatient settings with advanced medical technologies and prescription drugs. Life expectancy has increased by nearly ten years. Death rates associated with heart disease have been cut in half, and new treatments and diagnostic tools have improved survival rates for prostate, colon, and breast cancer. Our medical and scientific knowledge and, along with it, our ability to treat illness and disease has improved dramatically over the past four decades. Yet, Medicare itself has not kept pace with these dramatic changes. It has been too inflexible and bureaucratic. Designed for the 1960s health care system, it has been unable to adapt to changing medical practice. Medicare does not provide true preventive coverage, disease management, or protection against catastrophic health care costs.

As a result, we have today glaring and unacceptable gaps in the coverage that is available to seniors and individuals with disabilities—the most obvious of which is the lack of prescription drug coverage.

Over the past three decades, for example, the death rate from atherosclerosis has declined by over 70 percent and deaths from ischemic heart disease have declined more than 6 percent, largely due to the advent of beta blockers and ACE inhibitors. During the same period, death rates from emphysema have dropped nearly 60 percent due to new treatments involving anti-inflammatory medications and bronchodilators.

Today, over six hundred medicines are under development to treat or prevent diabetes, cancer, heart disease, stroke, neurological diseases, and other debilitating illness. Nearly four hundred drugs have been produced during the past decade alone. But, under today's Medicare, these drugs simply are not available to seniors.

We must act to ensure that this generation of seniors, and the next, has access to the healing miracles of modern medicine. And we must act to provide our seniors, and the next generation of seniors, with true health care security: quality preventive care, affordable prescription drugs, protection from catastrophic health care costs, better coordinated care, disease management, and access to modern technology.

As voluntary prescription drug coverage, the bipartisan bill we are debating today takes a major step in that direction. It devotes four hundred billion dollars over the next decade to adding a new, voluntary prescription drug benefit to the Medicare program. And it takes concrete steps to speed less expensive generic drugs to the market to help make prescription drugs more affordable for all Americans.

Within months after this legislation is signed into law, seniors will be able to get a voluntary Medicare-approved prescription drug discount card that will reduce the costs of their drugs by an estimated 10 to 25 percent. Lower income seniors will get an additional subsidy of six hundred dollars on top of these discounts to help them purchase needed medicines. Thus, seniors will get immediate relief even before the comprehensive drug benefit is fully implemented, with additional help for those who need it the most.

Beginning in 2006, seniors will have access to the new drug benefit. Those who wish to add the new prescription drug benefit to their traditional Medicare coverage will have that choice. The new drug benefit is completely voluntary and available to all seniors. Appropriately, it provides the most generous help to lower income seniors and those with catastrophic drug costs.

## Substantial Assistance for Lower Income Seniors

Seniors with incomes below 135 percent of the Federal poverty line ($11,648 for individuals and $14,965 for couples) will pay no premiums, no deductibles, and only a modest co-payment for their comprehensive coverage. Beneficiaries with incomes below 150 percent of poverty ($12,942 for individuals and $16,327 for couples) will pay only a portion of the premium and a fifty–dollar deductible. After that, the government will subsidize 85 percent of their drug costs.

In my home state, over 430,000 low income Medicare beneficiaries—nearly half of all beneficiaries in Tennessee—will have exceptional prescription drug coverage under this bipartisan plan. One quarter of a million Tennessee seniors who today have no prescription drug coverage at all will gain access under this proposal, along with millions more across the nation.

## Improvements to Traditional Medicare

The legislation also strengthens and improves the traditional Medicare Fee for Service program. It adds new preventive coverage for diabetes and cardiovascular disease. For the first time, Medicare will cover initial preventive physical examinations. And this agreement responds to the 6 percent of seniors with chronic disease who account for about 50 percent of all Medicare spending. The legislation will launch a series of major pilot programs on disease management and quality payment incentives that could result in dramatic improvements in the care of the most ill and the most needy. This will help us better target health care resources to those who require it most.

The legislation also puts in place national standards for electronic prescribing, along with incentives for doctors to fill prescriptions electronically. These reforms should dramatically improve medication therapy management, reduce medical errors, and improve patient safety.

As the Senator from Montana, the Ranking Member of the Senate Finance Committee, has said so eloquently during these past several days, this bill does nothing to destroy the existing Medicare program. In fact, it immensely strengthens the traditional Medicare program.

As my colleagues know, this legislation has received broad support from well over 350 organizations, including the AARP—which represents thirty-five million seniors. In its letter of endorsement last week, the AARP also makes clear that, at a result of this legislation, "millions of older Americans and their families will be helped by this legislation." In addition, AARP writes: "The integrity of Medicare will be protected."

## New Health Care Choices

Today, most seniors choose to enroll in the traditional Medicare Fee for Service program. But this may not be the best choice for all seniors, and it may not be the choice of all seniors in the future.

There are about five million seniors who are covered by private health plans under the Medicare program today. Beginning immediately, the legislation will strengthen Medicare's local HMO coverage. It will help stabilize and improve the coverage of those five million seniors in the current Medicare + Choice program. As a result, Medicare + Choice will become a more stable, secure, and strong option for those seniors who have already chosen to enroll in coordinated care plans.

This bipartisan plan also provides seniors with even more choices—the choice to enroll in regional preferred provider organizations, or PPOs. The majority of Americans under age sixty-five get health coverage through PPOs. Most members of Congress, Federal employees, and Federal retirees also get coverage through PPOs. Employees covered by PPOs report high levels of satisfaction with their coverage. PPOs typically provide coverage for preventive care, chronic care management, disease management, and access to a broad range of doctors and hospitals.

Under the bipartisan agreement, seniors will have the opportunity to participate in these innovative plans if they choose. Moreover, beginning in 2010, we will test on a limited basis whether these private health plans provide higher quality than traditional Medicare. We will also test whether Medicare private health plans are most cost effective than traditional Medicare. All beneficiaries will be protected during this test. And the demonstration cannot be expanded or extended unless Congress acts to do so.

Throughout, seniors will always be able to stay in the traditional Medicare program. And they will have the option of adding prescription drug coverage. Meanwhile, tomorrow's seniors, many of whom are covered through PPOs now, may choose to continue private coverage when they retire. We are looking down the road to prepare for the baby boom population. We need to be ready now, not scrambling when it is too late.

## Strengthening Health Care in Rural America

This bill contains the most sweeping and strong rural provisions ever in a Medicare bill to come before this Congress. It also makes improvements to payments for graduate medical education and takes concrete measures to protect seniors' access to physicians.

For example, hospitals in my home State of Tennessee will receive 655 million dollars under this legislation. Physicians, who otherwise would face real cuts next year of 4.4 percent, would instead see a 1.5 percent payment increase in both 2004 and 2005. I am very proud that the American Hospital Association, the Tennessee Medical Association, the American Association of Medical Colleges, and the Alliance for Specialty Medicine strongly support this legislation. The bill has also received strong support from the Rural Health Care Association, the Rural Hospital Coalition, and the Coalition for Geographic Equity in Medicare.

## Controlling Prescription Drug Costs

Some of my colleagues have said that this legislation does nothing to control prescription drug costs. I respectfully disagree. First of all, under this bill, seniors will be able to get a drug discount card right away. They will be able to present their Medicare discount card to their pharmacist and receive a 10 to 25 percent cut right off of the top.

This bill also works to contain drug costs before the drugs get to the pharmacist's shelf. It does so in a number of ways. The bill speeds generic drugs to the market. It encourages competition to lower prices, and it gives the Medicare recipient new power to comparison shop.

Let's start with the generic drug provisions. In 1984, Congress passed the Hatch-Waxman law to encourage cheaper generic drugs to come onto the market. Under that law, generic competition has flourished. When the law was passed, generic drugs were less than 20 percent of the market. Today, generic drugs represent nearly 50 percent of the entire market.

The Hatch-Waxman Act has been incredibly successful in allowing consumers to get low-cost alternatives. But there have been some abuses. Therefore, we are moving to close loopholes in the system through this bill. And the core of the provisions build on the work of Senator Gregg and Senator Schumer.

Under the new system, a new drug applicant will receive only one

30-month stay of approval of a generic drug's application. This is a major change. Under the old system, drug companies could receive multiple stays of approval for generic rivals. Now, they will get one stay only.

The agreement takes additional steps to get generic drugs to the market faster, through which patients will get safe, effective, low-cost generic drug alternatives to brand name medicines.

That is why this bill is supported by the Generic Pharmaceutical Association and the Coalition for a Competitive Pharmaceutical Market.

The bipartisan Medicare agreement also empowers drug plans to negotiate discounts from drug companies. The Congressional Budget Office says that this approach will enable drug plans to significantly control drug costs for their beneficiaries.

Moreover, the savings they negotiate will not be subject to federal limits. They will be able to get the lowest prices possible, even if those prices are lower than those negotiated under Medicaid. The Congressional Budget Office has estimated that this provision alone will save eighteen billion dollars.

Not only will the Medicare agreement help lower prices, it will help give consumers more information about their medical options. This bill expands federal research into the comparative effects of different drugs and treatments.

With this new information, seniors will be able to comparison-shop in the medical marketplace, just like they would for any other product or service. Patients and their doctors will be able to compare treatment options and choose the course of action that best addresses their medical needs. And Medicare and health consumers will get better value for their money.

## Health Savings Accounts

I am also very pleased that this legislation will make tax-preferred Health Savings Accounts available to all Americans. HSAs will help control costs over time, and give individuals the ability to better control their health care dollars and health care decisions.

I wish we could have gone even farther. I wish we could have added provisions from the House bill that would have allowed individuals to roll over some funds each year from their flexible spending accounts. I also believe we must do more in the coming years to allow individuals to invest funds on a tax-free basis to meet their health care needs in retirement, just as we do with 401(k) plans and Individual Retirement Accounts. I am committed to coming back and addressing these issues in the years ahead.

## Demographic and Structural Challenges

Our first priority must be to provide seniors with health security. But, at the same time, we know that Medicare also faces serious financial and demographic pressures in the coming years. Between now and 2030 the number of seniors will nearly double from forty million to seventy-seven million; the program's costs will more than double to nearly 450 billion dollars annually, even before we add prescription drug coverage or improve other benefits; the number of taxpayers paying into the system to finance health coverage for seniors will drop from four today, to 2.4 by 2030; seniors, who represent 12 percent of the population today, will represent 22 percent of the population in 2030; and one last fact: each senior will be in the Medicare program longer. Life expectancy at age sixty-five will increase approximately 10 percent over the next thirty years.

The demographic underpinning has been defined: more seniors, each senior living longer, and fewer workers to support each senior. So, while we need to act to provide prescription drug coverage to seniors, we also need to do so responsibly. This legislation takes an important first step in linking Medicare payments to quality. It also relies on competitive market forces to help control health care spending.

Moreover, for the first time in Medicare's history, we will ask those seniors who can afford to pay more for their coverage, to do so. And we will put in place more accurate and more transparent measurements of Medicare's fiscal strength—as well as special procedures for attempting to better control Medicare spending growth in the future.

These reforms do not go far enough for some of my colleagues. At the same time, they go too far for others. Overall, however, I believe this is a balanced, bipartisan bill that is worthy of the support of the United States Senate.

It is not a perfect bill. But, it is a meaningful step in the right direction. It will provide substantial relief from high prescription drug costs for millions of seniors. It will help rectify payment inequities for rural health care providers. And it will begin to inject into the Medicare program new health care choices and much needed flexibility so that seniors will have the option to choose the kind of health care coverage that best suits their needs.

Today, America is one step closer to being a more caring society for millions of seniors and individuals with disabilities struggling with high prescription drug costs and outdated, often inadequate, medical care. Today, we are one step closer to providing real health security to seniors all across the nation.

As a physician, I have written thousands of prescriptions that I knew would go unfilled because patients could not afford them. With this bill, that will change. As a senator, I have watched as a decades-old Medicare program has operated without flexibility, and without comprehensive and coordinated preventive care, disease management, and catastrophic protection against high out-of-pocket medical costs. With this bill, that will change also.

This legislation is historic. By dramatically expanding opportunities for private sector innovation, it offers the possibility of genuine reform that can dramatically improve the quality of care available to seniors. At the same time, the legislation preserves traditional Medicare for those who choose it. It combines the best of the public and private sectors and gives today's seniors innovative health care options and positions Medicare to serve tomorrow's seniors as well.

This legislation is possible because of the work and dedication of every member. I would like to take a moment to thank those whose commitment was critical to this effort. First and foremost, Chairman Charles Grassley and Ranking Member Max Baucus deserve credit. As does Senator John Breaux who joined me six years ago on the Bipartisan Commission on Medicare and again on this Conference Committee. All Members of the Conference Committee showed a degree of dedication and resolve seldom seen in either Chamber, especially Senators Hatch, Nickles, and Kyl. But we wouldn't have reached this point without building on the strong foundation laid by Members over the last several years, especially Senators Snowe, Jeffords, Gregg, Hagel, Ensign, and Wyden. Finally, the Senate could not have done this alone. The House Leadership, Speaker Hastert, and Leader DeLay, deserve special recognition, as does the Chairman of the Conference, Chairman Bill Thomas, and the Chairman of the House Energy and Commerce Committee, Chairman Billy Tauzin.

In closing, I would like to thank again every member of this body who has worked so hard on this legislation—not just in this year, but in the previous six years of our most recent effort to strengthen and improve Medicare. I urge every Senator to support this bill. I implore every Senator to avoid filibusters and other partisan political maneuvers that threaten the prescription drug coverage and health care security our seniors need and deserve.

I yield the floor.

# On Conservativism

*January 23, 2004*
*Remarks to the Conservative Political Action Conference Reagan Banquet*

## "Press on to Win the Prize"

Thank you, Art, for your generous introduction, and for the privilege of being with you tonight.

I'm profoundly grateful to stand before not only fellow conservatives, not only fellow patriots, but also friends who believe that one of the great presidents in American history was Ronald Wilson Reagan.

I'm here tonight because I believe in you. Because I believe in the ideas we share as conservatives. Because I recognize the vital role of our cause in the glorious past and even more glorious future of America.

And because I—as Majority Leader of the United States Senate—want our ideas, our cause, and our concerns heard in the United States Senate.

You have listened to many distinguished speakers these past two days: the Vice President, cabinet secretaries, senators, and members of the House. Each plays a unique role in our democracy.

But just so you know that I understand the real role I play, I want to read to you the most accurate description I've heard of my job as Majority Leader.

This is from Alan Murray—the host of CNBC's *Capital Report:* "Being Senate Majority Leader is akin to being groundskeeper at a cemetery: you have a lot of people under you, but they aren't paying much attention."

This is a decisive time for America. Our nation stands at a crossroads. And with the upcoming elections in November, we will soon choose a path: either we will adopt the pessimism and negativity of the Democratic contenders for president, or we will affirm the bold and positive leadership of President George W. Bush.

Tonight, I want to touch upon three issues that will be at stake in this election and concern our cause: the protection of human dignity, the family as the bedrock of a healthy society, and the defense of liberty.

C.S. Lewis saw decades ago the dangers facing human dignity. In his essay "The Abolition of Man," he warned that in conquering nature, nature is actually conquering mankind.

The question facing us in this postmodern era is: "Are we eternal souls made in God's image or just flesh and blood with only darkness at the end of our lives on Earth?"

If human beings are special—if we are truly sacred—then we must devote ourselves to a better world. But we must not do evil to bring about good.

My own profession is medicine. And a good physician must, I fundamentally believe, also be a very good scientist.

I can tell you from my own experiences that without revolutionary advances in medical science and technology, my own heart transplant patients of a decade ago simply wouldn't be alive today.

Indeed, we reject an irrational fear of technological advance.

But the secret of human dignity is living within limits—ethical limits, moral limits that don't hamper human advances, but preserve them and promote them.

We strongly support ethical stem cell research. But we reject the cloning or the patenting of human beings.

The practice of brutalizing a baby the very moment she is ready to emerge into the world is an affront to my whole medical and surgical experience. And even more profoundly, it is an affront to values that America has held so dearly for more than two and a quarter centuries.

For almost a decade we worked to ban this brutal, barbaric, and morally offensive procedure—partial birth abortion. But our opponents blocked us. It's hard to imagine they tried to block us right up to the very end in the Senate.

After years of hard work, we elected a Republican Senate, a Republican House, and a Republican President. And we *finally* banned the gruesome procedure of partial birth abortion. Thank you my fellow conservatives for keeping the faith. And thank you, President George W. Bush.

That's what happens when you work to align the stars and get good people together to accomplish a great goal.

And that's why I'm so excited to be with you tonight. The stars really are aligned in the executive and legislative branches to make great things happen. But I think we must all admit we've not done as well with the courts. It's the courts that have put a hold on banning partial–birth abortion. Maybe that's also why Democrats have launched the unprecedented filibuster of the President's judicial nominees—to retain control of the third branch of government.

For the first time in our history, a minority of Senators—all Democrats—have used the filibuster to deny a bipartisan majority the opportunity to vote up or down—yes or no, for or against—the President's nominees. A minority is denying the majority its constitutional duty to give "advice and consent."

This is wrong.

It is wrong to apply religious or ideological litmus tests to qualified nominees. It is wrong to use the confirmation process to curry favor with special interest groups. It is wrong for Senate Democrats to verbally assassinate the President's nominees.

President Bush, thank you for courageously standing up to Senate Democrats and appointing Judge Charles Pickering to the bench.

Let me assure you: our party will stand its ground until the Senate does its duty. We will not cut a deal. We will not blink. And we will not back down. The President's judicial nominees will get the vote they deserve.

To further preserve human dignity, the Senate will soon take up the Unborn Victims of Violence Act. This bill recognizes that when a criminal attacks a pregnant woman and kills her unborn child, he has claimed not just one, but two precious human lives. And it ensures that those who prey upon a pregnant woman and her child will pay a heavy price.

There's a second critical question facing our nation: "What is family?"

Our Founders assumed the answer was obvious. They didn't write into the Constitution the definition of family, because it wasn't even an open question. For them, and for all of us here today, we know the strength of our society rests on the foundation of strong families.

But the issue before us today is that activist judges in Massachusetts are intent on destroying the traditional definition of family.

It's true that respect for marriage has seen better days. That's all the more reason not to abandon or radically redefine the God-ordained institution of marriage.

I do want to be very clear: we reject hatred and intolerance. We must treat all our fellow citizens with kindness and civility. But marriage should not be redefined by activist judges. And we won't let it.

Marriage should remain the union of a man and a woman. We will do whatever it takes to protect, preserve, and strengthen the institution of marriage against activist judges. If that means we must amend the Constitution, we will do it.

The President has announced a bold initiative to promote healthy marriage in the welfare reauthorization bill. We promote home ownership to reduce poverty and stabilize communities. We should do no less for marriage.

There's a third pressing issue facing our nation, and that is the defense of liberty. America is a peaceful nation. We do not want war. We abhor it.

But there are times when justice and freedom are so threatened, that we must act—and we must act with overwhelming force. As we have come to realize as a nation, we have a choice: either we take the battle to terrorists on their soil and on our terms, or the terrorists will bring the battle to us on our soil and on their terms. Baghdad or Boston? Kabul or Kansas City? The choice is ours.

As long as George W. Bush is President, America will take the battle to the terrorists. Yes, we will search every cave, raid every safe house, destroy every training camp, and freeze every bank account that terrorists may use to plot their evil ways. We will make the world safe from terrorists because terrorists will no longer feel safe in the world.

The question of defending liberty is not just about taking up arms, but also about creating a vibrant economy.

Upon taking office, President Bush immediately went to work to revive our economy. We've cut taxes every year he has been in office. Combined, the President's tax cuts are the largest in American history.

Have they produced results? All across America businesses are investing now more than ever. Housing starts are at their highest level in twenty years. Worker productivity is at an all-time high. The stock market has broken through the ten thousand point barrier. And the unemployment rate has dropped to a fourteen-month low.

This is the fastest growing economy since Ronald Reagan was president. And that, my friends, is no coincidence.

Tax cuts are not just about the size of government, but the size of our freedom. More government leads to less freedom. We must preserve freedom. We must make the American people's tax cuts permanent.

We must also curb frivolous lawsuits that stifle economic growth. We'll begin with class action reform and then rapidly move to medical liability reform. Americans are already spending too much money for health care. They don't need reckless trial lawyers pushing huge awards to pad their own pockets.

On spending, Congress has heard you loud and clear. We must reduce the deficit. Beating back more than a trillion dollars of Democratic amendments last year is not enough. The President understands this. Republicans in Congress understand this. We must tame the explosive growth of government spending. And we will. Liberty is also more than just restraining government growth.

Edmund Burke, the father of our movement, wrote: "Men are qualified for civil liberty in exact proportion to their disposition to put moral chains on their own appetites." George Washington said much the same in his farewell address, when he noted: " . . . religion and morality are indispensable supports" for a healthy society.

We are a pluralist nation, as we should be. But it was our Framers who believed that our Constitution was designed for a virtuous people. Government can't make people religious or devout, but it can and must get out of the way and let religion flourish. Attempts to denude the public square of all religious expression betray a misunderstanding of the role of religion in a pluralist nation.

The Founders intended a form of separation of church and state. But they did not intend any form of separation of God and state.

When it comes to education, many parents do not have the same freedoms wealthier parents have. In Washington, D.C., and other places around our nation, too many of our kids are trapped in troubled schools. And too many of my liberal colleagues are willing to tolerate this disparity. They oppose school choice in our nation's capital while they send their own children to private school.

This is about to change. Yesterday the Senate passed—and today the President signed—legislation to give Opportunity Scholarships to thousands of the poorest students in failing D.C. schools.

This will change thousands of lives forever. And it will give children a down-payment on hope.

It is true that America stands at a crossroads.

The election next November is about more than just which party controls the White House and the Congress. It's about human dignity. It's about the family as the bedrock of our society. And it's about the liberty endowed upon us all by God.

While these issues go to the foundation of who we are as a people, they will find expression in the leaders we choose . . . and those we reject.

I can tell you that George Bush is a man of character, courage, and moral clarity. He is the clear choice, the best choice and, for me, the only choice to lead our nation.

As Americans, we must faithfully serve the cause of freedom. It is our duty. Did the hundreds of thousands of patriots who have laid down their lives, so that we may live free, do so in vain?

I'm confident that Americans have found a new love and respect for our freedom since September 11th. We have learned anew what too many had forgotten, that the price of liberty is eternal vigilance.

At the Normandy commemoration in 1984, President Reagan vowed: "We will always remember. We will always be proud. We will always be prepared, so we may always be free."

Together, let us protect human dignity, let us preserve family, let us promote liberty, and let us, my fellow conservatives, press on to win the prize.

# On Jobs and Democratic Partnership

*March 24, 2004*

Mr. President, I am very disappointed by the vote here today and especially by the actions of my colleagues on the other side of the aisle.

This legislation is essential if we are to accelerate the rate of job creation. The JOBS bill will bring our trade and tax laws into compliance with our trade agreements. It will also provide badly needed reforms to further stimulate manufacturing growth.

This bill was developed in a strong bipartisan fashion under the leadership of Chairman Grassley and Senator Baucus. It was voted out of the Finance Committee, on which I serve, by a vote of 19 to 2. Every single Democrat on the Committee voted in favor of the bill, including the junior Senator from Massachusetts.

That is why I am very concerned that the Democrats have now decided to filibuster yet another bill for election-year, partisan purposes. I think this is a terrible mistake. This is a mistake that will have a detrimental impact on the recovery of U.S. manufacturing jobs.

Every day we delay actions is another day where American jobs are put at risk. Every day of delay is inexcusable. European tariffs have already been imposed. These tariffs are a European tax on U.S. manufacturers. By voting against cloture, our Democrat colleagues have voted in support of a Euro-tax on U.S. manufacturing.

I had hoped my colleagues on the other side of the aisle would have been able to find the courage to do the right thing. This legislation would pass the Senate by a wide margin if we could get past election year posturing.

Mr. President, we compete in a global economy. Some have suggested we close our borders to the world. Some think we can retreat into economic isolationism. But we can't. And we should not.

That would be a declaration of defeat. We are the most innovative society in the world today. Our workers lead all others in productivity. If allowed to compete on a fair playing field, U.S. manufacturers can lead the world.

In my home state of Tennessee, we compete well in that world economy. Exports have risen 26 percent since 1997. And those exports support 232,000 jobs in Tennessee. That's about 10 percent of Tennessee's workforce.

The EU is Tennessee's second largest trading partner, accounting for 21 percent of all Tennessee exports. One hundred seventy-seven million dollars in Tennessee exports are on the sanctions list. That amounts to 7.2 percent of Tennessee's exports to the EU and 1.5 percent of its global exports.

As many as 3,450 Tennessee jobs could be affected by this filibuster. This filibuster could have an estimated economic impact of 700 million dollars in my state. And no state is immune from these sanctions.

The Europeans are ready to impose 4 billion dollars in sanctions. So far, they have not done so. They have chosen to begin with a 5 percent tariff which increases 1 percent each month. They acted with restraint because they believed we would act quickly and responsibly. This vote can only lead to steeper sanctions.

Mr. President, this bill was approved by every Democrat in the

Finance Committee. Now it is being filibustered by some of those same members. Sadly, this is yet another example of flip-flopping.

My colleagues on the other side of the aisle say they're for manufacturing jobs. Well I say, "Here's your chance." The National Association of Manufacturers, representing ten thousand small and medium manufacturers, strongly supports immediate passage of this bill. The U.S. Chamber of Commerce, the world's largest business federation, has urged us not to delay passage of this bill.

My colleagues on the other side of the aisle say they support manufacturing. But when it comes time to actually help U.S. manufacturers, their actions say "Sorry, we're not interested." Instead of being serious, they're being frivolous. Instead of being responsible they're being political. And it's just shameful.

It's shameful that anyone would play politics with our manufacturing jobs and it's even more shameful that anyone would do so after having spent so much time saying that they actually cared about U.S. manufacturers.

U.S. manufacturers today are increasingly burdened with unnecessary costs. In December, the National Association of Manufacturers released a study on the effect of rising costs to U.S. manufacturers. That study found that excessive taxes, frivolous lawsuits, high energy bills, and health, pension, and regulatory compliance costs were damaging U.S. manufacturing.

That study concluded that, while U.S. manufacturers have many challenges in today's global business environment, domestically imposed government costs are damaging U.S. manufacturers and harming workers more than any foreign competitor.

Let me repeat: government imposed costs are damaging U.S. manufacturing and harming workers. The study found that these imposed costs added at least 22.4 percent to the cost of doing business in the United States. These costs place American businesses at a significant competitive disadvantage as compared to our largest trading partners.

Meanwhile, our foreign competitors do not have these burdens.

Further, they have cut corporate tax rates to stay competitive. The combined average U.S. federal and state tax burden is 40 percent. The average tax rate for the top thirty industrial countries is 31 percent. There are even some socialist countries, Denmark and Sweden for example, who have lower corporate tax rates than we do. We simply cannot afford to add more costs to manufacturing.

And yet this new Euro-tax on U.S. manufacturers does just that—it adds yet another cost to U.S. manufacturing. Survey after survey of U.S. businesses confirms the same thing. The incentive to move jobs overseas is the direct result of the escalating costs of doing business at home. If we want to reverse the trend towards outsourcing, we have to address the issues that are motivating American companies to go offshore.

There is some irony here: government imposes these enormous costs and then demands that businesses reduce the outsourcing that inevitably results. If you want to stop businesses from moving offshore, then stop burdening their ability to create new jobs in the United States. The Euro-tax on manufacturing is just another incentive to move jobs offshore. Unfortunately, this is just one in a series of many bills that would help U.S. manufacturers that the Democrats have seen fit to filibuster.

Mr. President, for months, we have tried to move legislation that addresses the concerns of manufacturing. We tried to move a class action reform bill but it was filibustered. We tried to move an energy bill but it was blocked by our colleagues on the other side of the aisle. We tried to move a bill to help preserve doctors from frivolous lawsuits but it was filibustered.

We tried to reauthorize the workforce investment act to provide worker education and job retraining. But after approving this legislation unanimously, our colleagues from the other side chose to stop the bill by blocking the appointment of conferees.

And next month we are going to try to bring some justice and fairness to the current asbestos litigation lottery, but I fear that too will become yet another victim of the obstructionism that has come to characterize the opposition.

But every time we get a different excuse as to why strongly supported legislation gets filibustered. Mr. President, the time has ended for excuses. The time is over for playing politics with American workers. The time has come to move this legislation.

# On Dale Earnhardt

*February 2001*

MR. PRESIDENT, I rise today to pay tribute to an American legend, a working man who rose from his roots to the top of his profession, indeed to the top of the world, the racing world, that is. And that's why we loved him.

Like all legends, he was the best at what he did, the greatest race car driver in the history of NASCAR; perhaps the greatest driver that ever lived. With an uncanny feel for his car and a take-no-prisoners attitude on the track, he brought millions of fans into the sport. And that's why we loved him.

He was the People's Champ, the Last Cowboy, Ironhead, the Intimidator, but most of all he was just like us, funny and warm, human and accessible, and that's why we loved him.

But, Mr. President, Dale Earnhardt was much, much more. When a young fan was dying of cancer, Dale spent fifteen minutes on the phone with him, and flatly rejected any attempt to publicize it. When a local pastor came around seeking donations to pave his church's parking lot,

Dale wrote out a check for the full amount on the condition that the pastor never reveal that all the money came from one person, and especially not who that person was.

He routinely aided high school bands, and church groups, and once gave John Andretti a motor so he could qualify. When the doctor who tended drivers injured at the track had to travel cross-country, leaving his pregnant wife behind, Dale called to make sure she was all right, and then sent two men with a pick-up to the mountain retreat where they lived just in case she needed a fast trip to the hospital. His favorite charity was the Make–a–Wish Foundation, perhaps because he knew what true magic was all about.

Describing the tough racer with the tender heart, one NASCAR publicist said, "He'd do nothing for you on the track, but anything for you off it." And that's why we loved him.

Mr. President, as we all know now, Dale Earnhardt died a week from last Sunday, on the final lap of the Daytona 500, doing what he did best—racing for victory. Victory eluded him, but death did not.

After 281 finishes in the top five, 428 in the top ten, and 76 wins, including nine at Bristol, Tennessee where he also won the first of seven Winston Cups as a young rookie in 1979, Dale Earnhardt passed from living to legend. His death, like his life, transcending his sport.

To the hundreds who knew him and the millions who did not, he was John Wayne, Humphrey Bogart, and James Dean all rolled into one. He was a husband, a father, a mentor and a friend. But most of all he was like America, caring, big-hearted, open and free. And that's why we loved him.

## Graduation Address at St. Albans School

*June 2002*

Ralph Waldo Emerson, over 130 years ago, wrote: Hitch your wagon to a star. This now famous maxim is great fodder for inspirational and commencement speeches. Today, most people interpret Emerson to say: if you hitch your wagon—that is, the stuff that makes up you—to a star, you set a lofty goal for yourself and focus your life (or, your wagon) on reaching that goal (your star). It suggests goal setting, discipline, competition, drive, focus. That is not my message today. With sons Bryan, Jonathan and Harrison all at St. Albans, I'm confident that St Albans has taught you that.

Before I get too far, I'm a dad. All the moms here tell their sons you don't communicate enough. As you guys know, the moms say the same thing about the dads. So while I have floor, I want to communicate to Harrison Frist as directly and simply as I can, Harrison, please, please, over the next thirty minutes, don't even think about water.

Don't do anything with water; please don't squirt water, and in the future keep dad's squirt guns at home.

When you first set foot on these grounds—for many of you it was four years ago, for most of you it was eight, and for a bunch of you it has been 12 years—you hitched your wagon to this very day. Your star, which joyfully will be realized in a very few moments, has been to climb these steps, accept your diploma from the Bishop, and minutes later burst through the West Front doors. You committed the wagon of your youth to this day.

Think back nine months to the opening exercises in this magnificent cathedral. It was probably a blur to you, but to those of us as family who watched, we saw you process, each individually paired with a C-Former, the huge size and mass of your being (your wagon) juxtaposed to the tiny, wide-eyed, nervous yet hungry new students. Your wagons were separated by two feet in height, a ton of hormones, but also importantly the twenty thousand hours of spiritual, physical and intellectual St. Albans experiences with the seventy-one friends in your class.

You will never, ever in your life, spend this much time so intimately with one set of friends. You have built friendships and relationships that will endure your lifetimes. Yesterday at Prize Day, I flipped to the back of the current St. Albans Bulletin where alumni post their addresses. On page forty-two are the class notes from David Vauthier who writes that alumni can reach him in Catonsville, Maryland. He's a member of the Class of 1928. That is like you writing your class notes in the year 2076.

Indeed, you have been there with each other in the classroom, but you have been there for each other outside the classroom—in creative and performing arts, and in the choir and singing groups, and at lacrosse, crew, voyager, or track and field.

You have won and lost together. You have cheered and jeered together. You have received awards and ovations at Prize Days, and at Performing arts and athletic banquets.

You have shown your buoyant spirit for this school in the Dog Pound and at homecoming—congrats on beating Landon. And your steadfast love for each other comforting friends—at times of losses of parents and loved ones, and in times of failure.

You have shown your love for God in chapel. You came together in the Little Sanctuary to worship God and to learn His teachings, but also to share life intimately with each other. Your wagon bed has been fortified with the interlocking foundation of faith and family. And that will be with you—it must stay with you—your whole life.

And you have shared your experience at St. Albans with your families—from the annual holiday Lessons in Carols in this magnificent cathedral, to baseball spring training eating swamp cabbage at a pig roast in Okeechobee.

"Hitch your wagon to a star." But that is not my message today. You have learned that at St Albans. In fact, my friends, I think Ralph Waldo Emerson was wrong, or perhaps he was only half right.

My message to you today is not "hitch your wagon to a star"—but rather "hitch a star to your wagon." Yes, it's those everyday blessings of life that bring lasting joy and fulfillment.

An example. Three weeks ago on a beautiful sunny day, I rushed from the floor of the U.S. Senate, asked the majority leader to hold whatever votes were pending, in order to make my last three-legged races at Field Day. But the Field Day I most remember is the one with Harrison four years ago. It was a hot day, full of semi-organized chaos. There were hundreds of parents and blue and white paint spattered across faces. Mr. Herman was working the crowds. At the last moment I told Harrison that we should really try to win our sack race. So I set our star. I could smell victory!

I studied the technique of the winners in the earlier classes; we practiced for five minutes, counting out loud to synchronize our steps. We tightened the itchy burlap sacks around our legs. I specifically noted the exact position of the large orange cones that marked the finish lines.

Bang! We got off to a great start. We stayed out front. We counted out loud. We crossed the orange cones ahead of the pack. Victory!! Or so I thought. I felt Harrison's leg straining to pull me forward as I slowed down. Harrison said, "Don't stop!" Then the other teams rushed passed us.

I'd stopped too early. I stopped at the orange cones at the finish line for the lower school, twenty yards short of the real finish line. We lost. We never reached our star!!!

The lessons are many:

1. A sack race is more important than votes in the US Senate.
2. It is the wagon that counts, not the star.
3. When you pick your star, define it well. Don't pick the wrong orange cones. After today you will be doing most of your star picking on your own.
4. Your stars will change. Your generation will see more change than any generation in history. Man will walk on Mars. Scientists will develop a cure for HIV/AIDS. Billions of people still living under tyranny will taste the sweet fruit of democracy—freedom. Keep yourself open to change, be willing to take risks, and to explore opportunities as they arise. And you can only do those things if you are consumed not with reaching a single star, but by focusing on the wagon of everyday life. You will lose more sack races than you will win. You may never reach your star. History is full of brilliant artists who never sold a painting, gifted composers whose genius was never heard, and all-star athletes who never won a championship. Their joy comes not from the star they never reached, only from the wagon of their everyday lives.
5. Traditions—like Field Day—matter. The Class of 2002 leaves new traditions. They become your legacy. McDonalds Week, the performing arts banquet, epiphany, nationally ranked crew, beating Landon at homecoming, initiation of the School of Public Service.

I am confident that you will succeed in life. As the wisest man I ever knew, my dad, once told me: A life is made up of peaks and valleys. But the thing to remember is that the curve is always going up. The next peak is a little higher than the previous peak; the next valley isn't quite so low. St. Albans has prepared you to climb to the peaks and rise from the valleys of life. We are proud of you, and you should be proud of yourselves.

But without meaning and without a sense of moral duty, you could never realize the full potential of your education. St. Albans has given you the values and the traditions, to take what you have learned here and what you will learn in the future and turn it all into a fulfilling and glorious life.

This philosophy is so well expressed in the school motto—For Church and For Country. As graduates of St. Albans, you now have a duty, a responsibility, to take your foundation of knowledge, honor, courage and leadership and use it to serve God and the United States. This is your duty; it's also your destiny. It is captured beautifully by your class window unveiled at breakfast yesterday morning—the American flag warmly embracing the school.

Where were you on September 11th? This is likely to be the most frequently asked question of you over your lifetime. The terrorists attacked. The Towers fell. The Pentagon was set aflame. And with uncertainty and little information at the time, you went to the Little Sanctuary to learn, to pray, to cope, to heal. Never in the history of St. Albans has "For Church and For Country" meant more than at that moment.

As you exit this cathedral with diploma in hand, glance up one final time at the glorious stained glass window and commit to serve others. You have a duty to do so.

It is written in Proverbs 16:9, "In his heart a man plans his course, but the Lord determines his steps." Choose your stars wisely; today we parents formally relinquish that responsibility to you. Fill your wagon in abiding love for God and for country. And, as you sprint down this isle and burst through the West Front doors, hitch the stars you choose to your wagon and capture the magic and the boldness and the genius of the moment, the rest of your lives.

You are grown men. Harrison, we love you. Congratulations and God bless St. Albans.

# On the Occasion of Christmas

*December 10, 2002*
*A Christmas letter to fellow Senators*

Dear _______:

The holiday season is here, and it's a wonderful time to pause and express appreciation to our loved ones, to reflect on the past, and to anticipate the grand opportunities ahead. Each of us in our Senate family serves others, too often casually neglecting to take care of ourselves and those closest to us. Take sixty seconds to serve yourself (and your family) by addressing each of the nine items below. Age-appropriate screening and regular check-ups *will* improve your health. You owe it to those around you. Most of the following are age-specific to the "typical" senator, and thus please don't extrapolate to the entire population. I include suggestions for both men and women, in the hopes that you will share these tonight with your loved ones.

1. Have you had a colonoscopy in the last five years? If not, do! Every year since I've been in the Senate except one, someone in the

Senate family has had colon disease diagnosed this way. And cured! (It's not as bad as you might imagine!) If you are older than fifty and have not had a colonoscopy, a fecal occult-blood ("hemoccult") test (requires a stool sample, but can be done from home!) yearly helps screen for polyps and cancer.

2. Do you have any moles that are changing in size, shape or color? If so, have them biopsied immediately. In addition, any mole greater than the width of a pencil eraser needs to come off (or seen by a dermatologist).
3. What is your blood pressure? If elevated (one in five men over fifty-five have high blood pressure = "hypertension"), treat it. You typically *don't* have any symptoms with hypertension!
4. For women (over fifty), have you had a mammogram since last December? A PAP smear in the past three years?
5. What is your PSA (Prostate-Specific Antigen blood test for cancer)? It should be checked annually, along with that digital rectal exam by your doctor. Remember, prostate cancer is the leading cause of cancer in men (one in eight over sixty years old are at risk). You will be cured if detected early. If I had to guess, I'd say that two of us in the Senate family will be diagnosed with new elevation of PSA this year!!
6. Consider a treadmill exercise (or other stress) test for your heart, especially if your parents had heart disease or if you have smoked—it can be life-saving. You will typically develop significant heart disease with a perfectly normal resting EKG. There are a bunch of new heart imaging tests you can discuss with your doctor.
7. Get a good old-fashioned physical exam annually, which will include the routine screening blood tests.
8. Don't forget your shots: flu shot annually, and ask for Pneumovax and tetanus booster (to prevent "lockjaw") every ten years.
9. Wear your seat belt, don't smoke (lung cancer is the number-one

cancer killer in men), and exercise for at the very least thirty minutes three times a week (it's stress reducing!).

Karyn and our three boys wish you and your family a healthy and joyful holiday season.

With warmest wishes,
Bill Frist, M.D.

## On Being Elected Senate Majority Leader

*December 23, 2002*

LAST NIGHT, recognizing that our lives as a family would likely today take a direction radically different than what I had asked for or even anticipated just seven days ago, Karyn and I went to the same church I've gone to on the eve of my elections in 1994 and 2000. While there my mind kept returning to that passage in Proverbs: "In his heart, a man plans his course, but the Lord determines his steps."

I've been given responsibility before, as a physician, to listen, to diagnose, to treat, to heal. Until today, I've always regarded my most profound professional responsibility in my professional life the blessing I had to hold in my hands the human heart, recognizing all its glory and all its potential, and then technically seating it into the chest of a dying woman to give her life and a future she would not otherwise have.

A few moments ago, my colleagues gave me a responsibility equal to that—some would even say a heavier one. I accepted that responsibility with a profound sense of humility. They gave me their confidence, their support, their trust—and elected me to serve as their leader in the United

States Senate. In that capacity, my intentions are to serve, not be served, so we together can capture the remarkable potential, and express the full will and purpose of the institution of the United States Senate on behalf of the American people.

I pledge to take this opportunity to strengthen the institutional integrity of the Senate and to work with members of both parties, in both chambers, to make the lives of all Americans more fulfilling. I want to say how very proud I am of my Republican colleagues. We have risen to the challenges of the past two weeks, and we will rise to the challenges of the next two years. We stand united; we speak as one team; and we will transform this moment into a catalyst for unity and positive change.

These are trying times for America. In the coming days, I will be working with the entire Senate so that together we can address the daunting challenges we as a nation face: Our brave men and women in uniform and the President need our continued support to win the war against terror; our economy needs a boost. Every American who wants a job should have the opportunity to find one; we will improve and strengthen Medicare, address prescription drugs for our seniors and individuals with disabilities, and focus on the uninsured and the obvious health care disparities I've witnessed first hand; and we must dedicate ourselves to healing the wounds of division that have been reopened during the past few weeks.

Still, just as critical as what we decide to do is how we decide to do it. The unprecedented way all this has happened gives me personally the tremendous opportunity to join a recently elected leadership team that is experienced and energetic and committed. Senator Stevens, McConnell, Santorum, Hutchison, Kyl, and Allen—elected six weeks ago—have already begun planning for the next Congress. I will rely heavily on their counsel, their ideas, and their expertise.

I have asked the leaders, as I will every Republican Senator, for their ongoing input and counsel. As Majority Leader I will seek the wisdom to put the strengths of each and every one of us to the best possible use for all of America. Minutes ago, I called Senator Tom Daschle. I committed to work with him and the Democratic Caucus to make this a positive and productive Congress.

What is required of us—members of the leadership, senior members and junior, conservatives and moderates—as Republicans and as Democrats—is to work together as a team. My Republican colleagues witnessed my commitment to working as a team in my leadership role as chairman of the National Republican Senatorial Committee—rallying around a common goal to achieve what many said was impossible.

And my closest team—the one that is my family. Karyn, my wife, and my three sons.

On our call a few moments ago, I pledged to my colleagues that as majority leader I will do all within the power and responsibility they so generously granted me to ensure the Senate stands united, our party stands united, and our country stands united. These are extraordinary times. We have a duty—an historic duty—to lead the whole of America, and together we will.

Now let's all go home and have a safe and happy holiday with our loved ones.

## Acknowledgments

A WEEK PRIOR TO Christmas, 2003, I was sitting at my desk working on my third novel when my agent, Chris Ferebee, called and said that he'd been approached by a publisher wondering if I'd write the biography of Bill Frist. From that phone call to today's deadline, has been a whirlwind of mythical proportions. Having survived, I am indebted to several people.

My publisher, David Moberg, thank you for offering me this assignment and providing the resources needed to allow me to cover the story. My editor, Kate Etue, for walking through this with me and for willingly granting me an extension when the project began to grow legs. My research assistant, Jody Hysler. It is no exaggeration to so say, quite honestly, I could not have arrived here, and on time, without you.

Mark Tipps offered firsthand insight that I'd never have gained without his willingness to share it.

To the many people who shared their time and reflections with me—Tom Nesbitt, John Gibson, Barry Banker, John Eason, David Charles, Tracy Frazier, John Morris, Karl VanDevender, Gordon Inman, Walter

Merrill, Gilchirst "Gick" Berg, Uwe Reinhardt, Ed O'Lear, Jan Muirhead, Kim Jett, Dick Furman, Franklin Graham, Lloyd Ogilvie, Phil Brown, Bernard LaFayette, Fred Thompson and others—thank you for entrusting me with your stories.

To be truthful, when I lifted rocks and looked for the story behind Bill Frist's closet door, what I found surprised me. Instead of finding a man who, on his way to the top, trampled the people beneath him and left them drowning in his wake, he took them on board, even rescued a couple, befriended them, equipped them and valued them—no matter their position or title. I was once told that you can tell who the leaders are by the line of people following them. As I studied Bill Frist, I saw this in action. I was amazed at the number of people—and the varieties in their backgrounds and political persuasions—who stood behind or alongside him, called him friend and who were willing to follow him most anywhere.

My life as a writer is a gift—a privilege—and I am grateful. Several family and friends have contributed to this. Briefly:

Sealy, again, thank you for everything. Chris, I'm indebted to you. Allen and Jenny, thank you for your encouragement of me, your belief in me and for allowing me flexibility in my writing schedule.

Charlie, John T. and Rives, the stories of great men are worth reading. Maybe as you get older, you'll add this one to your library. Between now and then, there's baseball, fishing and tender moments too numerous to count.

Christy, I really don't know how you hold it all together. How you handle the boys, me, our life and your work is a mystery on the level of the eighth wonder. The last few months have been as tough or tougher on you than me. Thank you for allowing me this and for so unselfishly taking up the slack. You amaze me.

Lord, thank you for this. I pray that I have dealt justly with this man's life. Where I have not, please make up the difference.

# Chronology

| | |
|---|---|
| February 22, 1952 | William Harrison Frist, born |
| 1968 | At the age of 16, Frist obtains his pilot's license |
| 1974 | Graduates from Princeton University |
| 1978 | Graduates with honors from Harvard Medical School |
| 1978–1984 | Residency and surgical training at Masachusetts General Hospital and Southampton General Hospital in England |
| March 14, 1981 | Marries Karyn Jean McLaughlin in Lubbock, Texas |
| May 6, 1983 | William Harrison Frist Jr. born in Southampton, England |
| 1985–1986 | Serves as Senior Fellow and Chief Resident at Stanford University |
| October 11, 1985 | Jonathan McLaughlin Frist born in Stanford, California |
| 1986 | Starts Vanderbilt University's heart and lung transplantation program |
| April 29, 1987 | Bryan Edward Frist born in Nashville, Tennessee |
| 1989 | Founds and becomes surgical director of the multi-organ Vanderbilt Transplant Center; publishes first book, Transplant |

| | |
|---|---|
| 1990 | Howard Baker tells Frist the Senate would be the best forum for his talents and expertise |
| November 1992 | Chairs Governor Ned McWherter's Medicaid Task Force |
| January 1, 1994 | Takes a leave of absence from Vanderbilt Hospital to organize his campaign for senator |
| March 1, 1994 | Announces his candidacy for United States Senator |
| November 8, 1994 | Elected US Senator for the state of Tennessee |
| 1997 | First medical mission trip to Africa |
| October 25, 1998 | Runs first official marathon (Marine Corps Marathon) |
| 1999 | Serves as deputy whip of the US Senate |
| November 7, 2000 | Re-elected US Senator for the state of Tennessee |
| May 24, 2001 | Jim Jeffords leaves the Republican Party |
| October 2001 | Anthrax attacks on Senate offices in Washington, D.C. |
| December 12, 2002 | Sen. Trent Lott toasts Sen. Strom Thurmond at his 100th birthday |
| December 20, 2002 | Sen. Trent Lott steps down as US Senate Majority Leader |
| December 23, 2002 | Unanimously elected Senate Majority Leader, 108th Congress |

# Notes

*Introduction*

1. Douglas Waller, "Capitol Grudge Match," *Time*, June 10, 2002.
2. "Person of the Week: Tom Daschle," *Time*, June 7, 2001.
3. Gloria Borger, "A Bad Good Ol' Boy," *U.S. News and World Report*, December 23, 2002, 25.
4. Ibid.
5. Transcript, *Fox News Sunday*, FOX, March 4, 2001.
6. Colbert I. King, "Sen. Byrd. The View from Darrell's Barbershop," *Washington Post*, March 2, 2003, A23, http://www.americasvoices.org/avarc2002/archives2002/WallaceM/WallaceM_052402-Part-IX-Section2.htm (accessed January 2, 2004).
7. Prov. 16:9, NIV.
8. Dr. Karl VanDevender, (Internist, The Frist Clinic), in discussion with the author, April 22, 2004.

*Chapter One*

1. J. Lee Annis and William H. Frist, *Tennessee Senators* (Lanham, MD: Madison Books, 1999), 243.
2. David Brooks, "Bill Frist's New South," *Weekly Standard* 8, no. 19 (January 27, 2003).
3. Mark Tipps, (Attorney, Walker, Bryant, Tipps & Malone), in discussion with the author, April 6, 2004.

4. Bill Frist, "Frist Receives Court TV 'Everyday Heroes' Award," Bill Frist, United States Senator Website, http://www.frist.senate.gov/index.cfm?FuseAction=PressReleases.Detail&PressRelease_id=1385&Month=4&Year=2003.
5. Barry Banker, in discussion with the author, April 22, 2004.
6. Dr. Kim Jett, (Cardiothoracic Transplant Surgeon, Dallas, Texas), in discussion with the author, April 28, 2004.
7. Jimmy Moore, (Police Officer, University of Clemson), in discussion with the author, April 29, 2004.
8. Bill Frist, Untitled Speech (Keynote address, George Washington University School of Medicine and Health Services Commencement, Washington, D.C., May 18, 2003).
9. Mark Tipps, in discussion with the author, April 6, 2004.
10. Ibid.
11. Barry Banker, in discussion with the author, April, 22, 2004.
12. Mark Tipps, in discussion with the author, April 7, 2004.
13. Ibid.
14. Brooks, "Bill Frist's New South."
15. Douglas Waller, "Is Frist Just What the Doctor Ordered?," *Time*, January 13, 2003.
16. Ibid.
17. Ibid.

*Chapter Two*

1. Brooks, "Bill Frist's New South."
2. Jeffrey L. Rodengen, *The Legend of HCA* (Fort Lauderdale, FL: Write Stuff Enterprises, 2003), vii.
3. Brooks, "Bill Frist's New South."
4. Ibid.
5. Frist and Wilson, *Good People Beget Good People*, 106.
6. Ibid.
7. Ibid.
8. Ibid.
9. William H. Frist, M.D., *Transplant* (New York, NY: Fawcett Books, 1990), 115.
10. Dr. Karl VanDevender, (Internist, The Frist Clinic), in discussion with the author, April 22, 2004.
11. Brooks, "Bill Frist's New South."
12. Annis and Frist, *Tennessee Senators*, 245.
13. Frist and Wilson, *Good People Beget Good People*, 107.
14. Dr. John Morris, (Trauma Surgeon, Vanderbilt University Hospital), in discussion with the author, April 21, 2004.
15. Dr. Karl VanDevender, in discussion with the author, April 22, 2004.
16. Rodengen, *The Legend of HCA*, 15.

17. Frist and Wilson, *Good People Beget Good People*, 108.
18. Frist, *Transplant*, 121.
19. Ibid.
20. Dr. Karl VanDevender, in discussion with the author, April 22, 2004.
21. Gordon Inman, in discussion with the author, April 19, 2004.

*Chapter Three*

1. Frist, *Transplant*, 116.
2. John Gibson, in discussion with the author, April 21, 2004.
3. Frist, *Transplant*, 122.
4. Frist, *Transplant*, 126.
5. John Gibson, in discussion with the author, April 21, 2004.
6. Frist, *Transplant*, 127.
7. William H. Frist, ed., *The Bell Ringer* (yearbook, Montgomery Bell Academy, 1970).
8. John Eason, (Business owner), in discussion with the author, April 21, 2004.
9. Frist, *Transplant*, 128.
10. John Gibson, in discussion with the author, April 21, 2004.
11. Frist, *Transplant*, 128.
12. Gilchrist Berg, (Princeton Classmate), in discussion with the author, April 26, 2004.
13. Ibid.
14. Ibid.
15. Ibid.
16. Ibid.
17. Ibid.
18. Annis and Frist, *Tennessee Senators*, vii–viii, 247.
19. Frist, *Transplant*, 130.
20. Ibid.
21. Ibid.
22. Frist, *Transplant*, 132–133.
23. Ibid.
24. Ibid.
25. Frist, *Transplant*, 131.
26. Frist, *Transplant*, 132.
27. Dr. Kim Jett, in discussion with the author, April 28, 2004.
28. Frist, *Transplant*, 40.
29. Frist, *Transplant*, 136.
30. Frist, *Transplant*, 136.
31. Franklin Graham, in discussion with the author, April 13, 2004.
32. Frist and Wilson, *Good People Beget Good People*, 154.
33. Dr. Richard Furman, in discussion with the author, April 28, 2004.
34. Dr. Lloyd Ogilvie, (Former Chaplain, United States Senate), in discussion with the author, May 5, 2004.

35. Gilchrist Berg, in discussion with the author, April 26, 2004.
36. Dr. Lloyd Ogilvie, in discussion with the author, May 5, 2004.
37. John Eason, in discussion with the author, April 20, 2004.
38. Frist, *Transplant*, 141.
39. Jan Muirhead, in discussion with the author, April 30, 2004.
40. Annis and Frist, *Tennessee Senators*, 249.
41. Frist, *Transplant*, 53.
42. Frist, *Transplant*, 89.
43. Ibid.
44. Ibid.
45. Frist, *Transplant*, 82.
46. Frist, *Transplant*, 92.
47. Ibid.
48. Frist, *Transplant*, 111.

*Chapter Four*

1. Dr. Walter Merrill, (Transplant Surgeon, Vanderbilt Transplant Center), in discussion with the author, April 18, 2004.
2. Ibid.
3. Dr. John Morris, in discussion with the author, April 21, 2004.
4. Dr. John Gibson, in discussion with the author, April 20, 2004.
5. Frist, *Transplant*, 101.
6. Jimmy Moore, in discussion with the author, April 29, 2004.
7. Ibid.
8. Frist, *Transplant*, 234–235.
9. Annis and Frist, *Tennessee Senators*, 252.
10. Ed Cromer, "Frist's Knockout Punch Defies Political Experts," (newsletter, Montgomery Bell Academy, 1994-5), 2-3.
11. Dr. John Gibson, (Internist, Private Practice), in discussion with the author, April 20, 2004.
12. Barry Banker, in discussion with the author, April 21, 2004.
13. Annis and Frist, *Tennessee Senators*, 253.
14. Annis and Frist, *Tennessee Senators*, 136.
15. Mark Tipps, in discussion with the author, April 6, 2004.
16. Ibid.
17. Ibid.
18. Dr. Karl VanDevender, in discussion with the author, April 22, 2004.
19. Mark Tipps, in discussion with the author, April 6, 2004
20. Ibid.
21. Senator Frist of Tennessee, speaking at proceedings, on July 11, 1995, 104th Congress, 1st sess., *Congressional Record* 141, no. 6.
22. Annis and Frist, *Tennessee Senators*, 255.
23. Dr. Lloyd Ogilvie, in discussion with the author, May 5, 2004.

24. Mark Tipps, in discussion with the author, April 6, 2004
25. Paulette V. Walker, "Senator, Formerly a Medical Researcher, Gets a Key Role in Setting U.S. Science Policy," *The Chronicle of Higher Education*, February 28, 1997, A38.
26. Henry W. Foster with Alice Greenwood, *Making a Difference* (New York, NY: Scribner, 1997), 158.
27. Mark Tipps, in discussion with the author, April 6, 2004
28. Frist and Wilson, *Good People Beget Good People*, 109–111.
29. Ibid.
30. Franklin Graham, in discussion with the author, April 13, 2004.
31. Dr. Richard Furman, in discussion with the author, April 28, 2004.
32. Ibid.
33. Lloyd Ogilvie, *Perfect Peace* (Eugene, OR: Harvest House, 2001), 153–154.
34. "Frist Reaction to HIV/AIDS Signing," US Senator Bill Frist Website, http://frist.senate.gov/index.cfm?FuseAction=PressReleases.Detail&PressRelease_id=1413&Month=5&Year=2003.
35. Lloyd Ogilvie, (sermon, First Presbyterian Church, Nashville, TN, May 25, 2003).

*Chapter Five*

1. William H. Frist, M.D., *When Every Moment Counts* (Lanham, MD: Rowman & Littlefield, 2002), 91.
2. Frist, *When Every Moment Counts*, 23.
3. "When Every Moment Counts," When Every Moment Counts, http://www.wheneverymomentcounts.com/author/author.html.
4. Ibid.
5. Ibid.
6. Frist, *When Every Moment Counts*, 9.
7. Frist, *When Every Moment Counts*, 15.
8. Frist, *When Every Moment Counts*, 16.
9. Frist, *When Every Moment Counts*, 38.
10. "Frist, Kennedy Introduce Bipartisan Bioterrorism Response," US Senator Bill Frist Website, http://frist.senate.gov/index.cfm?FuseAction=PressReleases.Detail&PressRelease_id=1115.
11. Michael Lemonwick, "Homegrown Terror," *Time*, February 16, 2004.

*Chapter Six*

1. Mark Tipps, in discussion with the author, April 6, 2004.
2. Mark Tipps, in discussion with the author, April 30, 2004.
3. Ibid.
4. Barry Banker, in discussion with the author, April 21, 2004.
5. Dr. John Gibson, in discussion with the author, April 20, 2004.

6. Mark Tipps, in discussion with the author, May 3, 2004.
7. Mark Tipps, in discussion with the author, April 6, 2004.
8. Barry Banker, in discussion with the author, April 21, 2004.
9. Dr. John Morris, in discussion with the author, April 21, 2004.
10. Dr. John Gibson, in discussion with the author, April 20, 2004.
11. Ed O'Lear, (Princeton Classmate), in discussion with the author, May 1, 2004.
12. Gilchrist Berg, in discussion with the author, April 26, 2004.
13. Ed O'Lear, in discussion with the author, May 1, 2004.
14. Dr. John Gibson, in discussion with the author, April 20, 2004.
15. Tracy Frazier, (former Assistant to Bill Frist), in discussion with the author, April 20, 2004.
16. Dr. Richard Furman, in discussion with the author, April 28, 2004.
17. Dr. Walter Merrill, in discussion with the author, April 15, 2004.
18. Franklin Graham, in discussion with the author, April 13, 2004.
19. Dr. Lloyd Ogilvie, in discussion with the author, May 5, 2004.

*Chapter Seven*

1. Dr. Karl VanDevender, in discussion with the author, April 22, 2004.
2. "Frist Comments on Civil Rights Pilgrimage," US Senator Bill Frist Website, http://frist.senate.gov/index.cfm?FuseAction=Speeches.Detail&Speech_id=53.
3. Dr. Karl VanDevender, in discussion with the author, April 22, 2004.
4. Rev.Bernard LaFayette, (Civil Rights activist), in discussion with the author, May 3, 2004.
5. Rev. Bernard LaFayette, in discussion with the author, May 3, 2004.
6. Senator Fred Thompson, (Actor and former Senator), in discussion with the author, May 12, 2004.
7. "Frist Address to Congress of Racial Equality," US Senator Bill Frist Website, http://frist.senate.gov/index.cfm?FuseAction=PressReleases.Detail&PressRelease_id=1340&Month=1&Year=2003.

# Index